DISCARD

13.75

LB
1029   Devaney, Kathleen.
.06   Developing open education
D48   in America.

Developing Open Education in America

A Review of Theory and Practice in the Public Schools

By Kathleen Devaney

National Association for the Education of Young Children
Washington, D. C. 20009

This book was developed under a grant from the National Institute of Education, Department of Health, Education, and Welfare. However, the opinions expressed herein do not necessarily reflect the position or policy of that Agency, and no official endorsement should be inferred.

Developing Open Education in America was created by the Far West Laboratory for Educational Research and Development, a public non-profit organization supported in part by the National Institute of Education, Department of Health, Education, and Welfare. The Laboratory was established through a Joint Powers Agreement in February, 1966. Present signatories include: The Regents of the University of California; The California State Board of Education; The Trustees of the California University and State Colleges; The Board of Education of the San Francisco Unified School District; The Regents of the University of Nevada; The Nevada State Board of Education; The Board of Regents, University of Utah; The Utah State Board of Education.

The Laboratory's goal is to contribute to the improvement of educational practices. Through research about new ideas and practices in schools and through development of new educational products and methods, a staff of 220 works to help children have more and better opportunities to learn.

Copyright © 1974 by the Far West Laboratory for Educational Research and Development. All rights reserved. No part of this book may be reproduced or transmitted in any form or by any means, electronic or mechanical, including photocopying, or by any information storage and retrieval system, without permission in writing from the Publisher.

Copyright is claimed until 3 years after date of copyright. Thereafter all portions of this Book covered by this copyright will be in the public domain.

Library of Congress Catalog Number 74-78803

Printed in the United States of America.

*No great thing is created suddenly,
any more than a bunch of grapes or a fig.
If you tell me that you desire a fig,
I answer that there must be time.
Let it first blossom, then bear fruit,
then ripen.
Since, then, the fruit of a fig tree
is not brought to perfection suddenly,
or in one hour, do not you think to possess
instantaneously and easily
the fruit of the human mind.*

–Epictetus

Photo Credits

Cover: photo—Carol Baldwin, John Muir School, Berkeley, California; design —Johnny DeLeon, Corporate Press, Inc., Washington, D.C.
Center for Teaching and Learning, University of North Dakota: 137
Community Resources Institute, New York City (Herb Mack): 3, 12, 57, 61
Creative Teaching Workshops (Wendy Holmes): 70, 77
Education Development Center, Follow Through, Philadelphia Advisory Center (Lora Haus): 75, 115, 123
Ford Foundation (Bob Adelman): 8, 16, 24, 40, 81, 93, 117, 128; (Bruce McAllister): 4, 43, 49, 63, 83, 100, 110, 112, 133
Grape Street School, Los Angeles, California: 29
John Muir School, Berkely, California (Carol Baldwin): 142, 152
Olive Elementary School, Arlington Heights, Illinois (Eileen McCarty): xii, 26

Table of Contents

Foreword	vii
Preface	ix
Acknowledgements	xi
Chapter 1 **Open Education in America: Native or Transplant? Process or Model?**	1
Chapter 2 **A Different Role for the Principal**	17
Chapter 3 **Creating the Curriculum**	41
Chapter 4 **A New Resource— The Advisor**	71
Chapter 5 **The Teacher as Learner**	101
Chapter 6 **Relationships with Parents**	129
Chapter 7 **Evaluating Children's Growth**	143
Appendix 1 **A Short Bibliography of References and Curriculum Materials**	165
Appendix 2 **Questions for Review, Discussion, School-Profiling, or Problem-Solving**	179
Index	187

Foreword

The documentation, organization, and analysis of open education as practiced in America today was sorely needed. Kathleen Devaney and the Far West Laboratory for Educational Research and Development have filled the gap with clarity, insight, and excellent timing. They have produced a synthesis of the developments in open education which have proliferated in many forms in recent years. Though distinctions between American and British styles of open education are noted, the dominant emphasis in this book is addressed to the diversity of programs and sponsors, both public and private, as only comprehensive coverage in American educational ventures authentically should do. This publication gives focus to the fact that strong supportive people and mechanisms are essential if programs advocating open education are to be effective for America's children. It further documents that in order for the change to open-endedness to occur, the dynamics of whole school-community participation and support OVER TIME are essential.

If you are one of the prophets of doom about open education, an analysis of failures is included. If you are a firm advocate, you will find clear definitions and descriptions of open education practices which can enable you to energize your efforts. NAEYC is pleased to publish this thoughtful analysis for all who wish to provide young children with viable alternatives for learning—each in his own unique style.

Evangeline H. Ward
President, NAEYC

Preface

This book is for teachers, prospective teachers, principals and other administrators, and parents. It is not intended to describe the appearance or the benefits of an open classroom or to give directions and inspiration for the task of creating one. Rather, it is intended to stimulate thought about the conditions required within a school *system* if teachers are to be able to move toward openness.

Substantial and lasting change—affecting many teachers and children, not just a few classrooms—calls for substantial, long-term help for teachers from others in the school community. This need is amply demonstrated by the experience of the open education movement in England, where the principal, the curriculum, the advisor (or resource teacher), teacher education, and relationships with parents all function to energize—or at least to minimize interference with—the teacher who resolves to change. In the United States, wherever open education is practiced on a scope broader than the single classroom, one also finds reliance on one or more of these "enablers" for teachers. This book is a report of the varied ways in which several open education projects in American public schools have provided more than token support for teachers as they strive toward real change.

The book results from a one-year nationwide study by two staff members of the Far West Laboratory for Educational Research and Development, San Francisco. The work was sponsored by a grant from the Task Force on Dissemination, National Institute of Education.

Acknowledgements

Gretchen Thomas gathered much of the material for this book during visits to schools and interviews with teachers, principals, advisors, and project directors. Thus she provided evidence and insights which, combined with those gained by the writer in similar visits, underlie the information and the ideas of the book.

A panel of consultants helped the project staff to select the descriptors of open classrooms which appear on pages 3 and 4, and they helped to select the schools and projects to be visited. The panelists clarified the staff's conception of the roles played by "support agents" within school districts—from principals to parents—who enable teachers to change toward open education. The panelists also critiqued the reviewers' draft of the manuscript. Panel members were the following:

James Browne, Coordinator
The Associates Program
Institute for Educational Leadership
Washington, D.C.

Robert B. Davis, Director
University of Illinois Curriculum Laboratory
Urbana, Illinois

E. Babette Edwards, Co-Chairman
Harlem Parents Union
New York, New York

Carrie A. Haynes, Principal
Grape Street Elementary School
Los Angeles, California

Judith Hayward, Resource Teacher
John Muir Elementary School
Berkeley, California

Theodore Manolakes, Professor
Elementary Education
University of Illinois
Urbana, Illinois

Charles H. Rathbone, Director
The New City School
St. Louis, Missouri

J. Richard Suchman
Institute for the Study of Human Learning
HumRRO
Monterey, California

Chapter 1
Open Education in America:
Native or Transplant?
Process or Model?

Ever since Americans began reading, five years ago or more, about the British infant schools' "open" classrooms—homey and humming with happy and above all, busy children—individual American teachers have moved to make their own classrooms less austere. They have pushed desks out of straight rows and made lessons out of objects from nature or the neighborhood. Bit by bit—perhaps a few hours a week, perhaps most of the time—they have replaced whole-class lessons and textbook assignments with individual, child-appealing or even child-chosen learning projects.

Certainly some American teachers worked this way for years without thinking they were borrowing from the British. This kind of teaching is not uniquely English. It has roots in American as well as European theory and practice: in Dewey, Erikson, Bruner, in child development psychology and humanistic psychology. It has branches in the nursery school and kindergarten movement, progressive private schools, and the alternative school experiments of Holt, Kohl, Kozol, and others.

But such ideas have flowered in England in high-quality, self-disciplined, yet intensely personal student work in many state-supported primary schools, while in the United States, the same ideas have taken root only in private and preschool education and in scattered public school classrooms and not firmly enough to generate an opening-up of schooling for a significant number of American children.

American reform—blunted but dogged

Some of the writing that came out of the curriculum reform movement begun in the late 1950s in America, described *aspirations* that sound very similar to today's descriptions of the actual *achievements* of the best English open schools. John Goodlad's 1969 "checklist of expectations"— practices he had hoped to see in his survey of 100 American primary schools—included the following: diagnosing and prescribing learning according to each child's cognitive level, and providing for many differing styles and interests among children; emphasizing "process" learning and active involvement with a variety of materials and natural, out-of-school experiences; small group, child-directed discussions and projects rather than teacher-dominated lessons; and flexible physical environments and groupings of children.[1]

As Goodlad noted, such practices had been the aim of an American reform movement dating back to 1957.[2] Recurring efforts to change schooling so that it is at once more child-centered, more humane, and more intellectual, are part of an old tradition, often frustrated, but stubbornly persisting in the United States as well as in England. The history of these efforts refutes the charge that open education in the United States is a passing fancy, even though it is true there have been faddish implementations—classrooms in which furniture and schedules have been rearranged, but children's and teachers' activities have stayed basically the same.

The reforms that Goodlad described as being "blunted on the classroom door" were attempted in the United States in the 1960s mainly by means of the research-based invention and dissemination of new curriculum materials. Dozens of studies and descriptions that Americans have written about the substantial, if partial, success of reforms in England show that the English made their changes in a markedly different way. The differences do not seem to stem from differing educational goals or differing needs in children, but from an educational system which differs from ours in several important ways.

Differences in the British system

The English schools are smaller, the pressures less. English principals see themselves as educational policy makers and leaders, not just as building and personnel managers. The curriculum can be heavily influenced— if not created—by principals and teachers, whose judgment is considered equal—if not superior—to district supervisors, university scholars, research and development experts, and textbook writers. Teachers receive long and practical classroom experience before they become professionals, and as professionals they receive frequent in-classroom help from master teachers. English teachers enjoy higher status and respect in the community than do their American counterparts. And so on.

Because our system is so different, Americans wishing to change not just a single classroom but a whole school or district toward open education must be prepared to move much more than classroom furniture and furnishings. Wherever one finds American schools with more than an occasional open classroom, one finds administrators creating new services for the teacher and redefining the teacher's role and relationships. These are the most trustworthy signs that a school administration is not just riding the bandwagon: that it understands open education and is serious about achieving it.

Characteristics of open classrooms

Confusion and disagreement about the definition of open education may impede even the most serious and practical administrator's planning. To define what open education means in this book, we collected descriptors from writings of American educators who proceed from the same premises about children's learning as their British counterparts. Books, articles, and research papers that contributed to this definition are referenced in Note 3 following this chapter. The eight consultants named in the *Acknowledgements* helped select the following statements as descriptors of teachers' and children's work in American classrooms where the opening process has moved beyond the beginning stage. The reader should keep in mind that few teachers beginning to open their classrooms will be able to focus on all these aspects at once, and that even those American teachers with relatively long experience in open education may not be doing all these things. (As William P. Hull has pointed out, the language about open education has developed faster than the practice.[4]) Related to this is the fact that there is no "model" of what an open classroom ought to look like and no single set of behaviors which all teachers strive to produce in all students or in themselves. (The reader is asked to substitute the pronoun "he" for "she" wherever appropriate.)

> The teacher divides her time into small, concentrated periods in which she attends to children working singly or in small groups, rather than addressing the whole class as one group all day. Groups may be formed according to children's interests rather than ability levels, and groupings may change frequently.

3

The teacher works with students as a stimulator, advisor, consultant, and resource, rather than as a giver of knowledge. She listens and watches a lot more than the traditional teacher, and talks a lot less.

The teacher does not merely set out lumps of content or skills to be mastered by students, either as a group or individually. She also (or mostly) leads and encourages them to be aware of things and happenings around them as sources of information, to express and combine ideas, to test how things work, and to solve problems. There is little or no pressure to "get through the book."

Each child can choose frequently from among several appealing alternative kinds of school work. The teacher guides these choices both by her selection of materials and by her counseling with children. Children's and teacher's own personal interests provide many of the starting points for lessons. Work in (or leading to) reading, writing, and math are always included among the alternatives. Almost always there also will be science and creative expression—painting, crafts, music, drama, movement. The teacher also may assign work, depending on her assessment of children's needs.

The teacher conveys to children standards of quality that she expects from their work. These standards are tailored to individual children—and they may be quite demanding. Work is not praised simply because it is completed, but because it is especially good, original, or indicates that the child has taken unusual care.

In diagnosing and prescribing for learning, the teacher considers the child's style of learning and his background and interests as well as his ability level. In evaluating the child's progress, goals set for the individual child are considered more useful than standardized achievement tests. The teacher's notes and collections of each child's work are valued and discussed with parents as evidence of learning.

The teacher regards the child's whole range of experiences—including his interests and feelings—as consequential for learning.

The teacher makes curriculum decisions and develops many of her own materials on the basis of the needs of her own class and in collaboration with other teachers, the principal, resource teacher, or parents.

The teacher provides several activity centers within the classroom (and there may be more available to her children in neighboring classrooms). Typically, she develops over time a math center, a library corner, a writing area, a science workshop (usually with living plants and animals), space for painting, clay, cooking, woodworking, a store, etc. These areas change as children's interests develop and change, and they are furnished and maintained by children as well as by the teacher. The learning centers contain natural and homemade materials as well as books, games, kits, worksheets.

Parents are welcome in the school during the school day and frequently work in classrooms as volunteers. Volunteering is a clue that they understand the educational goals of the open classroom and have chosen to place their children there.

It's important to note that two educational innovations many Americans associate with open education are not included at all in these descriptors: nongradedness, and open-space school architecture.

Many innovative educators believe that, especially in primary years, children greatly benefit from being in mixed-aged classes—for instance, a class with five-, six-, and seven-year-olds. But this "family grouping" or "vertical grouping" is seldom considered an essential condition of an open classroom.

Similarly, open-space architecture, which does away with classroom walls and clusters several learning groups, each with a teaching team, in "pods" or "bays" around a central "media center," is not a necessity for open education. In fact, many who have evolved open methods prefer the self-contained classroom, because it provides the security of familiar structure, small scale, privacy, and quiet in which the teacher can adjust to the difficult changes that open education requires in her relationships with children. This is not to say that open educators disdain handsome new buildings with modern equipment and ample space. Rather they believe that teachers, like children, learn in different styles and at different paces, and need space organized in such a manner that they will feel secure when trying new things.

There are several more sophisticated conceptualizations of open education, which grew out of combined theories from philosophy, sociology, and several branches of psychology. The definition of Bernard Spodek, of the University of Illinois, illustrates this combination.

1. School activities are goal oriented rather than ritual oriented. Goals include developing intellectual, language, and social skills, developing values, developing ways of dealing with affect, and developing personal autonomy.
2. School activities presented are developmentally appropriate for the children in the group.
3. Children in the classroom are involved in the decision-making process of the group. Respect for children underlies the decision-making process as well as all teacher-child interactions.
4. Learning is viewed as taking place as a result of the child's acting on the environment, abstracting information, and operating on this information in some intellectual manner.
5. Learning is viewed as taking place as a result of dialogue.[5]

Virgil Howes's description of the role of the student in the open classroom shows a similar combination of ideas. (1) "The child is central"—whereas in the traditional school (and even in individualized programs) the texts and knowledge are central. (2) "The child is whole" —development does not occur in the brain alone but in the whole physical and emotional being and in active interaction with the world. (3) "The child grows in his feelings of control over his own learning." (4) "He functions on the basis of open rather than closed systems:" teachers do not have predetermined ends for the child.[6]

Since open education requires no specified school organization, curriculum materials, or behaviors for teachers or children—in short, no "treatment", Educational Testing Service evaluators compare it to other currently popular kinds of teaching on the basis of how much input teachers contribute to decisions about what is learned, and how much input comes from the children.[7]

The table below especially highlights the difference between open education and "free schools." In the free, or "laissez-faire" school the children choose what they will do in school, and the teacher will seldom interject

	input:	*general type of classroom*
child	high	open education
teacher	high	
child	high	"free" school
teacher	low	
child	low	traditional
teacher	high	
child	low	programmed instruction
teacher	low	

decisions. This reflects the free-school philosophy that a child's first-hand spontaneous experiences with freely chosen subjects will be sufficient, over time, for learning whatever he truly needs to know. In this view, the teacher who places herself between the child and his learning is more hindrance than help. In contrast, open educators believe a three-way relationship—child-teacher-materials, or what David Hawkins calls *"I-Thou-It"*—defines the essence of education.

> When *you* give a child a range from which to make choices, *he* then gives you the basis for deciding what should be done next, what further opportunities you should give him—materials and suggestions that are responsive to his earlier choices and that may amplify their meaning and deepen his involvement. That is *your* decision. It's dependent on *your* goals, it's something you are responsible for . . . The investment in a child's life that is made in this way by an adult, the teacher in this case, is something that adds to and in a way transforms the interests the child develops spontaneously . . . [The child's deep involvement with things *provided by the teacher* is terribly important]. . . . For the child this is not merely something fun to play with . . . it's also a basis for communication with the teacher on a new level and with a new dignity. Until a child is going on his own . . . thinking his own thoughts and making his own unique individual kinds of self expression out of them, there isn't anything for the teacher to respect, except a potentiality. So the first act in teaching, it seems to me, . . . is to encourage this kind of engrossment. Then the child comes alive for the teacher as well as the teacher for the child. They have a common theme for discussion, they are involved together in the world.[8]

The curious teacher—a curiosity?

By emphasizing the high level of choice open education demands of both children and teachers, the Educational Testing Service conception highlights the most important difference between the way an open education teacher works and the way most American teachers do their jobs. Even the idiosyncratic, star-performer teacher, who is not ruled by textbook or

curriculum and is acclaimed for her own highly personalized style, is traditional, according to the ETS concept, if she fails to consider children's choices as well as her own judgment. The ETS researchers stress that open education implies a new job description for the teacher—relating one-to-one, not one-to-thirty; inviting and respecting decisions made by children; learning as well as teaching; and continually designing or revising learning materials to fit the children. Such a teacher sees the elementary classroom as a place of learning for herself as well as for children. There she studies the child as well as the subjects that appeal to the children's and her own curiosity.

It is hard for a teacher to be open, curious, and creative if she has spent her career trying to dispense knowledge and control behavior, and if her own professional education and experience have consisted of knowledge dispensed and decisions controlled by superiors. But the evidence that American public school teachers can change can be found in open classrooms from Harlem to Watts; from Minot, North Dakota, to Lenoir, North Carolina; from Old Glastonbury, Connecticut to Huntington Beach, California—in inner city, small town, and suburban schools.

How have they been able—or enabled—to change? As mentioned above, the reports of the English open education movement describe several factors supporting change in English school systems. These are:

1. Educational leadership by the principal or headteacher.
2. The availability of a resource teacher (or the principal) to advise a teacher in her own classroom.
3. Individualized curriculum developed in each school.
4. Pragmatic professional education, especially inservice.
5. Mutually supportive relationships with parents.

The literature on the change process in American schools suggests these factors must be provided if similar change is to occur here.

In the early 1960s, Louis Rubin and his colleagues at the University of California, Santa Barbara, wrote about the barriers to change they experienced in a five-year project to innovate schools, and especially to develop correspondences in curriculum and teaching methods from kindergarten through high school in Santa Barbara County. Rubin concluded that change pursued for the sake of being fashionable or to attract funding does not take hold. Innovation should not be attempted until administrators shake off their "orthodox conceptions" about how they work, how teachers work, and how they work together; and until learning goals are studied, understood, established, and commonly accepted by the whole staff. Change requires "self-renewal" in both principals and teachers.[9]

In the 1969 Goodlad survey of "blunted reforms," the failure to change was attributed to absence of factors such as those above:

—Lack of leadership by the principal: "Because they are rewarded for maintaining the [status quo], administrators are not likely either to challenge it or to reward subordinates who do."

—Lack of in-school help for teachers: "If teachers are to change they must see models of what they are to change to; they must practice under guidance the new behaviors called for."

—Tired curriculum: "The schools are bogged down with routine trivialities and the lesser literacies."

—Poor professional education: "General failure to [educate teachers for self-renewal] constitutes the greatest failure of our educational system."

—Alienated parents: "Educators who push at the forefront of innovative practice stand ready to show their community-inflicted scars."

Goodlad concluded that the individual school, operating as an independent educational unit, *can* generate change, as curriculum programs and methods imposed from above cannot. But first principals and teachers must "fashion new norms, roles, supports, and rewards for themselves."[10]

This point is emphasized in Seymour B. Sarason's *The Culture of the School and the Problem of Change* (1971). During ten years of helping teachers deal with students' emotional and learning problems, Sarason and his colleagues in Yale's Psycho-Educational Clinic observed and analyzed the social system of the individual school. They concluded that the dynamics of a whole school, not any individual persons or products within it, control the results of innovation. Good ideas and missionary zeal are sometimes enough to change the thinking and actions of individuals; they are rarely, if ever, effective in changing complicated organizations (like the school) with traditions, dynamics, and goals of their own.[11]

Sarason spotlights the bulkiest change barriers in a school: the role of the principal, the attitudes and capabilities of teachers, the curriculum (which not only evades, but appears to defy the needs of children), the lack of supportive personnel for teachers, and the strained relationships with parents.

Sarason disagrees with sociologists who construct theories about the change process in all schools and then put forth a "model" of how to change. He believes sociologists know far less than they think they do about the actual functioning of schools as systems, and that existing models for school change derive far too much from the psychology of the individual and the experience of industry. Sarason says there is no one way to start innovation in a school; every would-be school innovator must design his own plan, taking the following precautions: (1) Untangle the strands of *role* relationships (not personality relationships), rules, traditions, and educational values that make up the web of community life in your school. (2) Identify and plan how to deal with sources of opposition. (3) Figure out how you're going to make decisions: you *have* to have leadership; do you also have to have complete representativeness in the decision-making group? (4) Face up to how long it's going to take—not how long to see results but how long *just to get started*.

The main function of a plan for innovation should not be techniques for persuading others to accept the changemaker's ideas, Sarason says, but rather techniques for gathering information about the basic "regularities" in children's and adults' behavior in the school, and the written and unwritten rules everyone seems to acknowledge. All of this should focus on the whole setting, not on individual personalities. Such information is usually surprising, even to insiders in the school, and it generates many practical alternative change strategies.

> I would suggest that where one starts [the change process] has to be with a problem that is presented to and discussed with the target groups—not as a matter of empty courtesy or ritualistic adherence to some vague democratic ethos but because *it gives one a more realistic picture of what one is dealing with. An obvious consequence of this is that in different settings one may very well answer the question of where to start rather differently,* a consequence that those who need to follow a recipe will find unsatisfactory. . . . [12]

The purpose and plan of this book

Such different starts in different settings are reported in this book. All together they show that, just as there is no one model for conducting an open classroom, neither is there a recipe for introducing open education. Thus the different beginnings here reported are not recommended as models to be copied but as studies of factors which have enabled teachers to change toward open education. These factors may well be crucial to change in the reader's situation: The role of the principal, the resource of an in-classroom advisor, new curriculum, inservice education for teachers, and relationships with parents. The following five chapters focus on these factors, as they have been used to support teachers in different American public schools. The final chapter describes problems in evaluation which open education poses for teachers, administrators, and parents, and which thus relate to all of the support factors. This organization of the book is intended to focus the reader's attention on his own situation, first identifying support factors that will be necessary and then locating potential sources of support. (Appendix 2 provides some study questions for each chapter, designed to help the reader—or a group—estimate the potential for changing their own school.)

Informal reports such as this are intended to communicate experience among professionals and concerned laymen pursuing common objectives, rather than to recruit new adherents to a cause or to announce research findings. Addressing American educators just entering or midstream in open education projects, this book suggests that their plans can be informed and enriched by news and commentary about promising practices elsewhere, even though the work reported is still in development. Lillian Weber observed that the richness of English practice was in large part produced by the cross-fertilization effect of informal communications among experimenting infant school teachers, head teachers, county and national ad-

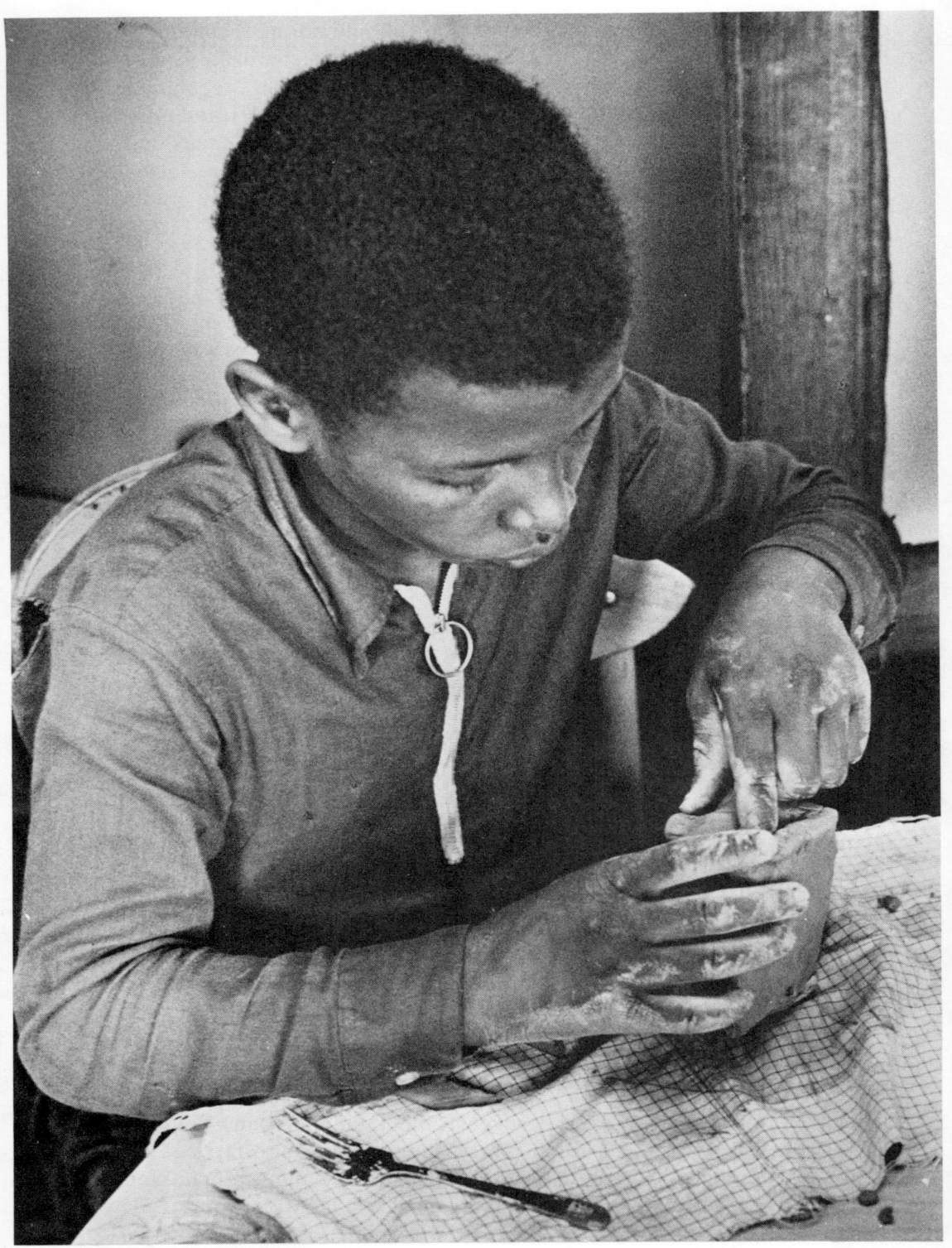

visors. Emulating them, Weber makes frequent reports of her own work in New York City, emphasizing experiences rather than expertise.

> We are learning. Of course, we don't know all about it . . . but we don't wait for a shining completeness. We publish and say what we believe today. Further assessment and thought is our constant responsibility.[13]

Such communications also suggest promising paths and places for research. Thus they may tend to reverse the recent relationship existing in the United States between school people on the one hand and academicians and researchers on the other. The American curriculum reform movement of the 1950s and 1960s was one of theories and programs initiated by scholars and then tried out on teachers and children. (As one observer put it, the university mathematicians invented the new math, and then they discovered they would also have to invent children that it would fit.) American advocates of open education—many of them associated with universities and with research and development organizations—insist that teachers' experiences should be the mother of scholars' invention, not the other way around.

William P. Hull, who brought Americans the first reports of Leicestershire schools, is one who says the American curriculum reform movement now should be investing in research into the nature of children's complex thinking as it develops in informal classrooms. But a teacher who manages an open classroom could not do such research well, Hull believes, because he or she is like a juggler who can't stop to analyze his performance for fear he'll drop the balls. On the other hand, researchers—people with "advanced skill in playing with a limited number of variables"—are mostly unable or unwilling "to face the daily complexity which confronts the classroom teacher."[14]

Thus David Hawkins, an American philosopher of science and education and an open education theorist and curriculum developer, calls for academic researchers to tie themselves to the classroom—not in order to "certify" what goes on, but to learn.

> For it will turn out, at least today, that the authorities [in the study of the intellectual development of young children] are persons who have made a great investment in working with the unformed child who in turn is happily involved with the unformed clay or sand. . . . Thus it is my plea to the intellectuals . . . who would contribute to the practical improvement of education . . . that they first seek out the best existing practice and apprentice themselves to it.[15]

Footnotes

1. John Goodlad, "The Schools vs. Education," *Saturday Review of Literature*, April 19, 1969, pp. 59-60.
2. *Ibid.*, p. 59.
3. The following books, articles, and research papers contributed to our definition.

a) David Armington, "A Plan for Continuing Growth," *Open Education: A Sourcebook for Parents and Teachers*, ed. E.B. Nyquist and G.R. Hawes (New York: Bantam, 1972).

b) Roland Barth, "Assumptions About Children's Learning," *Open Education: The Informal Classroom*, ed. C. Rathbone (New York: Citation Press, 1971).

c) Anne Bussis and Edward Chittenden, *Analysis of An Approach to Open Education* (Princeton, N.J.: Educational Testing Service, 1970).

d) *Conditions for Growth*, Education Development Center Follow Through Program, 53 Chapel St., Newton, Mass.

e) Ruth Flurry, "Open Education: What Is It?" *Open Education: A Sourcebook for Parents and Teachers*, pp. 102-108.

f) Theodore Manolakes, "What is of Most Worth to the Child? A View of Modern British Infant Education." (Speech presented at the National Association of Elementary School Principals, Miami, Florida, April 11, 1972.)

g) Hermine Marshall, "Criteria for an Open Classroom," *Young Children* 28, no. 1 (October 1972): 13-19.

h) "People and Parameters," *Insights* 4, no. 7 (April 1972). The newsletter of the New School for Behavioral Studies in Education, University of North Dakota, Grand Forks, N.D.

i) Excerpts from the Plowden Report, *Open Education: The Informal Classroom*.

j) Charles Rathbone, "The Implicit Rationale of the Open Education Classroom," *Open Education: The Informal Classroom*.

k) Vincent Rogers, *Teaching in the British Primary School* (New York: Macmillan, 1970).

l) Herbert Walberg and Susan Thomas, *Characteristics of Open Education: Toward an Operational Definition* (Newton, Mass., 1971).

m) Herbert Walberg and Susan Thomas, "Open Education: An Operational Definition and Validation in Great Britain and the United States," *American Educational Research Journal* 9, no. 2 (Spring 1972): 197-207.

n) Lillian Weber, *The English Infant School and Informal Education* (Englewood Cliffs, N.J.: Prentice-Hall, 1971).

4. William Hull, "The Case for the Experimental School," *Insights* 4, no. 1 (September 1971): 2-11.
5. Bernard Spodek (Speech presented at the National Association for the Education of Young Children Annual Conference, November 1972, Atlanta, Ga.).
6. Virgil Howes, personal communication. This material is included in a different form in *Informal Teaching in the Open Classroom* (New York: Macmillan, forthcoming).
7. Taken from a chart in Bussis and Chittenden, *Analysis of An Approach to Open Education*, p. 23.
8. David Hawkins, "I-Thou-It," *Open Education: The Informal Classroom*, pp. 91-92.
9. Louis J. Rubin, *Synergetics and the School* and *The Nurturance of Teacher Growth* (University of California: Center for Coordinated Education, 1966).
10. John Goodlad, "The School vs. Education," pp. 60-61, 80.
11. Seymour Sarason, *The Culture of School and the Problem of Change* (Boston: Allyn and Bacon, Inc., 1971), p. 213.
12. *Ibid.*, p. 217.

13. Lillian Weber, personal communication.
14. William Hull, "The Case for the Experimental School," pp. 2-11.
15. David Hawkins, "Childhood and the Education of Intellectuals," *Outlook* 7 (Winter 1972): 29. (Mountain View Center for Environmental Education, The University of Colorado, Boulder, Colo.)

Chapter 2

A Different Role for the Principal

Hoping to start and sustain an American open education movement that would not slavishly follow the English model but might parallel its achievements, Lillian Weber wrote:

> We search for clues to organization and there seems to be a special clue in the *active* participation of English [head teachers with] teachers . . . in the development of method and curriculum. English heads remain teachers, actively participating in the educational life of the school.[1]

Moreover, English principals are teacher trainers first and foremost, observe Ann Cook and Herb Mack.

> [They see themselves] as supports for staff, as catalysts, as innovators. . . . *All [give] priority to their role in the classroom, alongside of the teacher, subtly communicating style.* In practicing teacher training, [they have] a framework within which they want teachers to work—a definable direction, a philosophy—clearly demonstrated in action and usually articulated in words.[2] (Emphasis added.)

The English head—a teacher of teachers

Such a role is possible in schools which are, by urban American standards, so very small—200 to 350 pupils and eight to ten teachers—and in which the head teacher hires the new teachers. The English head can be a teacher of teachers rather than a director of teachers and building manager. As another American observer, Mark Heyman notes:

> Promotion to Head, usually preceded by service as Assistant Head, is a recognition of talent for teaching and for leadership among teachers; the assignment is not "a promotion out of teaching."[3]

An English educator emphasizes that the head teacher position is located at the top of the English educational career ladder. After a year observing the American public schools, Peter Raggatt wrote:

> [The English head] is a successful and experienced teacher who regards teachers, not the local administration, as his reference group. Usually a headship is the end of a career line; the American principal, however, identifies fairly early in his career with the local administration. . . . The principalship is a qualification that can lead to the central office and perhaps to a superintendency.[4]

Americans assume that English head teachers have more freedom from central office interference than do American principals. Whether this is strictly true is not clear: not all English heads act as independently as do the heads who have pioneered open education. Such head teachers would say that they are "autonomous" in relation to their local education authority, but this would be an exaggeration, reports Maurice Kogan.

> British education is characterized by the freedom of the schools to create their own curriculum, modes of internal grouping and organization, and style and attitudes in relationship to children. . . . That freedom is sometimes exaggerated and misunderstood. But it is real, and, in comparison with that of any other major educational system, emphatically unique.[5]
>
> [However] it cannot be true that heads are entirely autonomous, because, if this were so, one would find far greater variations within local authority areas [comparable to our school districts]. Instead, there is a degree of congruity of style and approach . . . the areas best known for their achievements have common features that imply a common source of policy and inspiration.[6]

This common source of inspiration for innovative heads has been the local education authority (L.E.A.), presided over by an energetic and innovative chief education officer. Where open education flourishes, the climate for change has been created by such officials, and the new ideas carried by advisors from the L.E.A. headquarters going into schools to assist and train teachers. In addition, the national department of education has contributed strongly to a climate of change through the work of Her Majesty's Inspectors who visit schools to maintain standards, and through the influence of the prestigious Plowden Committee (of which Kogan was the secretary), which published its detailed endorsement of open education in 1966. However, the manner in which new ideas are to be implemented in schools is not prescribed, nor is change required. Such decisions belong to the head.[7] As Kogan puts it, "What can be said about the British headteacher is that he enjoys discretion, and that he believes in it. . . . "[8]

The American principal—a building and personnel manager

The average American principal, in contrast, views himself not as a senior teacher but as a junior administrator, and commonly looks to superiors or to outside experts to make educational policy. This is a central observation made by Mary Bentzen as she led an I/D/E/A research group investigating the process of change in several Southern California schools associated as the League for Cooperating Schools.[9]

> The principals were faced with the premise that they were to be the key agents of change. Though they did not understand what was meant by "key agent," the principals at least recognized that they, and not their superintendents, were going to be on the front line of educational change. . . . [But] the principals expected League meetings to [not only] provide them with oppor-

tunity to exchange ideas about improving schooling, they really assumed from the outset that I/D/E/A would provide answers and direction.[10]

That principals view themselves as followers rather than leaders is an unmistakable impression from surveys of principals themselves, carried out within the past five years by the Department of Elementary School Principals (formerly affiliated with the National Education Association), and by the Center for the Advanced Study of Educational Administration at the University of Oregon.

The D.E.S.P. study, based on 2,318 replies from American principals to a 1967 questionnaire, shows that the great majority of them did not experience close involvement in the learning program in their schools.

They did not do regular classroom teaching. (Less than 20 percent said they spent half time or more in the classroom, and nearly 60 percent said they spent no time in classrooms.)[11]

They did not act as teacher educators. (There was not a single entry on the questionnaire that suggested that an activity of the principal might be to provide inservice education for his or her staff.)

Most did not control hiring of staff. (Only 29 percent said they had a major hiring role, while 38 percent said they had nothing to say about hiring faculty.)[12]

They did not control their school budgets. (Only 24 percent said they "plan, recommend, and defend" expenditures for their schools.)[13]

By and large their central offices did not invite them to participate in district-wide policy making. (Only 27 percent said they were "invited to participate.")[14]

They did not shape their own instructional programs. They replied that they could "modify and adapt" the district curriculum plan (54 percent), "exert some influence" (40 percent), or "follow closely" (6 percent).[15] Among principals in districts larger than 25,000 pupils, 41 percent said they worked with staff "to list the instructional materials needed for our program;" while 59 percent had to accept what the district provided.[16]

From its interviews with 270 principals in 1971 the Oregon Center concluded:

> Principals typically are concerned about the imbalance of managerial and educational responsibilities inherent in their position . . . [and] are uncertain about how they might delegate . . . "housekeeping chores" . . . to obtain more time for supervision, planning, and evaluation. . . . [17]

Yet the American principal has a wide area in which to operate if he or she is alert enough to claim it, Seymour Sarason contends.

> Any job description of a principal consists essentially of a set of generalizations, which, if anything, states or implies the minimum limits or scope of the position. It does not describe the maximum limits. . . . The range in practices among principals within the same system is sufficiently great so as to suggest

that the system permits and tolerates passivity and activity, conformity and boldness, dullness and excitement, incompetence and competency.[18]

Deterrents to leadership

Given that the door to educational leadership, if not wide open, is at least not tightly locked, why do so few American principals walk through it? The reasons Sarason, Goodlad, their colleagues, and others suggest have to do with working conditions, professional background, working style, view of self, and view of the system.

American urban schools are so large (the median size of school in the D.E.S.P. survey was 490 pupils) in comparison to those in England that even a principal with the will to emulate an English head teacher finds this difficult. Sarason generalizes from the Yale Psycho-Educational Clinic staff's observations of many principals whom one might think were in favorable positions to begin change—having just been appointed to head a new school.

> From the time of appointment until the formal opening of the school the new principal spends almost all of his time in what can only be called housekeeping matters: ordering books, supplies, and furniture, assigning rooms, arranging schedules, negotiating the transfer of students from other schools, interviewing and selecting prospective personnel, making up bus schedules, etc., etc., etc.[19]

In this era of declining budgets and disappearing assistant principal positions these housekeeping burdens are increasing. Educational decisions do not get priority attention.

> [W]hat life in the classroom should be, how teachers will be related to decisions and planning about educational values and goals . . . tend not to be issues about which he is set to do anything, or very much. It might be more fair to say that the principal is concerned with these issues but he is acutely aware that he does not know what to do about them.[20]

The average American principal's training and experience has not led him to encounter new learning theory relating to young children, much less practice it with real children, or to lead teachers' investigations of new methods.

Both the D.E.S.P. and the Oregon surveys of principals underline this point. The former shows that whereas the majority of principals valued a college course in "child growth and development" as the most important study area for the preparation of beginning principals,[21] the questionnaire did not even list child development as a "major area of undergraduate or graduate study by principals."[22] Nearly 75 percent of the respondents took their graduate work in some form of administration; only 7 percent in elementary instruction and 10 percent in "elementary supervision and curriculum."[23]

As the Oregon survey concludes:

> Because of the traditional nature of preservice programs in elementary school administration, principals tend to view their roles in "old-fashioned" managerial terms.[24]

Sarason,[25] Goodlad,[26] Bentzen and Tye[27] observe that since American school systems primarily value and reward orderliness and conformity in teachers, those principals who have come up through teaching ranks are likely to be short on creative ideas and leadership.

The conventional principal's style of working is likely to increase his handicap in dealing with educational policy matters, because this style prevents the principal from learning from and with the teachers, who are directly in touch with children. (The D.E.S.P. questionnaire, asking principals to choose their most frequent source of innovative ideas, does not even provide "teachers in my school" as a possible choice.[28]) Furthermore, Sarason believes that the average principal feels powerless to change classroom teaching practices he disapproves of. He is keenly aware that he is viewed as a judge in the classroom rather than as a colleague and teacher of teachers, and is thus resented. Sarason says the principal therefore may avoid classroom observation of teachers, feeling incapable of offering corrections or suggestions in a manner that an inadequate teacher could accept undefensively.[29]

This view of himself as supposedly powerful but actually impotent in relation to teachers is mirrored in the average principal's view of his relationship with the system.

> [T]he bulk of the meetings in which the [new] principal participates are with administrative personnel not only for the purpose of setting up house but in order [for him] to learn the rules and regulations relevant to whatever decisions he must make and plans that he has. The principal views these meetings . . . in terms of accommodating to the roles and power of others . . . and not in terms of using the system to achieve his purposes.[30]

All of these reasons—professional background, working conditions, working style, and view of the system—suggest why an average American principal does not innovate, even though in charge in an institution—the individual school—which in Goodlad's view is *the* strategic unit for change in American education.[31]

Sarason offers his diagnosis of the principal's problem not in despair, for he also encounters effective principals, but in hope of change. Schools can improve, he believes, if the people in them concentrate objectively and nonjudgmentally on the unproductive rules, roles, programs, and social patterns they're following unthinkingly, and stop blaming personalities—namely each other.[32]

Analysis of a failure

Such a modest, unimpassioned approach is not in the American reformist tradition. However, Roland Barth has written a case study of a failure in school reform, which suggests that the reformist tradition itself needs reform. In *Open Education and the American School* (1972) Barth cites the following reasons for failure of a project reforming elementary schools in a black district of a big Eastern city. Several of these reasons are characteristics common among current educational innovations: too much money, too little time, too vague goals, the arrogance of the reformers, their failure to understand and involve existing staff, parents, and children, and the complexity of the new administrative structures.

In the project Barth describes, the new administration abandoned the role of the elementary school principal and distributed authority and duties among a half dozen new executives responsible for two neighboring, but socioeconomically different schools. However, none of these new executive positions was designed to give the grass roots leadership Barth deems vital for a project aiming toward open education. As a result, Barth recounts:

> The central office and university designed program was implemented without consulting parents or existing staff.
>
> The program had no specific instructional goals relating to the children in the two schools, but only commitment to rescue them from academic failure and self-rejection and to try out, in a part of the project, the new ideas of open education.
>
> There was no sharing of policy and administrative decisions with faculty, but also no visible clear leader who could and would say "the buck stops here."
>
> The project hired new teachers for the open classrooms who did not understand the educational implications of the physical set-up, had had minimum teaching experience, had not had experience with black children, and had not "resolved their own authority problems."
>
> Parents were not consulted about assigning children to the open rooms.
>
> The project sprung open classrooms suddenly on the children and "violated the expectations of the school" held by children who could conceive only two alternatives—strict control or chaos.

Although the project failed, the idea of open education survived and Barth reports a fresh start is making headway in the same community. Even without that hopeful postscript, Barth's study would have a silver lining because it serves so admirably as a cautionary tale. It suggests that even though the old-fashioned role of the principal represses innovation, the solution is not to abandon that role. Also, Barth's report calls into question Americans' notions about the scale and pace of change. We are used to the idea of change being expressed in words like "task force," "massive intervention," "thrust," "exogenous shocks to the system." These terms are appropriate for the transcontinental railroad, major surgery, moon shots, and Super Bowls, but they may be too threatening to institutions like schools, which are no longer young and do not respond well to shock therapy. Fear of forced change may cause people to be more change-resistant than they might otherwise be.

Educational reformers who have relied on leadership by outsiders with reputations as experts, star performers or, worse, mavericks have encountered this resistance. As one teacher in an apparently hopelessly bogged down school system commented, "Probably the maverick image is the worst possible one for a principal wanting to bring about change here."[34]

The determined innovator who decides, with these cautions in mind, that he can neither bulldoze nor bedazzle the system with a new project, begins instead to look around for cracks to infiltrate, boats to rock gently. As Barth notes, it is not usually necessary to *control* the central office but to *understand* it, in order to exploit opportunities and/or circumvent frustrating procedures.[35]

An understanding of the central office is, in fact, indispensable for the principal of an innovating school, for principals are caught in the middle between teachers and parents—and the district bureaucracy. They must know district policies and personalities in order to know how much they can maneuver and how to react in a crisis. A principal of a California suburban school, determined to continue the open program he and his teachers had started, but facing the hostility of conservative parents who had tried to have him fired, defined his job as taking the heat off teachers, and also off the central office. He expected no support from the superintendent. "He's in a survival role. He doesn't come to observe the school, because if he comes he'll have to take a position. As long as we try to change, I'll be vulnerable," he said.[36]

Ingredients of success: timing, scale, space, and pace

A number of central office actions can be used by a principal as opening wedges for open education: his own appointment as a new principal; a new or a remodeled school building; federal grant money; desegregation; decentralization; student teacher programs; year-round scheduling; etc.

An example of such an opportune way of beginning open education is provided by Open Corridor in District 3 of the New York City public schools. Although it was initiated not by a principal, but by City College professor Lillian Weber, who was placing and supervising student teachers within the public schools, Open Corridor's experience illuminates many of the problems a principal initiating change must face. First of all, Weber understood the system well enough to recognize and seize the opportunities of the diffusion of power created by parents' activism and district decentralization. Then she developed the program on the basis of her understanding of the social relationships that control whatever happens in New York schools. As Weber describes the beginnings of Open Corridor in 1968:

> I decided to take a small piece of a school because I could not wait for consensus about the whole issue of decentralization and community control. When you begin to believe something is possible—then you begin. I did not ask the Board of Education. I did not begin with a whole school of 40 teachers. Growth would come from the delicate thread of voluntarism. Four or five teachers in one school wanted to change. That was a good number to begin with. It was also a good number of parents—150 sets or individuals—to involve in planning meetings and in parent pressure on administration to support teachers.[37]

Weber points out that starting small also has the advantage of not needing large infusions of new money, for which the innovators must show early results.

> Our particular task was how to get open classrooms with the least possible amount of change. The idea that you can't make something good without funding was drummed out of me by my long years in early childhood education. Our standards did not depend upon dollars. I'm not opposed to life being made easier by getting money. I'm opposed to the notion that the children will wait. All our teachers make their own materials. They insist on spending their part of the school budget for supplies in their own way.[38]

Organized parents provided the clout to hire a principal who allowed the teachers to control this budget. Weber provided the know-how about what materials to make.

Starting small was a necessity that she used as a virtue. Weber had no choice but to start with the few teachers and parents who shared her commitment, and with the old-fashioned facilities that were available—several self-contained classrooms opening onto a corridor.

> We used our separate classrooms as a strength; an advantage over the new architecture of the "open plan" school. The points of teachers' starting toward openness are very different and their rates of growth are different. This is how we work with children; so it must be how we work with teachers. The separate classrooms allowed teachers to move toward community with each other according to their own styles and strengths, and to move very slowly toward common efforts like planning together, sharing materials, and exchanging teaching assignments.[39]

In the limited shared space of the corridor, Weber initiated the new open program by working for an hour a day or so with 25 children—five from each classroom. She provided manipulative materials, active-learning projects, games, and group activities. The teachers in their own rooms with their doors open could see what was going on. Bit by bit they learned their own active, open styles of teaching by working with Weber in the corridor, while their classes were "covered" by student teachers from Weber's program at CCNY. Because the children were so actively involved on the corridor and were a small group, discipline was not a difficult problem. Children accepted alternating their corridor activities with their controlled classroom work once they were sure that the corridor activities would continue.

Weber emphasizes that the exposure of the corridor had distinct advantages over a resource teacher in a resource room's "closed door situation," from which she thinks it is much harder to spread innovation into the regular classroom program. The work in the corridor served as "a public statement." It told the principal, parents, and other teachers what open education means. It resulted in other teachers voluntarily joining the Open Corridor program. The principle which Open Corridor upholds above all is "community," a commitment to common purpose by teachers, outside advisors, principal, and parents. Such solidarity can take form only on a small scale, and rapid or forced growth destroys it.

One hazard of starting small is that the beginning which is permitted for a small, self-made community of teachers may be restricted in influence by a principal who really wants only what Weber calls "encapsulated tokens" or "islands" in a school. For instance, the principal may permit only one first grade that's open, and one second grade. Weber believes it is essential for teachers to have channels for working together and for new teachers to join an open corridor community or to form new ones.

Another hazard is the tendency of Americans to regard small enterprises as being only tentative and experimental, as if only large undertakings can achieve the permanence of success. "I am against the conception of a change to open education as an experiment," says Weber. The decision to change ought to be made with caution but with no tolerance of the idea "that if it doesn't work you'll turn back the clock to what you were doing before."

To principals who have approached me I say, "Look, this is not a fad. It's something that cannot be done without a long-range commitment." A principal who wants to do open education should engage with his staff in discussions and reading, to understand the goals of open education, that may take many months. He should find out about available teacher workshops, to develop the practice of open teaching. It may be that six months after the inquiry period begins he will find three or four teachers that really want to try this. His role should be to facilitate their progress.[40]

"Remember that you are changing people. . ."

Facilitating was the role chosen by Mary Stitt when in the fall of 1967 she began her first job as principal at Clive Elementary School, a K-5 school with about 560 pupils in Arlington Heights, Illinois. During that year, an activity program evolved after an afternoon of brainstorming by the staff during a winter Institute Day. The entire school separated at 2:30 p.m. on Friday afternoons, and each child chose to go to a classroom that provided encouragement for his particular interest (pets, French, knitting, cooking, etc.). The teachers coordinated the interest groups and observed that for the first time children were excited about school, that children's interests in their projects inspired cooperation, and that they (the teachers) were gaining new insights into each child.

The next fall, some of the Olive teachers wanted to continue this multi-age, activity-style teaching, but others held back. Rather than continue the program without the support of the entire staff, the new program was dropped. But that year the school obtained a $1,500 grant under Title III of ESEA and used the money to pay for released time to allow the Olive staff to visit schools using multi-age grouping and to purchase consultant help from Bernard Spodek of the University of Illinois, Department of Early Childhood Education. Spodek wanted to help American teachers evolve their own form of open education rather than use British infant schools as a model. As Stitt wrote to her superintendent:

> I believe the teachers at Olive feel a sense of freedom so that they can try many things. However, I have not tried to cram new programs down their throats. Some things I would like to have started I didn't, just because they were my ideas.[41]

After this preparation, Olive School opened its first multi-age classroom in September 1969. Parents were asked to volunteer their children for this class. The new school year had hardly begun when the open classroom teacher became seriously ill, and the superintendent recommended closing the classroom and returning the children to the single-age, more traditional classrooms. The other teachers and the parents, however, refused to give up the new program. Stitt saw this as an indicator of a growing cohesiveness that was bringing the staff together.

Because the new program was a shared endeavor by the whole staff, the traditional teachers were alert to the changes in the children in the open classroom. They saw the school's most troublesome problem—hostile behavior—begin to recede. Plans were made to open five more multi-age, active-learning classrooms in fall 1970. Spodek and four graduate students from the University of Illinois spent three days working with the staff at Olive the previous spring, and one teacher attended a workshop at the University that summer. During the next school year university advisors continued to work every week with Olive teachers in the classroom and in workshops.

There are now seven multi-age open classrooms at Olive; four primaries (six-, seven-, and eight-year-olds), and three intermediates (nine- and ten-year-olds). There are also single-grade classes at each grade level. Parents decide with teachers which classroom to place children in. Stitt is part of a study group in the district investigating open education in the middle school—sixth grade and junior high.

During the transition to open education Stitt used the school district's decentralized budgeting system (PPBS) to involve the whole staff in deciding how the building's budget would be spent.

> We have learned to set the instructional goals for the whole building. We decide together what our priorities will be. Our staff has grown professionally because they've accepted the responsibility for determining what kind of educational program we will have here. As a result, when we are asked to make a presentation about our school at a meeting, one of the staff may go instead of me.

When asked what advice she would give to other principals who wanted to bring about a similar change, Stitt said:

> Let it grow very slowly. You must first trust and respect your staff if you wish them to trust the children. You don't have to be a rebel: I'm pretty conservative. But I'm never afraid to tell people what I believe is right.
>
> Remember that you are *changing people*, not just putting in a new program. You have to believe philosophically in what you're doing, and be willing to live it, and to change to new and better ways. It has to be what you believe—and live.

"If you tell too much, they lose the spirit. . ."

At Grape Street School in Los Angeles, Carrie Haynes began her first job as a principal in the spring of 1969 in a setting very different from Mary Stitt's white middle-class suburban school:

> Located in a most vulnerable ghetto-setting in the heart of Watts, Grape Street Elementary School is nested in a pocket surrounded on all four sides by railroad tracks. After the trauma of a competitive examination which placed me number one on the principal's eligibility list of the Los Angeles City Schools Unified District, I, a Black woman, was given this assignment. When the announcement was made, I heard that many teachers were dismayed. . . . When I endeavored to become acquainted by visiting classrooms, I found many of the doors locked.
>
> My observations revealed such bland and bleak efforts, except in a few classrooms, I decided to ask teachers to formulate plans for reading lessons. Only a few of the plans received were adequate.
>
> In the fall of 1969, [a longtime teacher in the school] Mayme Sweeney, returned from a leave and introduced open structure to our school. Teachers looked around in her classroom in amazement and disbelief. She had perfect attendance every day. Her pupils just could not stay away from school. They had important responsibilities and work to be done. In Room 5, you name it

and they had it. A menagerie, a cash register, a typewriter, a post office, a turn-stile book holder, soft chairs, awning, measuring utensils, math materials, and on and on and on. Some teachers ridiculed the fact that all this junk was being assembled in this classroom. Others passed, lingered, or stopped in to envy the orderly manner in which each pupil planned and performed purposeful and meaningful activities. A few teachers began to question how they could individualize their instruction in some similar manner, and attended an ESEA Title III workshop on individualization.[42]

During the summer of 1970, three other teachers sold Haynes and the rest of the staff who could be reached on the idea of joining three other schools —one in Inglewood, one in Chula Vista, and one in Manhattan Beach—in a three-year project in open education funded by the Ford Foundation and directed by the International Center for Educational Development, a Los Angeles consulting group.

Each school has developed its own brand of open education because this type of program must be developed from within. Becoming a part of a project where others were involved lifted the morale of most Grape teachers. But the first, most important thing we did as a school was to find time to dialogue among ourselves. At first our talking seemed aimless. Some sessions were diatribes. But we were talking. And that was progress.[43]

Haynes recalls that Grape teachers' first attempts to make classrooms informal and child-appealing depended almost wholly on games— "checkerboards, playing cards, race cars, jacks and balls, dominoes, dice, and almost any recreational game you could name." Children were involved and busy, but only a few classrooms showed evidence of any academic learning. The School-Community Advisory Board, which was the parents' organization working with the school, helped deal with parents' complaints. Teachers' learning of how to make children's reading and math grow out of their involvement with games and activity centers was accomplished through staff meetings devoted to sharing what worked and working on inadequacies. These sessions have become a permanent, staff-run inservice program. School is dismissed at 2 p.m. every Wednesday so that teachers can take part in whole-staff or small-group workshops they plan themselves. Haynes believes that this self-conducted teacher education has produced the success which teachers and children enjoy today—great gains in student achievement, high teacher morale, strong community support, a national reputation for open education.

Mayme Sweeney, the first open classroom teacher at Grape who has been a leader of staff development, says teacher choice is essential in inservice.

> We've learned that if you tell teachers too much they lose the spirit. You have to leave them free to find out and decide for themselves. You must be careful not to go in with answers.

Haynes requires Grape teachers to create their own answers, suitable to their own pupils. A principal source of ideas is listening to their own students, but teachers also draw from ICED advisors, from teachers in other schools in the Ford project, from each other, and from Haynes herself. She knows every classroom and does not hesitate to suggest that a teacher look for help with a problem or to ask a teacher to share a successful solution. She talks with each teacher about his or her philosophy of teaching, and does not set forth her own model. The decision to mix age groups within classes in fall of 1972 was made by the whole staff after experiencing success with cross-age tutoring and visiting their project partner school in Chula Vista.

Staff development vs. charisma

Comparing the experience of Carrie Haynes and Mary Stitt one notes that both principals gave their teachers substantial teaching help, as distinguished from purely administrative support. This was natural, for Mary Stitt had been a science curriculum consultant and Carrie Haynes a reading expert. In addition, both provided their teachers with assistance in understanding the principles and goals of open education, in organizing their rooms, and developing learning materials. This aid came from professional advisors outside the two school systems rather than from district supervisors or coordinators. Both principals, however, emphasize that the most important thing they accomplished was staff unity and staff acceptance of responsibility for decision making.

This careful and patient work to make new patterns in principal and faculty relationships, similar to Sarason's recommendations, offers a more logical and objective explanation of Olive's and Grape's successes than does the reason more frequently cited for the success of open schools—that a "charismatic" principal succeeds where mere mortals fail.

Even if it is not possible, in a very large and diversely staffed school, to seek unanimity of goals among a whole staff, a principal can facilitate change by supporting and reinforcing the cohesiveness and mutual planning of a small group of teachers. David Bowick did this when he assumed the principalship at 49th Street School in Los Angeles, a K-6 school with 1,000 students, predominantly Black and from low-income homes. In 1970, his second year at the school, Bowick encouraged his teachers to visit other schools and to read about educational innovations, "so they could decide what kind of school we were going to have." As a result, Bowick recalls:

> A group of eight very powerful, good, young teachers decided they wanted to try open education. After they had written a proposal spelling out what they intended to do, we assigned them an old wing of the building. There were these grades: 5-4-3-2-2-1-1-K. They started very slowly in fall, 1971.
>
> The vice-principal and I were "administrative over-seers" of the program. The minischool had its own separate staff meetings and determined what administrative policies they wanted; then we worked with them to bring them about. For example, they decided to have seven classes and release one teacher to set up a "discovery" (special resource) room which all the children could use. We worked with parents and downtown to get the money and labor to set up the room for them. When they began to function as a unit—to go on trips and eat lunch together—we worked out schedules so they could do it easily. We supported children moving in and out of the classrooms.
>
> By spring, we felt fantastic changes in attitude and in learning—more than a nine-month gain in reading, which is far above the state average. The biggest gain is in students' ingenuity. A major goal was getting students to come to school—to like school and look forward to it. As a result of our new policies, which were very different from the old ghetto school ideas—for example, the vice-principal wouldn't whip children when teachers asked him to—some teachers transferred. But other teachers started asking to be transferred in. We ask that teachers put in a lot of time on planning and meeting together to make decisions. At first they objected, but then they realized they *can* shape the school to be the way they want it and they got really involved in making it happen.

At the end of the first year, tensions had built up between the minischool and the rest of the school, some of whom complained that the administration had been favoring the minischool. Bowick's solution was to divide the school into four clusters, of which the minischool was one. Each cluster set its own learning objectives, conducted its own inservice program, and managed its own curriculum materials budget.

For the open classroom teachers, Bowick's style has been a model for their own teaching. As one minischool teacher observed:

Dave Bowick and Dave Peha treat teachers in an open way. They are supportive. Their door is open. Seeing how they are with us, feeling how it makes me feel, has taught me that I have to have time to talk with children. They don't come into the room to pass judgment and spy on you. They don't say "prove it" to me. Instead when they evaluate they come in and sit down and talk with the children.[44]

Growth for traditional teachers too

Bowick's attentiveness to staff members not involved in the minischool is another aspect of his style worth emphasizing. Mel Suhd, consultant with the Advisory for Open Education in Los Angeles, elaborates on this point:

> This country is skewed very much in the direction of the "directive" teacher. If some of us want to move toward what we think is a more healthy way, we have to find subtle ways to give *directive* people experiences in self-initiation. We don't do this by dealing only with people we agree with. We need schools which can tolerate all sorts of teaching and give supports for growth to different kinds of teachers, just as we expect open classroom teachers to respond to many different kinds of learners. I speak of "opening education" because this wording does not leave out the traditional teacher. It says that the traditional parts of schooling are opening up and growing too.

Another viewpoint on this matter, and a different way of handling it from Bowick's, come from the experience of Herbert Shapiro, principal of P.S. 152, with an enrollment of 1,200 students in a middle-socio-economic class Brooklyn neighborhood. He and a few teachers began lunch-time seminars on open education a few years ago, and followed this with curriculum development workshops—for the principal along with teachers—at the Advisory for Open Education's New York City affiliate, Creative Teaching Workshop. Shapiro's participation made clear to other teachers in the school that he wanted change. Shapiro recalls:

> Our big question was, should we do the Lillian Weber Corridor thing—a small group working intensively? But the other teachers in the school said, "Why are we not being invited?" They would not permit us to leave them out, perhaps because they felt they too had to please the authority figure. Everybody knows what I'd like to see. Not everybody is convinced it's right, or is willing to make the effort required to redesign a classroom and a manner of teaching. So what do I do with those teachers who consider themselves strong traditional teachers? Is the help I give them different from what I give people who are reaching out for change with both hands?

> What I do is not require "open education" but do require that there be opportunities in classrooms for more flexible, richer experiences—more than textbooks and workbooks. Everyone in the building is making some effort because they are feeling the pressure of others who are farther along. There is some resentment of me for pushing. I don't mind.

The help that Shapiro has brought into the school by means of a small Carnegie Foundation grant is available to the whole staff. This is a teacher's resource center stocked and staffed two afternoons a week by two advisors from Creative Teaching Workshop. The advisors give workshops and go into classrooms only in response to teachers' requests.

Abilities and attitudes of the principal who makes change

The vignettes above indicate strong differences in personality and style among the principals described. These differences tend to obscure the characteristics they share in common, so that observers have to search determinedly for basic likenesses. The Oregon study of principals found the following commonalities among the principals it viewed as "beacons of brilliance."

1. Most did not intend to become principals . . . . [T]hey had intended to teach but were encouraged to become principals by their superiors.
2. Most expressed a sincere faith in children. Children were not criticized for failing to learn or for having behavioral difficulties. . . . [T]he administrators emphasized their responsibilities toward the solution of children's problems.
3. They had an ability to work effectively with people. . . . They were proud of their teachers and accepted them as professionally dedicated and competent people. They inspired confidence and developed enthusiasm. The principals used group processes effectively; listened well to parents, teachers, and pupils; and appeared to have intuitive skill and empathy for their associates.
4. They were aggressive in securing recognition of the needs of their schools. They frequently were critical of the restraints imposed by the central office and of the inadequate resources. . . . [T]hey frequently violated the chain of command, seeking relief for their problems from whatever sources that were potentially useful.
5. They were enthusiastic as principals and accepted their responsibilities as a mission rather than as a job. They recognized their role in current social problems. The ambiguities that surround them and their work were of less significance than the goals they felt were important to achieve. As a result, they found it possible to live with the ambiguities of their position.
6. They were committed to education and could distinguish between long-term and short-term educational goals. Consequently, they fairly well had established philosophies of the role of education and their relationship within it.
7. They were adaptable. If they discovered something was not working, they could make the necessary shifts and embark with some security on new paths.
8. They were able strategists. They could identify their objectives and plan means to achieve them. . . .[45]

Sarason identified similar qualities in principals he judged able to initiate change: (1) having an objective, calculating view of the school system

—especially the ability to assess the system's capacity to tolerate diversity; (2) viewing him/herself as "the primary determiner of action;" (3) viewing "the interests, problems, and characteristics of children" as the primary determiners of the school program; and (4) viewing teachers as capable and deserving of intellectual growth and participating in decisions.[46] Sarason comments:

> The principal may be this or that type of personality, he may be experienced or inexperienced, he may be likeable or otherwise, he may be intellectually bright or average—if he is not constantly confronting himself and others, and if others cannot confront him with the world of competing ideas and values shaping life in a school, he is an educational administrator and not an educational leader.[47]

The Oregon "beacons of brilliance" characteristics and Sarason's distinction between leadership and administration may be useful criteria for teachers, parents, or central office administrators to use in assessing the capacities of principals to head "opening" schools.

Training programs for principals

Where there is central administration support for open education, a program for implementation should include training for principals as well as for teachers, as is the case in any well-mounted innovation effort. For instance, in 1970, when the Hartford, Connecticut, school district embarked upon an open program for all primary grades in the district, the administration designed a six-weeks summer training program for principals. This was not to equip them to train their teachers, for the district provided a release-time, three-weeks, full-time course for teachers opening up their classrooms. Instead the principal-preparation course, which was voluntary, emphasized basic child development theory and teaching experience in an open classroom, with the objective of placing principals back in a teaching frame of mind. The course also stressed the new kinds of curriculum materials teachers need for open classrooms, the work that paraprofessionals do, and understanding of the teachers' need for unusual administrative support because of the extra work they take on and the insecurity they feel during the change-over. Perhaps most important, the Hartford principal-preparation program encouraged them to evaluate teachers differently than in the past.

In North Carolina, the State Department of Public Instruction offers state funds to school districts to install kindergartens, provided that the district commits itself to change from traditional to child-centered education. The commitment involves summer preparation not just for kindergarten teachers but for all first-, second-, and third-grade teachers and school specialists. The Early Childhood Division of the state department of education and the Learning Institute of North Carolina conducted summer institutes in open education for 2,000 teachers and 400 principals in the summer of 1972. The heart of the principals' one-week institute was daily workshops for eight to ten people in active-learning mathematics, environmental science, and using the child's own language for reading and writing. Participants were expected to exercise their own choices of workshops, to undertake and complete projects as children do in open classrooms, and to develop curriculum materials in the way open classroom teachers do. Workshops were led by experienced open classroom teachers from North Carolina and from English open schools.

In New York City, privately sponsored teachers' centers working with public school teachers also reach out to principals, encouraging them to enroll in workshops alongside their teachers. There is enough response from administrators for the Community Resources Institute to provide a two-week summer program for administrators only (30 principals, assistant principals, and district supervisors). They develop curriculum and exchange solutions to administrative problems caused by teachers' change to openness. Similarly, the Creative Teaching Workshop has moved from exclusive concentration on teachers to partnership with their principals —helping principals to assess the possibilities for changing their jobs so that they can act as producers of new methods and materials rather than as consumers only.

Convinced that the catalyst for change in a school is the self-renewal of the principal, Californians Keith Beery and Alfred Brokes designed a group dynamics workshop which a group of principals can conduct by themselves. The design originated as part of Project Catalyst, a consortium of ten elementary schools around San Francisco Bay, funded by the Bureau of Education of the Handicapped in the U.S. Office of Education. The goal of the project was to change participant schools enough so that teachers could "mainstream" children with behavioral and learning problems into regular classrooms. It was assumed that mainstreaming requires that all regular classrooms be more active, rich in materials, and individualized. The design of the Catalyst workshop calls for ten principals to meet twice a month and, with assistance from Beery's and Brokes's guidelines, help each other identify and express their goals for their schools, solve problems, and critique each others' patterns of working with teachers and children. Designing inservice programs, and making decisions based on objective information and in concert with faculties, are emphases in the guidelines. But Beery writes:

> We are asking (not telling) the educators in a variety of elementary schools what *they* see as their personal needs as well as what they see as the pupils' needs. We are asking *them* to identify their own resources, their personal and group strengths. We are asking them to identify their personal and building goals. We are asking them to create their own means for meeting their professional and pupil goals. We are asking them, in short, to design their own growth environments.[48]

The project is being evaluated by teachers' ratings of principals' growth in management style—such qualities as interpersonal relationships, decision making, sharing of responsibility, resource finding, staff development—and by measuring the growth in standardized reading scores, interpersonal relations and personal feelings of children in the participant schools. It is designed to spread by having principals after a year or two in a catalyst group, then form a new group of ten, for which they act as facilitators. Transportability of the workshop design is being tested in a number of states under grants from state departments of education.

Support for principals

Besides formal training programs, there are several actions an administration can take to help principals prepare for open education.
1. Provide opportunities for study of child development psychology and Piagetian learning theory, and reward these efforts.
2. Provide opportunities for returning to the classroom to work with children, and reward such efforts.
3. Relieve the principal of some of the burdens of red tape and central office meetings.
4. Consider administrative restructuring that would provide "career ladders" for advancement in the system through continuing growth and leadership in *instruction* as well as through management.
5. Put principals in touch with each other for problem sharing, problem solving, idea exchanges, and professional growth, rather than for management duties.

Realistic expectations

What one concludes after comparing the English experience with that of the Americans who have begun open education is that it is most realistic for Americans committed to this kind of change to look for principals who are strong and forward-looking leaders and who are involved with teachers and children, even though they may not be skilled teachers or teacher educators.

In her master's degree thesis summing up an investigation of the roles played by eight American principals in implementing open education in their schools, Gretchen Thomas concluded that "getting their teaching staffs and/or parents to work together to form educational goals for the children" was the single most important contribution the principals made, in their own estimations.

> Staff development, sometimes in the form of child development training and sometimes curriculum development, has been frequent (at least twice weekly; in most cases daily) and continuous. Whether this training takes place under the principal's direction or through a special program, the principal is an active participant, not just a facilitator.

Involvement of parents in planning the program, in providing materials and other physical improvements, and in working in the classroom has also been a central focus of the principal's work.

In their relationships with staff and parents, all eight principals believe they must "work with them in the same open way we ask them to work with children." They share with staff and parents the responsibilities for program design and development, trust both to make their own thoughtful, responsible decisions, and offer them choices in the type of education the school provides for children.[49]

Theodore Manolakes writes that the good American open school principal

should be a person with a vision of what the school might become and the ability to communicate this to authorities, citizens, and teachers. He [should] play a primary role in bringing together the proper mix of people and resources, as well as in creating a positive building climate for educational growth. This important role for the principal may not require a professional who is himself a great teacher, but rather one who can identify with good teaching and encourage it.[50]

Edward Chittenden agrees with Manolakes that American principals should not try to copy the English.

To ask one of our American principals to act like an English head is unreasonable. Our schools are so large. Many of our principals have had relatively little teaching experience and so are lacking in intuitive knowledge of ways to work with kids. A teacher in an open school said to me, "My principal is a tremendous support but no *help*."

Footnotes

1. Lillian Weber, *The English Infant School and Informal Education* (Englewood Cliffs, N.J.: Prentice-Hall, 1971), p. 248.
2. Ann Cook and Herb Mack, *The Headteacher's Role* (New York: Citation Press, 1971), p. 11.
3. Mark Heyman, "Learning from the British Primary Schools," *The Elementary School Journal* 72, no. 7 (April 1972): 340.
4. Peter Raggatt, "Administration in British Primary Schools," *The National Elementary Principal* 52, no. 3 (November 1972): 26.
5. Maurice Kogan, *The Government of Education* (New York: Citation Press, 1971), p. 13.
6. *Ibid.*, p. 29.

7. Sir Alec Clegg, *Revolution in the British Primary Schools* (Washington, D.C.: National Association of Elementary School Principals, 1971), pp. 29-32.

8. Kogan, *The Government of Education,* p. 29.

9. Mary Bentzen, "Study of Educational Change and School Improvement: A History of the League of Cooperating Schools," *I/D/E/A Reporter*, Fall 1969, pp. 5-9. (Information and Services Division, P.O. Box 446, Melbourne, Fla.)

10. *Ibid.,* pp. 6-7.

11. *The Elementary School Principalship in 1968: A Research Study* (Washington, D.C.: National Education Association, Department of Elementary School Principals, 1968), p. 44.

12. *Ibid.,* p. 57.

13. *Ibid.,* p. 60.

14. *Ibid.,* p. 55.

15. *Ibid.,* p. 80.

16. *Ibid.,* pp. 80-81.

17. Gerald Becker et al., *Elementary School Principals and Their Schools: Beacons of Brilliance & Potholes of Pestilence* (University of Oregon: Center for the Advanced Study of Educational Administration, 1971), p. 6.

18. Seymour Sarason, *The Culture of School and the Problem of Change* (Boston: Allyn and Bacon, Inc., 1971), pp. 141-142.

19. *Ibid.,* p. 116.

20. *Ibid.,* pp. 116-117.

21. *The Elementary School Principalship in 1968: A Research Study,* p. 36.

22. *Ibid.,* p. 25.

23. *Ibid.,* p. 26.

24. Becker et al., *Elementary School Principals,* p. 8.

25. Sarason, *The Culture of School,* pp. 115, 118-119.

26. John Goodlad, "The Schools vs. Education," *Saturday Review of Literature,* April 19, 1969, p. 61.

27. Mary Bentzen and Kenneth Tye, "Effecting Change in Elementary Schools," *The Elementary School in the United States: The 72nd Yearbook of the National Society for Education, Part II,* ed. J. Goodlad and H Shane (Chicago: University of Chicago Press, 1973), p. 358.

28. *The Elementary School Principalship in 1968: A Research Study,* p. 88.

29. Sarason, *The Culture of School,* p. 120.

30. *Ibid.,* p. 116.

31. Goodlad, "The Schools vs. Education," p. 80.

32. Sarason, *The Culture of School,* p. 4.

33. Roland Barth, *Open Education and the American School* (New York: Agathon Press, 1972), p. 174.

34. Personal communication with a teacher who did not wish to be quoted.

35. Roland, *Open Education and the American School,* p. 177.

36. Personal communication with a principal who did not wish to be quoted.

37. Lillian Weber (Speech presented at the National Association for the Education of Young Children Annual Conference, November 1972, Atlanta, Ga.).

38. *Ibid.*

39. *Ibid.*

40. *Ibid.*

41. Mary Stitt et al., "Up the Staircase in Arlington Heights," *Open Education: A Sourcebook for Parents and Teachers,* ed. E.B. Nyquist and G.R. Hawes (New York: Bantam, 1972), p. 205.

42. Carrie Haynes, "A Happening in a Ghetto School," *The California Journal for Instructional Improvement* 14, no. 2 (May 1971): 79-83.

43. Carrie Haynes, "Humanizing Instruction in the Open Classroom," (paper presented at the Pi Lambda Theta Seminar on Humanizing Education, June 24, 1973, UCLA, Los

Angeles, Ca.) Pi Lambda Theta, National Honor and Professional Association for Women in Education, 2000 East Eighth St., Bloomington, In. 47401. Haynes's account of Grape Street is also available in "Personalizing Education in the Open Classroom," *Thurst* 3, no. 2 (November 1973), Association of California School Administrators, 1575 Old Bayshore Hwy., Burlingame, Ca. 94010. ($1.50)

44. Harvey Barrett, personal communication.
45. Becker et al., *Elementary School Principals,* p. 2-3.
46. Sarason, *The Culture of School,* pp. 110-150.
47. *Ibid.,* p. 147.
48. Keith Beery, *Models for Mainstreaming* (Dimension Publishing Co., Box 4221, San Rafael, Ca., 1972), p. 61.
49. Gretchen Thomas (Master's thesis, University of California, Berkeley).
50. Theodore Manolakes, "Introduction: the Open Education Movement," *National Elementary Principal* 52, no. 3 (November 1972): 15.

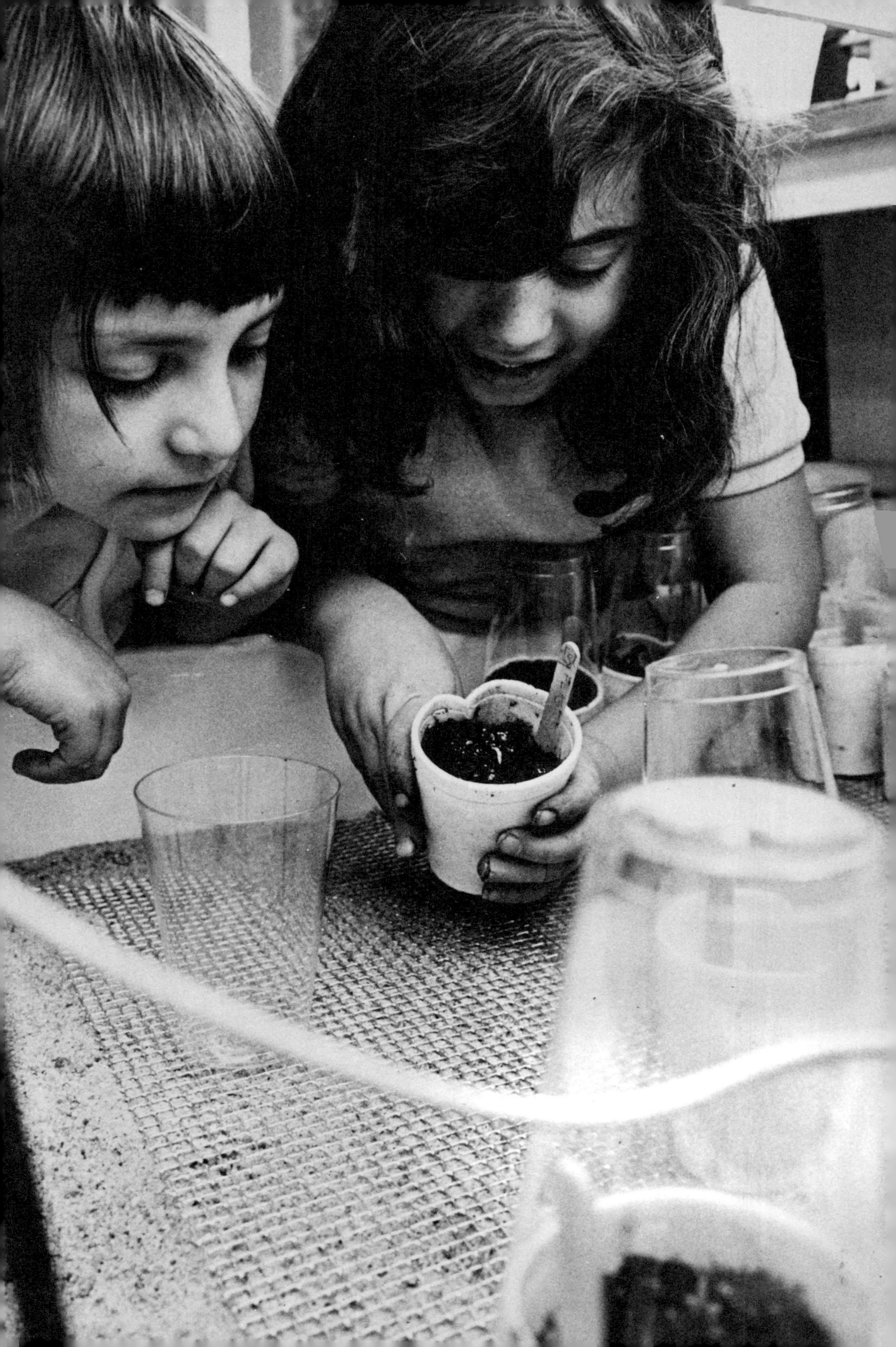

Chapter 3
Creating the Curriculum

The hallmark of open education is a belief about how children learn that challenges the conventional belief about curriculum and requires that, ideally, curriculum be created—not just presented—by the teacher, working with the principal or resource teacher, with fellow teachers, and with the students themselves. This conception of curriculum entails more than a different arrangement and scheduling in the classroom, more than individualization, and more than "active," manipulative learning materials. But it does not demand basic changes in the course of study: reading, writing, arithmetic, science, social studies, physical education, art, music are emphasized in the open classroom as much as in traditional education.

Curriculum change in England

In Alec Clegg's description of how experimenting infant school teachers slowly changed the traditional curriculum in England, he makes clear that they did not inject new subject matter into the traditional course of study but rather (a) emphasized the *purposes* for which skills are acquired in addition to the skills themselves, (b) sought to bring into the classroom children's experiences that can lead to self-motivated and continuing learning rather than facts which are easily forgotten or soon obsolete, (c) focused on individuals rather than groups, and (d) substituted themselves for the achievement test writers as decision makers about the specifics to be learned.

> And what about the "body of knowledge everyone should have?" How much of the knowledge crammed into us was fruitful and how much was sterile? How much of it moved our minds to activity and how much was merely acquired for the moment in order that we might make the grade or pass the examination?[1]

> We [had] allowed control of the curriculum to be handed over to the examiners, people who never [saw] the children. . . . Since some things can be measured more readily than others, we tended to emphasize what can be measured, and to undervalue what cannot. . . . [2]

Reading, writing, and arithmetic are still the crux of the curriculum. What is new, Clegg says, is that teachers "seized on" the third proposition in the saying: "What I hear, I forget. What I see, I remember. *What I do, I understand.*"[3]

41

Another English educator, David Pryke, describes the change in this way:

> The old idea of curriculum was: *Ram it in. Ram it in. Children's heads are hollow.* But today, four points reach a little beyond this maxim and demonstrate the change of emphasis:
> 1. The curriculum should enable the child to get to know himself and his possibilities.
> 2. It should provide opportunity for him to think for himself.
> 3. It should enable him to make his personal contribution. . . . intellectually, physically, spiritually, emotionally, morally, aesthetically.
> 4. It should allow him to understand (as fully as he is able) the world as he comes to know it.[4]

The results of these changes have been amply and glowingly described in this country by the flood of literature for teachers and laymen started by Joseph Featherstone's 1967 series of articles in *The New Republic*. Clegg's description of the curriculum situation in a good English primary classroom includes the following activities and materials:

> Somewhere in the room there would most certainly be a table on which were set out natural objects that were both beautiful and scientifically interesting. Elsewhere . . . might be a well-arranged display of fabrics and other objects of interest and beauty, designed to emphasize texture, colors, and shapes. There might be some small animals kept as pets. . . . And there would certainly be a generous and easily accessible supply of books of reference and fiction.
>
> One child might be painting; another might be arranging flowers. Two children with a stopwatch might be observing ball bearings rolling down a plank, while a third child tabulates the results. . . .
>
> After the initial activities period, it is likely that the class might . . . pursue a piece of work resulting from a recent visit to a water canal lock, a post office, a sewage works, a power station. . . . [S]ome would paint, some write, some calculate, some read and investigate. . . . [A]ll children would be engaged in something that in other, more formal schools would fall into the often arid compartments of history, geography, English, and mathematics.
>
> Such technical matters as spelling would be dealt with as adults would deal with them—by looking up in small dictionaries the word that is needed in the context of the moment. . . . There would, of course, be activities shared by the whole class as, for instance, when they sang together, or went into the [gym] for . . . a physical activity—sometimes gymnastic, sometimes dramatic. . . .[5]

Qualities of English open schools

All curriculum roads lead to or branch from reading. In England, as in the United States, children are expected to be able to read when they leave the infant school (age seven or eight). English teachers practicing open education do not believe that all children will learn to read by themselves, if provided only with the rich environment Clegg describes.

> Reading is not something that every child can absorb through his pores. Do not assume that if a child is placed in a cheerful environment with nice books at hand he will automatically become literate in time. . . . [6]

The English teachers do not wait for the spontaneous appearance of reading readiness, but provide an imaginative and varied repertory of classroom activities that enable children to make themselves ready: the "Wendy houses" where children can dress up and play out their own dramas of family life; puppet play; "movement"—the combination of physical education with drama and dance; choral singing and playing simple musical instruments; painting; arranging flowers and still lifes; the teacher's daily story telling and reading from books; her constant attentiveness and responsiveness to each child's questions and comments; and her encouragement of children's conversation together. All of these are conscious, carefully designed "instructional interventions" (as American educational technologists might put it) leading to the development of children's fine perceptual discriminations, spatial awareness, and spoken language. All of them undergird formal reading and writing.

Doris Nash, of Sea Mills School in Bristol, is officially speaking a headmistress but practically speaking a consummate teacher of reading and writing. She believes that if children learn to discern pattern and meaning and to express themselves in movement, music, drama, and painting, it will later be natural for them to find meaning in the written word and to express themselves by writing. The knowledge that some children do have difficulty learning to read spurs Nash and the best informal teachers to lay even more solidly in these children a foundation of natural expressiveness, on which speaking, writing, and reading will be built.

The English open educators have no concept of a different kind of education that would be "compensatory" for children with learning problems, Lillian Weber points out.

> In . . . English infant school educators' analyses, good compensatory education would be *good* education. . . . Activity methods and rich experience were not associated in their minds with private, progressive, middle-class education. Their state schools had been in the slums, and the methods had been developed there. . . . The variety of rich environment and individual pace and relationship were meant to allow for many possible starting points and different ways and paces of development.
>
> When the education of economically deprived children became a matter of international concern, the majority of English infant school educators reacted by reaffirming the applicability of informal education to these needs.[7]

Another quality of the English open schools that is striking to Americans, as David Pryke observes, is the way in which "British teachers seem to rely . . . on their own wit and creativity in gathering . . . teaching materials."

> How [do they] teach without packaged exercises and workbooks, without a basal reading series, without 30 social studies textbooks for the whole class, or without the magical, guaranteed successful, cannot-do-without You-Name-It Company's phonics (or other) program?[8]

Similarly, with some notable exceptions like the Nuffield teacher guides in math, school administrators do not depend on outside experts to develop "hierarchies," "strands," and conceptual schemes for each subject at each learning level, nor do they rely on the "instructional technology" with which to "install" these in classrooms. As Clegg describes this:

> At worst, a group of pundits remote from the classroom think great thoughts as to how improvements shall be brought about, and these are then accepted by the school authority and "required" by them from the schools. . . . The effect in many instances is a lack of conviction, a lack of sincerity, and inert and sterile results . . . [Real] progress in education is best brought about when it is drawn convincingly and sincerely from good practicing teachers. . . .[9]

The teachers in turn draw their classroom materials from the children, Edward Chittenden observes:

> Children are expected to assume an active role in creating a successful educational setting—they contribute materials and ideas, they make suggestions about better ways of doing things. . . . In other words they are producers as much as consumers of what the school has to offer. The open informal setting is not simply a cafeteria in which the individual child takes what he wants or finds interesting.[10]

Decision makers in England

American admirers of the infant schools have a tendency to attribute the English curriculum development to superteachers and superleaders in the educational establishment, beings far wiser and nobler than educators on this side of the Atlantic. If this is not entirely myth, it is at least exaggeration. As Ann Cook and Herb Mack describe British teachers:

> The great majority involved in the integrated day are not exceptional teachers. They are, rather, a mixed group—supported by a practical and philosophical framework and themselves encouraged to develop as people. If they are dramatically different from their more formal colleagues, it is not in training or intellectual gifts but rather in the way they order their priorities. These teachers focus on the child, *not on a standardized expectation, not on the material, or on the group.*[11] (Emphasis added.)

Mark Heyman blows away some of the halo surrounding the heads of English administrators by his observation that there is no social mandate in England to prepare all children for comprehensive high schools and even college entrance, as there is in the United States, and thus innovative heads have felt relatively little risk or restriction about changing the curriculum. On the contrary, the national department of education and several local education authorities endorse open approaches.

> Because of the national examination system (now undergoing major changes) which guarded the portals to higher education and to the type of secondary education that leads to higher education, there has been little interest in developing uniform curriculums or a mandatory program at the elementary-school level. Furthermore, the assumption is widespread that, in a civilized society, one knows what children should learn, particularly if one is a professional concerned with children's education. Under these circumstances, it was possible for compulsory elementary education to develop in a manner in which the teachers in each school, directed by the head teacher, make the decisions about curriculum and methodology.[12]

An English educator who has observed American education, Peter Raggatt, points out that this control by the head teacher grows directly out of English tradition, which is very different from American educational tradition:

> In America education has been the concern of the community since the early Puritans established their schools in New England. In England education was

historically bestowed on the masses by an elite. At no time did the community play any role in decision making. When control of the content of education passed out of the hands of the clergy following the implementation of compulsory education in the latter part of the nineteenth century, it was taken over by a relatively well-educated corps of teachers.

In England authority for curriculum decisions remains within the profession, while in the United States school teachers consistently need to go to the community to legitimize their goals and the content of their curriculum.[13]

Decision makers in America

While it looked to an English observer in 1972 as if the American public has frequent, potent, and stifling influence over curriculum decisions, Stanford educationists Michael W. Kirst and Decker F. Walker said a year earlier that "research has shattered the myth of lay control of schools, at least in the area of curriculum."

> Curriculum decisions have been very much an internal issue to be decided by school professionals . . . [often by bureaucrats] beneath the superintendent. . . . The key bureaucratic officers appear to be assistant superintendents for instruction and department chairmen, who work in committees with groups of teachers.[14]

In any event, Kirst and Walker agree with Raggatt and with elementary school principals themselves (See Chapter 2) that the curriculum decisions are not made at the local school level. As Bentzen and Tye observed in 1973, highly bureaucratized school districts implement "common means to accomplish common purposes."

> Standards of attainment are common for all or most pupils. Curricula and pedagogy are standardized. State or district syllabi and state or commercial textbooks dictate how and what is to be taught.[15]

Thus the most *practical* difference in curriculum policy between England and the United States is not that in England professionals control decision making and in America laymen do, but that local choice prevails in England and mass standardization is the present American pattern.

However, the American public's power is real, even if unused, and potentially significant, as Kirst and Walker point out:

> The increasing role of federal and state governments, the increasing willingness of elected officials to speak out on educational questions, the increasing willingness of mass media to publish achievement test scores of local schools, and the demands for community control are portents of an increasingly political approach to curriculum questions on the part of the general public.[16]

Open educators read these signs as well as anyone and observe that parents have cause to be dissatisfied, even angry. However, American open educators insist that the means chosen for school reform must not be more of the same—curriculum goals set and materials developed on a mass basis by people far removed from real children and actual classrooms. Whether the curriculum reformers are district or state or federal bureaucrats, textbook publishers, university professors, or new-breed educational technologists, the process is basically the same: people other than the local school staff are making the decisions. Harriet Talmage, education professor at the University of Illinois Chicago Circle campus, points out that under these conditions innovation is only apparent, not real.

> The McGuffy Readers of a century ago had three roles. They were the curriculum. They were the instructional materials. They dictated the instructional strategies and the approaches to grouping [of children in the classroom].[17]

Textbooks today perform these same three tasks, as do the instructional packages and systems developed during the curriculum reform movement of the late 1950s and 1960s, Talmage maintains: "However elaborate instructional packages have become, whether we use the term *textbook* or *instructional materials,* these materials serve as the arbiter of the curriculum of a school system."[18]

Seymour Sarason, describing the results of the new math developed by university mathematicians, finds that "the more things change the more they remain the same." He observes that a curriculum movement determined to make children enjoy mathematics, to want to become mathematicians, and to be able to be mathematicians, produced the same feelings of struggle, failure, rigidity, and boredom that were associated with the old arithmetic.[19]

These new curriculums are not harmful, they are just disappointing, says one of the scientists who was involved in the curriculum development—David Hawkins of the University of Colorado.

> I value the period very much and think it has produced some good curricular ideas and materials. But it did not really come face to face with the deeper problems. . . . We had our virtues and our vices: on the one hand a fresh view of subject matter and a willingness to try radical innovation; on the other, ignorance about children—and thus about the art of the possible—and arrogance about teachers' difficulties and schools' failures. From the combination we. . . . accepted very conventional ideas about the proper use of textbooks, [courses of study] . . . and lesson plans. . . .
>
> [Besides] us who were content-oriented, there has grown up another sort of expertism having to do *not* with subject matter primarily but with programming, testing, and evaluating of curricular materials, teaching strategies and educational technology. . . . Valuable as much of this work may yet prove to be for special purposes, it has often had the effect . . . of rigidifying the behavior of teachers and children even further. . . .[20]

The irony of such strenuous efforts for change producing such unbudging status quo was apparent to Lillian Weber after her 18 months in England. Looking at the British educational practices that resulted from teachers' concern for children who were poor, alienated, and nonlearning, she saw a basic strategy of creating the curriculum around the *children,* a strategy in which "prescribed curriculum and prescribed standard have no part." From this perspective it seemed to Weber that American compensatory education was not innovation—merely "an intensified and 'improved' form . . . of the *teacher* as central . . . controlling and imparting information . . . ."[21]

The feelings of disappointment about American curriculum reforms of the past 15 years are reinforced by the findings of the Rand Corporation's 1972 review of research about educational innovation.

> In general, evaluations have not led to many encouraging findings. . . . Oftentimes differences between [new math and new science] curricula and conventional ones are small and sometimes results favor the conventional method.[22]

> Programmed instruction is about as effective as conventional programs when student achievement is used as the criterion, but its superiority has not been affirmed.[23]

> [R]esearch has not discovered an educational practice that is consistently effective because no practice always "works" regardless of other aspects of the educational situation.[24]

> *Research tentatively suggests that improvement in student outcomes, both cognitive and noncognitive, may require sweeping changes in the organization, structure, and conduct of educational experience.*[25]

Open educators' beliefs about learning

To open educators the obvious way to begin sweeping changes is to change the definition—and the definers—of curriculum: of what is to be learned, and when, and how, and from whom. As Hawkins stated in 1965:

> The trouble with our educational system—profound and not superficial, difficult to remedy but as inescapable as failure—is that, in its ways of thought and in its institutional habits, it wrongly represents the nature of the human capacity to learn. . . .[26]

By defining curriculum primarily as knowledge—a given, almost as if it had physical properties—the present education system seems to view the student as "a passive vessel waiting to be filled," in the words of Charles Rathbone. He goes on to describe the way open educators think of the student.

> He is not one to whom things merely happen; he is one who by his own volition causes things to happen. Learning is seen as the result of his own

self-initiated interaction with the world. . . . Through "messing about" with his immediate environment, his manipulations advance from a general, nearly random *search* to a more planned and specific *search for*.[27]

The scholar who has influenced open educators most profoundly is the Swiss psychologist Jean Piaget, who has minutely observed the development of individual infants through childhood to formulate his theory of knowledge.

Piaget makes clear how different his theory is from our traditional idea of how the child learns:

> For traditional education theory has always treated the child, in effect, as a small adult, as a being who reasons and feels just as we do while merely lacking our knowledge and experience. Since the child viewed in this way was no more than an ignorant adult, the educator's task was not so much to form its mind as simply to furnish it; the subject matter provided from outside was thought to be exercise enough in itself. But the problem becomes quite different as soon as one [hypothesizes that] the child's principal aim of education is to form [his own] intellectual and moral reasoning power. And since that power cannot be formed from outside, the question is to find the most suitable methods and environment to help the child constitute it itself. . . .[28]

George E. Hein, former director of the Education Development Center's Follow Through program, writes that this view of the child's intellectual task as distinct from the adult's is fundamental to open education. So is

Piaget's method of *learning from* children by observing their natural actions in familiar settings and by informally interviewing them, rather than *judging* children against predetermined adult standards. From the interviews with children that have comprised his lifetime research, Piaget has conceptualized three major stages that all children everywhere go through as they develop intellectually. Understanding these stages is also fundamental to open classroom teaching in primary schools. Hein describes them as follows:

> [A]n early one in which children are concerned primarily with the things which are directly in front of them, that can be touched and heard and seen now (this stage lasts from birth to about five years old); a second stage, in which children will try to make connections . . . between things in their immediate vicinity and the rest of experience, but in which their thought is limited to ideas about things which are amenable to the senses (from about five to eleven, the "concrete" stage); and, finally, a stage in which children begin to . . . grasp and use our hypothetical-deductive system of thought.[29]

Educators like Hein and Rathbone, who set out to explain the rationale from which they operate, do not mean to imply that there is one doctrine handed down to all "opening" teachers or that all open classroom teachers who are successful in practice can theorize convincingly about what they do. Nevertheless, when teachers do go beneath the surface of classroom and curriculum management, they discover that their different methods arise naturally out of beliefs about how people learn which are different from the theories underlying other instructional strategies.

Three contrasting theories of education

A conceptual model that illustrates these differences is Lawrence Kohlberg's and Rochelle Mayer's conception of "three streams of educational ideology." In their conception, open education can be discerned in the "progressive" stream, which is defined by a cognitive-developmental learning psychology most strongly influenced by Dewey and Piaget and by the moral assumptions of ethical liberalism. Kohlberg and Mayer separate this "progressive" stream from what they call the "cultural transmission" stream, which includes both the classical academicians and the behaviorists, and from the "romantic" stream, shaped by the ideas of Rousseau, Freud, Gesell, and A.S. Neill.[30] (The writers imply "romantic" in the historic or literary sense rather than as meaning "impractical.")

Kohlberg and Mayer interpret the "progressive" (or open education) position as stating that *knowledge* is a temporary state of balance between "an inquiring human actor and a problematic situation," and learning is what happens between the actor and the situation up until this balance is achieved and whenever the balance shifts. Ordinary curiosity in the person and increasing complexity or change in the situation repeatedly tip the balance and trigger a search for a new balance—more knowledge. Thus knowledge is not built up like rungs on separate ladders, one for each scholarly discipline, but spreads out like a web, unique for each learner, connecting many different kinds of meanings.

In contrast to this "progressive" notion about knowledge here is how Kohlberg and Mayer describe the intellectual positions of the "romantic" and "cultural transmission" streams:

> 1. The "cultural transmitters"—both traditionalists and behaviorists—believe that knowledge is "repetitive" and "objective," with separable components that stay relatively constant and so can be singled out for transmitting and likewise can be detected in the receiver by means of scientific measuring instruments.[31]
>
> 2. The "romantics" are convinced by the maturational or "unfolding" psychiatry of Freud and psychology of Gesell, as well as by existential or phenomenological psychology, so that they consider that "knowledge or truth . . . is self-awareness or self-insight . . . [with] emotional as well as intellectual components."[32]

Kohlberg and Mayer also see differences in the way the three streams of educational thought conceive of children's development of *values*.

Philosophers in the "progressive" or open stream have stressed the "ethical universals," liberty and justice, as ultimate moral principles which should be upheld regardless of the immediate desires of children or the currently prevailing standards of the society surrounding the school. When American teachers have considered the theoretical underpinnings of opening up, values development has seemed less urgent than cognitive development. But a teachers's assumptions about values have deep implications for the organization, relationships, and order within a classroom which encourages a lot of choice for children. (More specifically, of course, the issue of values underlies the approach a teacher takes to social studies.) Kohlberg and Mayer point out:

> Not only are the rights of the child to be respected by the teacher, but the child's development is to be stimulated so that he may come to respect and defend his own rights and the rights of others.[33]

> A concern for the liberty of the child does not create a school in which the teacher is value-neutral [noninterference with the child's value decisions]. . . . But it can create a school in which the teacher's value-judgements and decisions involve the students democratically.[34]

In contrast to this "progressive" position, it seems to Kohlberg and Mayer that "cultural transmitters," especially behaviorists following Skinner, assume that all values are relative and there is no ultimate standard: They simply accept whatever values prevail in the society around the school.[35]

"Romantics" like A. S. Neill of Summerhill take their values from the child himself, Kohlberg and Mayer observe.

> Neill's faith in the "goodness of the child" is the belief that what children do want, when left to themselves, can be equated with what they should want from an ethical standpoint.[36]

Their concern for the rights of the child requires that they not interfere with his behavior.

Kohlberg and Mayer raise a provocative question about behaviorists and "romantics" alike: Is the teacher being "elitist" if he assumes that children are incapable of grappling with the intellectual and moral problems that the teacher himself confronts?

Curriculum: interactions of the student, the teacher, and the "stuff" of life

Because of their distinctly different view of the nature of the human capacity to learn, educators pursuing an open approach are gradually redefining curriculum and method. Instead of curriculum as a syllabus or framework of prescribed facts, concepts, and skills, organized for specific age levels, open educators think of curriculum as the whole developmental learning interaction that David Hawkins calls "I-Thou-It."[37] First, the existing and emergent conceptual structures, ideas, interests, and questions within the child's mind are an integral part of the curriculum. Second, materials come not only in forms of books and predesigned or packaged concrete manipulatives, but also from natural and familiar things, phenomena, and people in the school's environment. The third integral aspect of open education curriculum is the teacher's grasp of subject matter—though that is usually not conveyed in the formal manner of a lecture—and the teacher's understandings about the learning behavior of children in general, and each child in particular.

Eleanor Duckworth describes these three aspects of curriculum and how they are never separate, always intertwining, in an essay in which she narrates how she came to apply her clinical experience with Piaget in Geneva to her practical teaching in elementary classrooms.

> I had a certain skill in being able to watch and listen to children and figure out *how they were really seeing a problem* And this led to a certain ability to raise questions that made sense to them and to think of . . . new activities which might correspond better to their way of seeing things. I don't want to suggest that I was unique in this. Many of the excellent teachers with whom I was in contact had similar insights. . . . The point is that my experience with Piaget, working closely with one child at a time and trying to figure out *what was really in his mind,* was a wonderful background for being sensitive to children in classrooms. . . .[38]

> [T]*he right question at the right time* can move children to peaks in thinking which result in significant steps forward . . .; although it is almost impossible for an adult to know exactly the right time for a given question for a given

child—especially for a teacher who is concerned with thirty or more children—children can raise the right question for themselves when *the setting is right.* . . . And once the right question is raised, they are moved to tax themselves to the fullest to find an answer.[39] (Emphasis added.)

Duckworth refers to the child's attainment of a new skill or stage of intellectual development within Piaget's scheme, and the child's awareness of this, as "the having of wonderful ideas." She believes they do not just happen or unfold; rather, the child with the teacher's help builds them up from the foundation of other concepts and skills already in place. It is a custom-made design, not a prefab job. But new building requires both an existing foundation of content and the assistance of teacher and materials.

Duckworth says:

All kinds of things are hidden from us—even though they surround us—unless we know how to reach out for them. Schools and *teachers can provide materials and questions* in ways that suggest things to be done with them. . . . That is, one can familiarize children with a few phenomena in such a way as to catch their interest, to let them raise and answer their own questions, to let them realize that what they can do is significant—so that they have the interest, the ability, and the self-confidence to go on by themselves.[40] (Emphasis added.)

Such a program is a curriculum if you will, but a curriculum with a difference . . . the unexpected is valued. Instead of expecting teachers and children to do only what was specified in the booklets, without missing anything, the aim . . . is for children and teachers to have . . . unanticipated ideas on their own. . . .[41]

Both the Kohlberg and Mayer and the Duckworth essays help to clarify Piaget's theory of the learning stages that all humans go through. Thus they de-fog areas where American open educators' theory of instruction is vague. Duckworth's article is not a description of expediting automatic growth that might just as well have been left to nature, but rather the analysis of a teacher's alert, questing involvement to help create children's thought. On the other hand, she makes clear, "I do not, in any way, want to suggest that the important thing for education to be about is acceleration of Piaget stages."[42] Kohlberg and Mayer agree:

[A] concept of intellectual and ethical stages as "natural" [or universal] does not mean they are inevitable; many individuals fail to attain the higher levels of logical and moral reasoning. Accordingly the aim of the developmental educator is not the acceleration of development but the eventual adult attainment of the highest stage . . . the developmentalist is not interested in *stage acceleration,* but in avoiding *stage-retardation.*[43]

Further, they explain, it is not only important to help the child step up to a stage. It is equally and perhaps even more important to provide him with the scope and stimulation to explore widely at the level he has attained, applying his new understandings to many objects and phenomena. This *exercise* of his skills, grappling with a rich variety of subject matter, probably contributes more to later ability in school than does the *early attainment* of skill.[44]

As Duckworth concludes:

> The having of wonderful ideas, which I am suggesting is the essence of intellectual development, [depends] to an overwhelming extent on the occasions for having them.
>
> I think intelligence cannot develop without content. Making new connections depends on knowing enough about something in the first place to be able to think of other things to do, of other questions to ask . . . in order to make sense of it all.[45]

Curriculum materials—plentiful, playful "stuff"

The open classroom thus requires many and varied objects, happenings, and people, which stimulate children's purposeful activity, their thinking about this activity, and their concept-making and expression of their thinking.

As Hein writes:

> What we know about how children learn tells us that they must have "stuff." It's not just nice to have these things, it's not just that it makes children happy to play with pendulums and sand and gerbils, it is necessary that they do these things. It's not just that some of the discipline problems disappear when there are things in the classroom to occupy the children, but that intelligence will not develop fully unless children have the chance to test themselves against, and come to terms with, all sorts of chunks of the world of experience. Children must interact with people and balances, with animals and water. They must measure and count [real things, not just numbers on a page.] They must interact with others and solve problems, not just read about people and their problems.
>
> If we deprive children of real experiences in the school years, . . . we . . . make it harder for them to comprehend and learn from experiences later on. . . .[46]

It takes a great variety of materials to generate and support individualization of instruction, because children are individual not just in terms of the speed at which they can run the race to college, but also in terms of what Duckworth calls their whole "repertory of actions and thoughts"—the talents and techniques with which each child gets his learning act together.

Hein says that most of the materials should be familiar, natural, and open-ended things rather than objects which have no use anywhere except in the classroom—"pseudo-activities."

These pseudo-activities are ones which stress the result of the lesson, which are geared to *the* generalization to be learned to the detriment of the active experience. I have in mind activities that are structured so that they can lead to only one result. . . . There is nothing wrong in structuring something so that it illustrates what you wish it to illustrate. The only error is in thinking that it can serve in two ways at once: as an experience-enriching activity . . . and, at the same time, as a focused activity. . . .[47]

The belief, stated by Kohlberg and Mayer, and by Duckworth, that achieving a skill at an early age is not necessarily predictive of later academic success is characteristic of open educators. More than a decade of American research on the cognitive development of minority-group children growing up in slums and in families under severe economic stress had tended to the conclusion that these children would be permanently "disadvantaged," unless precisely engineered instruction in perceptual and cognitive skills could be administered to them in early childhood. However, Jerome Kagan, a Harvard developmental psychologist, now considers that children's spontaneous interactions in a natural environment which is accessible, appealing, and stimulating to them will enable them to make up for a late start.

He came to this position through his research on the children of a primitive Guatemalan village. In infancy these children were almost totally isolated from perceptual stimulation. As a result they were severely mentally retarded in early childhood. But by the age of 11, Kagan reports, "They're gay, alert, active, affective . . . *more* impressive than Americans in a set of 'culture-fair' tests. . . .[48]

Applying his conclusions to the schooling of American urban poor children, Kagan says educators should stop judging these children so early. He expresses confidence that even if they don't meet normative achievement standards in first and second grades, they will later. On the basis of their classroom experience open educators have long held the same conviction that Kagan bases on his Guatemalan research. They also are convinced that early frustration, boredom at being made to perform *ritually* skills they do not understand *purposively,* and their despair at being labeled failures, become emotional barriers blocking intellectual development.

For these reasons open educators fundamentally disagree with those whose first priority is early "skills" learning and who use modern educational "media" and behaviorist technologies to achieve it.

Better than skills: seeds, candles, pebbles . . .

Phillip Morrison, Massachusetts Institute of Technology physics professor who has been a participant in several science curriculum programs, believes that children today—"advantaged" as well as "disadvantaged"—need more old-fashioned, "stuff of life" experience in school and fewer processed materials because urban children are flooded with symbols—manufactured toys, television—rather than real things, and acquainted with parents' leisure time rather than with parents' work.

In earlier times, on farms and in villages, Morrison remembers, it was characteristic

> . . . that every child there, boys and girls alike, by the time he was ten or twelve had acquired a rich, nonverbal experience of such diverse things, such utilitarian things as . . . understanding how wheat was ground into flour, or possibly even using a crowbar as lever to lift some heavy load around the farm. Their experiences included not only a thousand different chores productive in their nature, but also a rich acquaintance with the affective side of life—with complex personal relationships, with birth, and death—all matters much closer at hand in reality than they are in our time, when indeed they are fully present, but outside the home, even mainly in symbol. Our present-day experience . . . is far reduced to a symbol flood which comes to you, a severely dependent social creature, for the most part nonparticipating and specialized away from all these experiences. *This tells me that the task of the school cannot primarily be the symbolic task.*
>
> We must try to undertake the replacement of these diverse experiences of early productive life by supplying in school context what is not available in everyday living. . . . A class must have much material, both physical and symbolic, but certainly largely physical, in the [lower] grades particularly. [Children need] a wealth of relationships with material; *not only must the children consume it,* but they must make it, destroy it, work on it with several people, work on it with one person, oppose it, support it—all kinds of relationships on the affective side.[49] (Emphasis added.)

David Hawkins believes the learning materials required for the elementary classroom are very simple and easily and inexpensively obtained. In a paper proposing open education as an approach for primary schools in developing African nations, Hawkins suggests:

> A large part of the material and equipment . . . will not be purchased at the insufferable prices of school supply firms, but will represent concrete materials from the city market, the village, the farm or the nearby forest or hillside. Plants are grown from seeds and cuttings, there is an aquarium in a cheap plastic bowl. . . . Small animals of the vicinity find their way [into the classroom] too, for study of their food habits and behavior. There are [flashlights], candles, mirrors, and a water prism. Mechanics is represented by inclined planes, unequal arm balances, springs and weights, and pendulums. There is water and sand. Geometry and arithmetic are represented by . . . pebbles, marbles in cups, small tiles. . . . There are books, some having been written by children, with pictures, to be read by other children. . . .

My point is that many of the essential materials already exist largely in the surrounding milieu, and are familiar to the adults of the surrounding community. Indeed they are often more familiar to the relatively uneducated than to

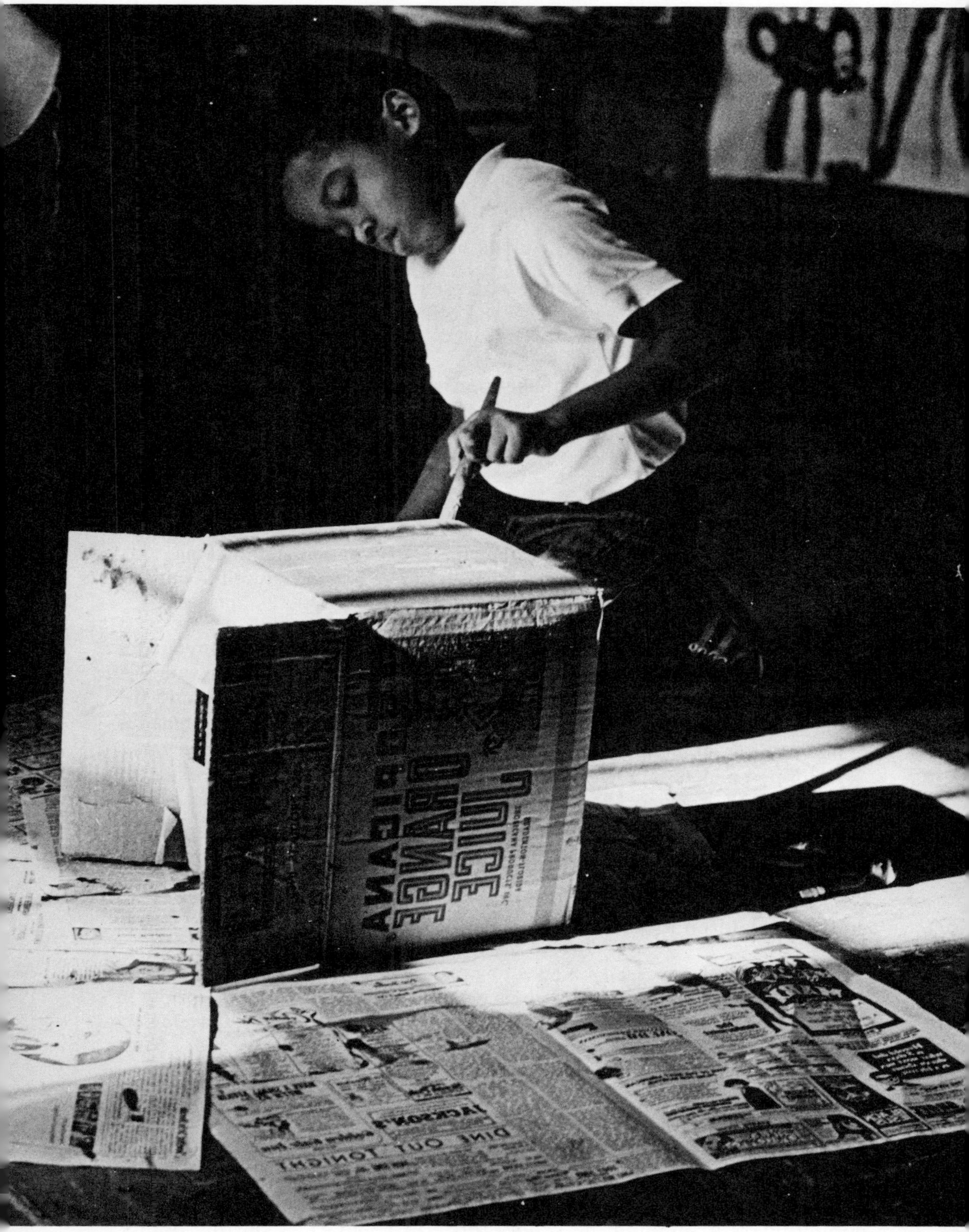
ORANGE JUICE
DINE OUT TONIGHT

the "educated"—yet these are the concrete embodiment of all the essential beginnings of the higher culture—of science, mathematics, literature. . . .[50]

Criteria for selecting materials

The open teacher needs some criteria beyond what is available and interesting to him or her personally for selecting materials from the environment to bring into the classroom. Roland Barth offers the following:

1. Things the children themselves bring in, or things they build.

2. People from the community who are informed about its history, natural features, economy; as well as the children's experiences during field trips.

3. Things that are common, inexpensive, familiar.

4. Things that have many potential uses and could lead to several paths of investigation rather than just one. Barth explains the importance of this feature of materials.

> Many manufactured educational materials have been designed to exclude all but one or two possible paths for the child's exploration and thinking. . . . The child . . . becomes dependent upon a source outside himself to initiate, sustain, and verify his own learning.[51]

> Many common materials exist which have not been designed by anyone for anyone, for any particular purpose, and yet which have definite structure. A magnet, sand, or a set of wooden blocks has definite structure and the capacity to influence and organize children's thought. But they are ambiguous and multi-programmed; they do not confine the child but, rather, offer him a major part in determining their use, depending on the questions they suggest to him. With the magnet he can make a motor, a test to see which materials are attracted to it, or a study of polarity with iron filing . . . and with sand he can build, measure time, draw, etc.[52]

5. Materials which seem likely to cause puzzlement, invite questions, and give children ideas.

> Fortunately, the necessity of selecting materials without benefit of observation of the children who will use them is short-lived. Yesterday, three children made robots out of cardboard boxes [the teacher thought they would use for a train]. Today he can provide paint, tin cans, and buttons . . . robot books, robot models, and robot pictures.[53]

Primary teachers may have had more experience than teachers of fourth-through-sixth-graders in selecting such materials. The upper grade teacher who has been textbook-bound all his career can rely especially heavily at the start on what the children themselves bring in and on his survey of the community surrounding the school (criteria 1 and 2) as starting points.

Preparation for using materials

An added criterion is perhaps the most important. It is *What the teacher knows about the material or can quickly find out*—whether the material is a toad, a broken alarm clock, or a collection of Indian arrowheads. This is because the learning environment is not just the materials but the interaction of the children and the teacher *with* the materials. Thus the teacher just beginning an open classroom must be careful not to have "too many materials with too little information on their use, potential, and purpose," writes Jennifer Andreae, an English open educator working with American teachers.

> [T]he quality of learning will be directly related to the teacher's understanding of what and how the children can learn from the materials.[54]

The teacher can count on the child's natural curiosity to lead him to try out interesting new materials, but this curiosity is not a permanent guarantee. The child will get bored and look for still another novelty *unless he starts learning*. A criterion for each material the teacher brings into the classroom is that the teacher know how to nudge curiosity along into learning. Floyd Page, of Creative Teaching Workshop in New York, believes the natural materials that the teacher brings in must first be investigated by the teacher.

> A practical knowledge of the physical properties of the materials is essential. Many teachers pick up an Elementary Science Study unit and use it without this basic knowledge of the physical properties of, say, water. Then they complain that the work of the children "doesn't lead anywhere." It's because they don't understand the concepts, and were expecting the kids to get them "from the materials."[55]

What Page recommends is that the teacher work with the materials on her own, and make a flow chart of what she learned from her investigations. This flow chart should serve not as a lesson plan on how to use the material with children, but rather as a guide to the knowledge that the material can reveal, and a preview of some responses that she should look for in children.

Once she has some personal experience and knowledge about some material the teacher can carefully select and present it to children and then closely observe what they do with it. Her observation should tell her what individual children already know and what they can learn, should indicate what her input into each child's learning should be, and should give her ideas of what to offer next. The teacher should use environmental materials not only as starting points or motivators for learning but as the continuing substance and sustenance of learning. That is, the terrarium home of salamanders and small green plants should not be a gimmick to lure children into textbook lessons on reptiles or on ecological systems: *the terrarium and the children and the teacher interacting should be the curriculum.*

The art of teaching in this way is learned only from experience. Vito Perrone, dean of the Center for Teaching and Learning at the University of North Dakota, observes it is one thing to enrich the environment and activate the children's study, but quite another to make curriculum subsist entirely on the interplay between children and real materials. To create curriculum in this way the teacher must have flexibility within any district-imposed formal curriculum, probably needs in-classroom advisory help, and certainly needs several years of experience.[56]

Many teachers beginning open education select only one area of curriculum to "open up" in; for some it's a collection of math workshop materials and activities fitted into nooks and crannies of the text; for others it's Elementary Science Study; for many others it's art. Barth comments that the English movement toward openness began with children's painting and crafts, while Americans have relied more on science—especially ESS, which was from its inception influenced by the English open teachers. The reading and language arts program may be the last to change.[57]

Reading in the open classroom

Developmental educators believe that reading, like all intellectual power, stems from the child's actions with objects, phenomena, and people in his environment. The student needs much to act upon, thus to symbolize in thought, then to talk about, and many opportunities to talk with children and with adults. As language experience (talking, listening, singing) is believed to be a prerequisite for reading, so are the abilities to discriminate minutely between letters, to perceive placement in space, to see the difference between wholes and parts. Thus developmentalists also believe the reading program should include many opportunities to refine these physical and spatial perceptions. They use the child's natural play, dance (or "movement"), painting, crafts, music, and dramatic play.

Lillian Weber writes that at Open Corridor schools teachers have been slow to accept this naturalistic way of teaching reading because of their anxiety to prove early success.

> The anxiety to "produce" success and the pressure on the teacher to use specific techniques were often greater than could be countered, even by the clear evidence that past use of these methods had been unsuccessful. Teachers continued, and continue, to use isolated-skill techniques,. . . . hoarded time for reading. . . .[58]

Because of this, Weber's priority in working with teachers is to show them how every activity she suggests within a Corridor will enhance children's language, and thus support reading.

> [W]e had to help teachers understand the relationship of aspects of the [Corridor] program that were not specifically reading but which *related* to its

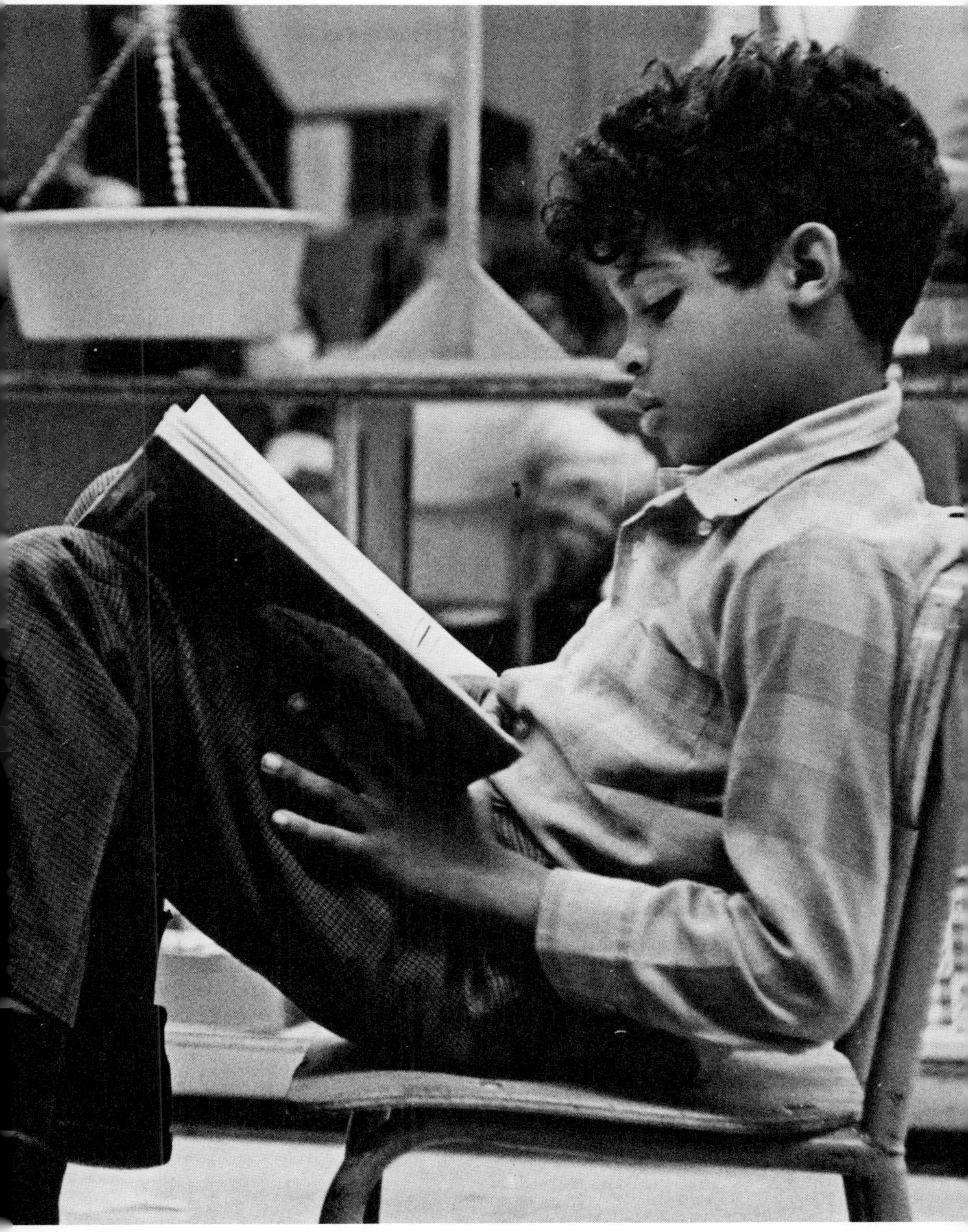

development. . . . dramatization, [art], and movement. We found that a teacher would make time for these things, but only if she saw that. . . . the classroom that lacked opportunities to dramatize and to represent is weak. . . . in support of reading.[59]

Such support is even more vital in Open Corridor classrooms than in the English classrooms where informal language methods were developed, because so many New York City children must learn to read in a language foreign to their native Spanish. Vera John, of the University of New Mexico, emphasizes that non-English-speaking children even more than native speakers need what the open classroom can provide: a continuity of setting between the home and the school and a feeling of being accepted and comfortable. The open setting also furnishes priceless opportunities for children to talk with each other and spontaneously to rehearse new language by themselves in solitary play, singing, and listening to music. John writes that, when singing in a foreign language the child, without feeling self-conscious, can "hear himself making sounds the way people who speak English make them, [and he] begins feeling his mouth, tongue, and teeth making new combinations." Singing also helps him learn to listen carefully.[60]

"Eclectic" is the word which Vito Perrone uses to describe reading programs created by North Dakota teachers who have received their open education preparation at the University's Center for Teaching and Learning (formerly New School for Behavioral Studies in Education). The teacher may use several kinds of basal readers and workbooks but not follow them in any particular sequence or consider any one set central to the reading program. Instead, the children's spoken language is the center of the program. North Dakota teachers are not doctrinaire about "whole word" or "phonics" methods. They use both techniques in informal ways. Individual and group practice in whole-word recognition on flash cards; informal training in phonics related to words from each child's own vocabulary; teacher's or parent volunteer's storytelling and book reading to the class; dictating stories to a tape recorder and listening to the play back; individual reading from commercial readers and story books—all are elements in the reading program each teacher designs for her class.

The classroom is a mini-library. "Classrooms without books and magazines in profusion can hardly be serious about reading," Perrone writes. "And a teacher [who] does not demonstrate her own love of language and books can hardly be serious about teaching reading."[61]

Many American open classroom teachers follow the practice of creating the first linkage between spoken language and print by having the child paint a picture each day and then tell the teacher what the picture represents so that the teacher can print a "key word" or short sentence under the picture. The child considers this "his word" and the collection becomes his own book, forming the first vocabulary he uses for reading. The Community Resources Institute of New York has developed a reading scheme for American urban schools incorporating such elements. It includes a

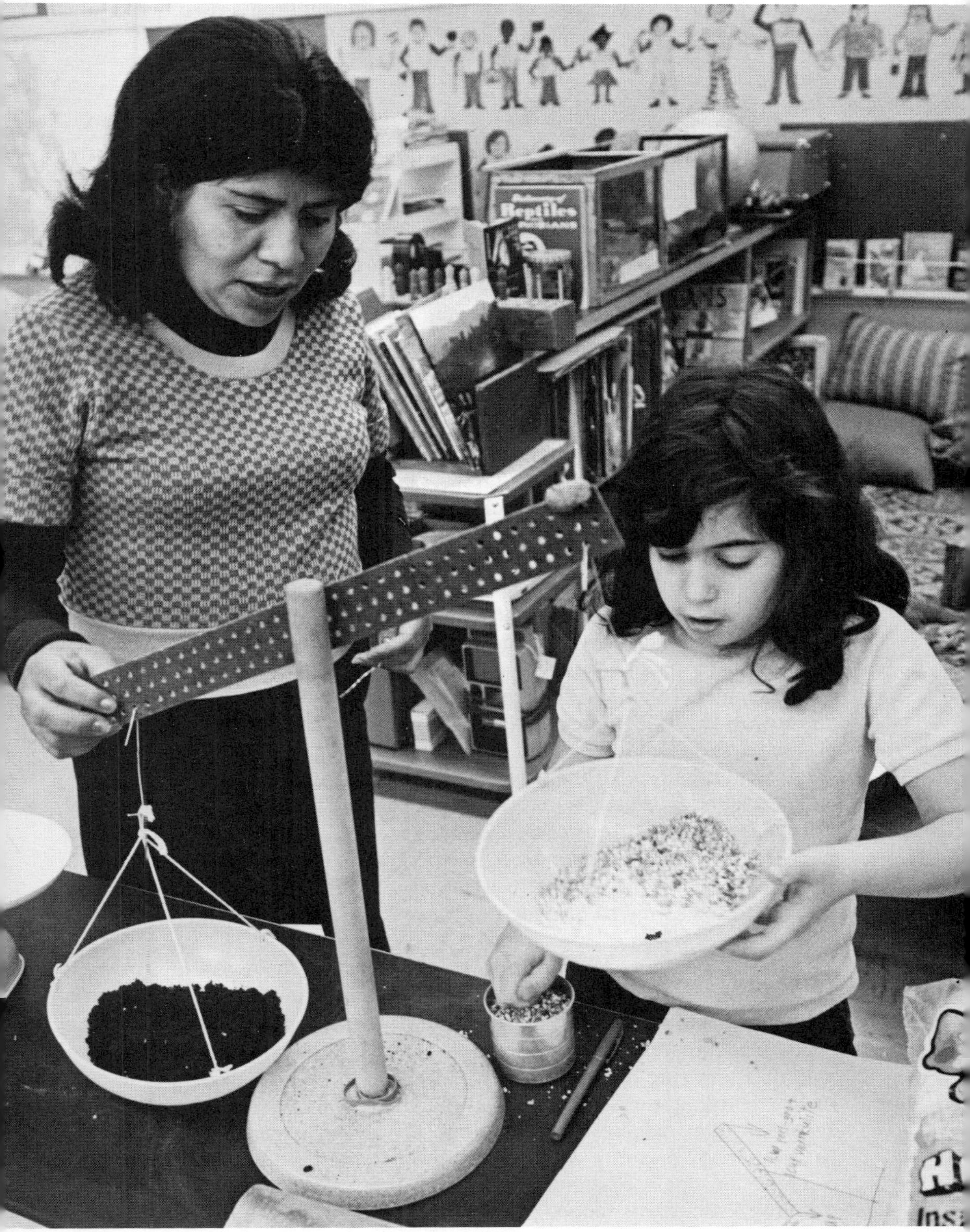
Reptiles

guidebook for the teacher on how to make the children's own books plus directions in the use of published series of readers.[62]

Math, science, and social studies

In mathematics, open educators do not take issue with the content of either old-fashioned arithmetic or the new math. No matter which math topics are taught, the open classroom teacher presents objects that the student can manipulate, investigate, and think about with the teacher, before presenting arithmetical symbols, algorithms, and paper-and-pencil exercises. The natural environment is used as sources of concrete objects and of problems, just as the child's own spoken language serves to provide reading material. The teacher also encourages children to write about their mathematical learning, as they are encouraged to find math in their everyday experiences, not just during "math period."

Since most American elementary teachers are ill prepared in math themselves, they need many concrete operational experiences of their own with the materials they will offer children. Thus the most natural activities for math, for teachers as well as for children, tend to be counting and recording results in number sentences and graphs, cooking, operating a store, using calendars, doing construction with wood or triwall cardboard (which requires measuring), calculating baseball averages, and the like—activities in which the teacher has had a lifetime of experience. Math games and uniquely mathematical equipment such as geoboards must be worked through by the teacher in advance so she herself understands the concepts they are meant to teach. The teacher's aim is to convey a view of math as a natural, purposeful human activity—finding order and patterns, solving problems. For many teachers, this means having their own math experiences which will make them enjoy instead of dread arithmetic.

The Madison Project in mathematics and the Elementary Science Study, both federally funded curriculum developments, were the first big importers of English ideas in mathematics. The manner of implementation of both of these curriculum projects is to upgrade teachers' own science and math understandings, and to provide or suggest classroom materials rather than textbooks.

Regarding science curriculum, open educators have no quarrel with either "concepts" or "process" as an approach to scientists' organizing the disciplines. However, they do not accept these sophisticated, intricately sequenced and interwoven schemes as being necessarily the *child's* natural way of organizing his learning. They think it more probable that the child makes learning webs—"trees," David Hawkins calls them—or that, as Jerome Kagan imagines, the child jumps from one lily pad of concept or skill to another lily pad in a way quite unpredictable by adults.

Thus, to open educators, some of the most innovative, "process oriented," materials-laden, packaged science programs exhibit the same shortcomings as textbooks: they lay out learning ladders that may not fit all children, they subtly imply that science is someone else's body of knowledge rather than the child's own experience plus his and the teacher's thought about it, and they imply that science is separate from other learning. These shortcomings, of course, can be overcome by the teacher who assumes that he or she—not the program or the text—designs the lessons, and uses encounters with everyday living things, familiar objects, and phenomena, as well as apparatus and experiments invented by experts.

Similarly, open classroom teachers look for themes for social studies in the local community—its civic and economic problems and natural resources, its geographic features, historical reminiscences of oldtimers, families' national origins, parents' occupations, and the like. Maps, local newspapers, landmarks and archives, museums, civic officials, tape recorders, cameras, products of local industries, biography, and historical fiction—these are preferred as resources and tools for social studies.

Especially pertinent to social studies is the character of the open classroom as a community. Over time the classroom ought to convey the essence of social living in a democracy—both problems and solutions. The child in a successfully evolving open classroom will have increasing experience of personal choice and will be required to respect fellow students' individuality and choice. At the same time, he will gain understanding of how cooperation can enhance individual effort, of how he can be both helper and receiver of help.

In a successful open classroom, the students' everyday experiences of choice and variety in school work, and of the interplay between knowledge and feeling, are expected to make their mark on his ideas about the way in which eventually he will earn his living. A classroom teacher communicates that she respects what the student does in school as his *work*, valuable because it fulfills a learning need or expresses a personal feeling. The teacher also conveys that the student is responsible for completing this work and for meeting standards that are appropriate to his capabilities. The teacher also urges the student to extend his capabilities. Such teacher actions are communications about work, and they can have subtle but deep influence toward students' later commitments to craftsmanship, professionalism, and self-fulfillment in their jobs.

The quality of open-endedness

Open educators' use of real-life objects, phenomena, and experiences differs from the "project curricula" familiar in the 1930s and 1940s, from laboratory-style science, and from many innovative learning materials featuring "concrete manipulatives." The difference, subtle but vital, has to do with "open-endedness"—that the open classroom teacher does not impose a single instructional purpose on "active" materials (seeds, blocks, animals, etc.) but rather discovers the child's own purposes for, or questions about, the material and capitalizes on them. Open educators recognize that some children will respond to the teacher's intention with eagerness and satisfaction, but other students will consider the teacher's idea not germane—no matter how concrete the materials—and so their learning will lack the propulsion of self-interest. Open educators also observe that imposing a single purpose on materials reduces opportunities for children to exercise their own resourcefulness and imagination and for the teacher to learn about students' capabilities and needs.

A federally funded curriculum project still in development has invented a systematic but flexible technique for the teacher to introduce a class project without specifying in advance what children should learn from it. The program is called Unified Science and Mathematics for Elementary Schools (USMES), but it involves social science and communications as well as science and math. It grew out of the 1967 Cambridge Conference on the Study of Mathematics and is sponsored by the Education Development Center with National Science Foundation support.

The project staff proceeds by posing open-ended "challenges" for participating teachers to work out over several weeks or months with their students in their classrooms. For instance: "How can you invent a new soft drink which will be popular and can be produced at reasonable cost?" "How would you improve the safety and convenience of a pedestrian crossing near your school?" "How would you improve the cafeteria service in your school lunchroom?" "How can you design and build a burglar alarm which would give effective warning and be reasonably priced?" Dozens of teachers have tried these challenges out with classes and kept journals of how they proceeded—what worked and what didn't, examples of students' work, results the students came up with, and suggestions for supplementary materials. Edited records are published as a learning unit. This allows that each teacher and class can approach the same challenge in their own way, but the teacher has available the considered experience of other teachers and consultants to aid his or her planning.[63]

The curriculum developers recommend that every school using this program provide a "design laboratory" where supervised children can work with tools to design and construct equipment they need as they work on the challenges. The program provides no texts, but rather sets of task cards for students to use only when they need to learn a particular skill in order to solve a problem. For instance, there is a set of "How To Cards" on using a stopwatch in the units, "Pedestrian Crossing," and "Lunchlines." The program requires teachers to take part in a summer workshop before it is initiated in a school and to participate in continuing seminars during the school year.

Successful open teachers use many texts and packaged materials in their classrooms simply by altering them to suit individual children. How much of the textbook structure a teacher can dispense with obviously depends on how much structure she has in her own head—about the subject matter and about children's learning behavior. Most teachers just beginning to open their classrooms feel vulnerable and overwhelmed by the task of designing their own curriculum materials. Thus inexpensive commercial materials specifically designed for open classrooms, evidencing more than a market-wise understanding of open learning principles, are enthusiastically received. (Some of these are listed in Appendix 1.) The progress of the open education movement need not, and probably should not, depend on such published materials, however. English teachers with no more training or ability than Americans and with impoverished school budgets have been creating their own curriculum materials for years with the help of their head teachers and school district advisors.

Footnotes

1. Sir Alec Clegg, *Revolution in the British Primary Schools* (Washington, D.C.: Association of Elementary School Principals, 1971), pp. 15-16.
2. *Ibid.*, p. 17.
3. *Ibid.*, p. 20.
4. David Pryke, "Helping Teachers Make the Transition from the 'Old' to the 'New'," *Teaching in the British Primary School*, ed. Vincent Rogers (New York: Macmillan Co., 1972), p. 272.
5. Clegg, *Revolution in the British Primary Schools*, p. 27.
6. Ann Fryer, "Teaching Reading in the Infant School," *Teaching in the British Primary School*, pp. 94-95.
7. Lillian Weber, *The English Infant School and Informal Education* (Englewood Cliffs, N.J.: Prentice-Hall, 1971), p. 221.
8. Pryke, "Helping Teachers Make the Transition," p. 286.
9. Clegg, *Revolution in the British Primary Schools*, p. 41.
10. Edward Chittenden, "Open Education—There and Here: What Makes the British Bandwagon Roll?" *Learning* 1, no. 6 (April 1973): 9.
11. Ann Cook and Herb Mack, *The Teacher's Role* (New York: Citation Press, 1971), p. 11.
12. Mark Heyman, "Learning from the British Primary Schools," *The Elementary School Journal* 72, no. 7 (April 1972): 339.
13. Peter Raggatt, "Administration in British Primary Schools," *National Elementary Principal* 52, no. 3 (November 1972): 27.
14. Michael Kirst and Decker Walker, "An Analysis of Curriculum Policy-Making," *Education Digest*, April 1972, p. 31.
15. Mary M. Bentzen and Kenneth Tye, "Effecting Change in Elementary Schools," *The Elementary School in the United States: The 72nd Yearbook of the Society for the Study of Education, Part II*, ed. J.I. Goodlad and H.G. Shane (Chicago: University of Chicago Press, 1973), pp. 355-366.
16. Kirst and Walker, "An Analysis of Curriculum Policy-Making," p. 31.
17. Harriet Talmage, "The Textbook as Arbiter of Curriculum and Instruction," *The Elementary School Journal* 73, no. 1 (October 1972): 20.
18. *Ibid.* p. 21.

19. Seymour Sarason, *The Culture of School and the Problem of Change* (Boston: Allyn and Bacon, 1971), pp. 45-46.

20. David Hawkins, *Statement on Environmental Education* (Testimony before the Committee on Labor and Public Welfare, U.S. Senate Education Sub-Committee, pp. 10-11, May 19, 1970). Available from Mountain View Center for Environmental Education, University of Colorado, 1511 University Ave., Boulder, Colo.

21 Weber, *The English Infant School*, pp. 232-233.

22. Harvey Averch et al., *How Effective is Schooling? A Critical Review and Synthesis of Research Findings* (Santa Monica, Ca.: The Rand Corporation, 1972), pp. 62-63.

23. *Ibid.*, p. 68.

24. *Ibid.*, p. 161.

25. *Ibid.*, p. 158.

26. David Hawkins, "On Living in Trees," *The Colorado Quarterly* (Boulder, Colo.: University of Colorado), Summer 1965, p. 19.

27. Charles Rathbone, "The Implicit Rationale of the Open Education Classroom," *Open Education: The Informal Classroom*, ed. Charles Rathbone (New York: Citation Press, 1971), p. 100.

28. Jean Piaget, *Science of Education and the Psychology of the Child* (New York: Viking Press, 1971), pp. 159-160.

29. George Hein, "Piaget, Materials, and Open Education," *EDC News* No. 1, Newton, Mass. (Winter 1973): 8.

30. Lawrence Kohlberg and Rochelle Mayer, "Development as the Aim of Education," *Harvard Educational Review* 42, no. 4 (November 1972): 451-455.

31. *Ibid.*, p. 460.

32. *Ibid.*

33. *Ibid.*, p. 473.

34. *Ibid.*, pp. 475-476.

35. *Ibid.*, p. 466.

36. *Ibid.*, p. 471.

37. David Hawkins, "I-Thou-It," *Open Education: The Informal Classroom*, ed. Charles Rathbone (New York: Citation Press, 1971)

38. Eleanor Duckworth, "The Having of Wonderful Ideas," *Harvard Educational Review* 42, no. 2 (May 1972): 220.

39. *Ibid.*, p. 222.

40. *Ibid.*, pp. 224-225.

41. *Ibid.*, p. 225.

42. *Ibid.*, p. 229.

43. Kohlberg and Mayer, "Development as the Aim of Education," p. 489.

44. *Ibid.*, p. 490.

45. Duckworth, "The Having of Wonderful Ideas," pp. 230-321.

46. Hein, "Piaget, Materials, and Open Education," p. 8.

47. *Ibid.*, p. 10.

48. Jerome Kagan, "A Conversation with Jerome Kagan," *The Saturday Review of Education*, April 1973, p. 41.

49. Philip Morrison, *The Full and Open Classroom*, The Education Research Center Occasional Paper No. 10 (Cambridge, Mass.: Massachusetts Institute of Technology, 1971), pp. 5-6.

50. David Hawkins, "Development as Education: A Proposal for the Improvement of Elementary Education," *Science Technology in Developing Countries*, ed. Zahlen and Nadar (London: Cambridge University Press, 1968), pp. 528-529.

51. Roland Barth, *Open Education and the American School* (New York: Agathon Press, 1972), p. 81.

52. *Ibid.*, p. 82.

53. *Ibid.*, p. 83.

54. Jennifer Andreae, *Theresa, Theatre and Terrariums: Open Education: ESEA Title I* (Albany, N.Y.: New York State Education Department, 1971), p. 23.

55. Floyd Page, personal communication.

56. Vito Perrone, *Open Education: Promise and Problems* Fastbacks No. 3 (Bloomington, Ind.: The Phi Delta Kappa Educational Foundation, 1972), pp. 32-34.

57. Barth, *Open Education and the American School*, p. 10.

58. Lillian Weber, "Letter from the Director," *Notes from Workshop Center for Open Education* 2, no. 1, Shephard Hall, City College, New York (March 1973): 1.

59. *Ibid.*, pp. 1-2.

60. Vera John, "Aspects of a Bilingual Classroom," *Notes from Workshop Center for Open Education* 2, no. 1, Shephard Hall, City College, New York (March 1973): 11.

61. Perrone, *Open Education: Promise and Problems*, p. 25.

62. Ellen Blance, Ann Cook, and Herb Mack, *Reading in the Open Classroom: An Individual Approach* (New York: Community Resources Institute of the City University of New York, 1971).

63. Unified Science and Mathematics for Elementary Schools, Education Development Center, 53 Chapel St., Newton, Mass. 02160.

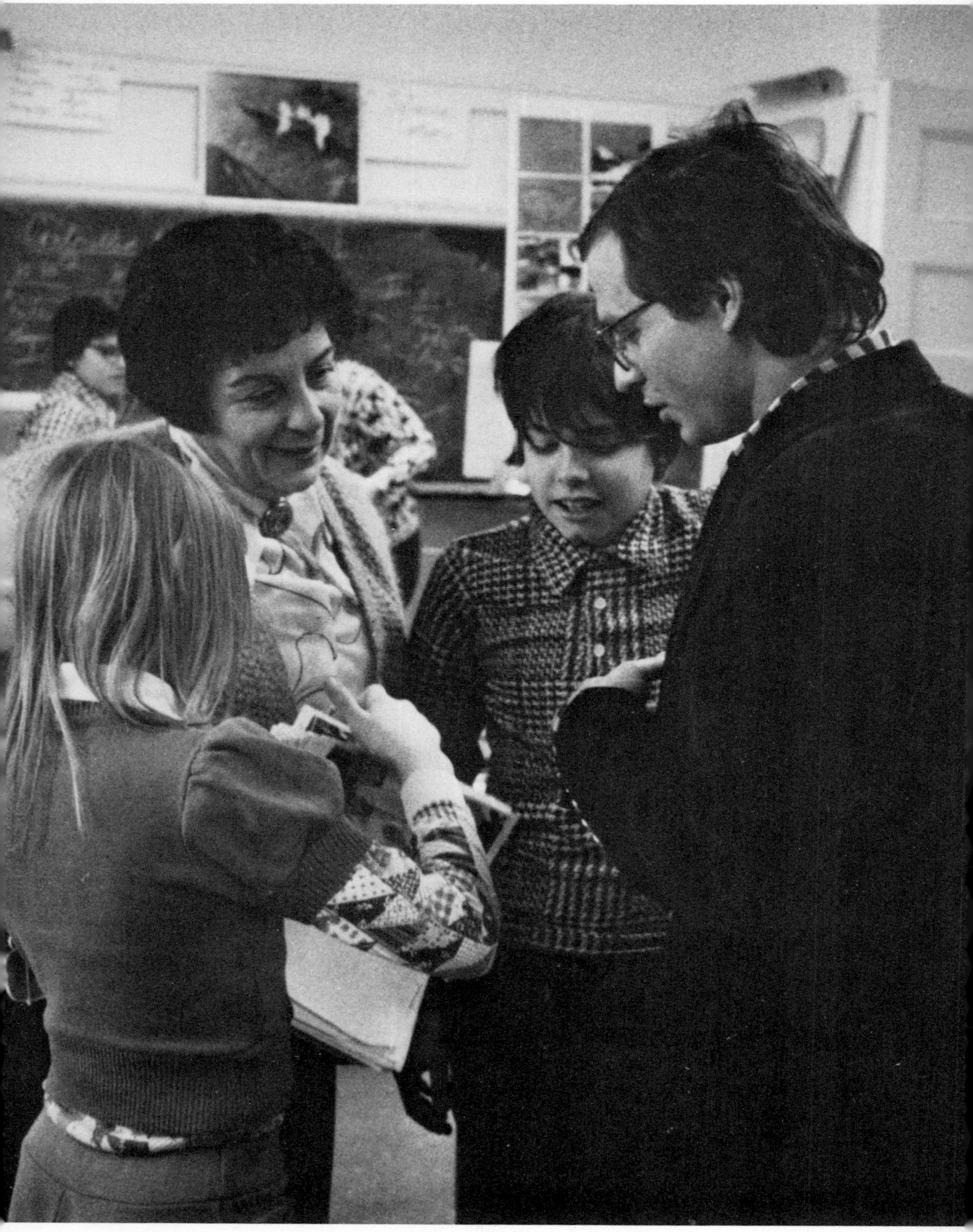

Chapter 4

A New Resource – The Advisor

An American who has worked both in English and in American schools names two minimum conditions for American teachers to open up their classrooms. The first is to remove from them pressures to conform to any particular classroom model or instruction method, and the second is to provide them with advisor teachers to work beside them in their classrooms. These prerequisites are stated by Tony Kallet, who was for eight years an advisor with the county educational authority in Leicestershire and now works at Mountain View Center in Boulder, Colorado. The two conditions are also cited by Alec Clegg, the Yorkshire chief education officer who was one of the initiators of the open movement in England.

Real change comes, Clegg says, not from the top down but from the bottom up, aided by advisors or "encouragers" who already have experience as open classroom teachers and who "avoid all temptation to impose rapid change on schools: rather they look for growing points in each school and move on from there."[1]

The position of the advisor seems similar to that of a curriculum coordinator or specialist, or a supervisor charged with maintaining standards of instruction. But there are two crucial differences: the advisor's objective is to "look for growing points" from which to develop the teacher's professional skill, rather than to evaluate the teacher; and the advisor's activities are the actual teaching of teachers and children rather than administering official policies and installing officially adopted programs.

An English teacher's description dating from the time just after World War II describes her feelings about the conventional curriculum "organizer" from the county educational authority. It will strike a familiar note with American teachers today.

> One morning, a circular letter from the education office contained the news that an art organiser had been appointed to the county's advisory staff. The news roused not even a glimmer of hope or excitement in me . . . any teacher worth his salt does not want to be "organised" himself, nor to have the subjects for which he is ultimately responsible "organised" over his head by someone who only sees the school for an hour or so a term, and who has only a fleeting glimpse of the individual character of the school in question. . . . It is true that most of them have been teachers themselves, but the very nature of their jobs demands that they should have been *specialists*. Their new jobs lift them to a position of some authority, and in doing so usually magnify for them the importance of the subjects to which they, personally, are attached. In turn

they visit every school . . . giving advice which is unsought and, what is worse, not understood anyway, tactfully refraining from either praise or candid criticism, but leaving behind them when the door closes the impression that they will expect to see a great improvement . . . by the time of their next visit. Now multiply the effect this treatment has on an overworked jack-of-all trades like the average school teacher by the number of [coordinators], and you will see that the general result is not one that is likely to make the teacher feel more capable of doing his job well.[2]

In contrast, Clegg describes the style of an advisor who worked under him.

The most gifted exponent that I know of the art of drawing the best out of the schools that he visited was an advisor who, when he entered a school, however poor in quality it might be, would look around until he could find something he could commend and that might, if developed, prove productive. He would praise the teacher for it, invite the head to see it, and leave the school with the idea that the school would be a better place if there was more of it. At his next visit, there *would* be more of it, and the teacher who had produced it would have begun to think why it was good, and his insight and understanding would deepen.[3]

The teacher's teacher

As important as personal style in the influence of the Leicestershire open education advisors is the official context in which they work—the fact that they are so very unofficial. As Browse and Kallet point out:

Because advisors are removed from any sources of power, the advice they offer is just that—advice; sometimes taken, sometimes not. . . . In a system characterized by a considerable degree of mutual trust among advisors, teachers, and administrators, there is an openness to new ideas, without a necessary commitment to them. Advisors . . . bring to the attention of teachers a wide range of materials and ideas, without anyone feeling that because these are suggested they must be used.[4]

When Kallet worked in Leicestershire, there were both specialists and general advisors. Because they had no official program to promulgate, advisors did not try to cover every school in their authority. They went only where invited and worked as long as they judged they were needed. Being unofficial, Kallet was not required to make evaluations and never reported to the headteacher his judgments of a teacher. His travels back and forth among classrooms and schools enabled him to collect and spread useful ideas rather than to compare teachers and schools. "A large percentage of what I was offering teachers was not my own ideas." He found a great variety of teaching styles and competencies and regarded them as a positive source of many ideas—rather than as an indication that he had failed to impart a standard practice. He was, in sum, not an administrator or a supervisor, but a roving teacher of teachers.

The Leicestershire advisor teaches teachers in two settings: in the teacher's own classroom and in inservice courses. The latter may be a workshop for all the teachers in a single school during release time or after school, an after-school series of classes at the county advisory center or some other central place for teachers from the entire district, or a one-week or longer residential institute. These two kinds of teaching enrich each other. The courses are designed by the advisor from his direct perceptions of teachers' needs as he works with them in their classrooms. And in classroom work which follows a course, the advisor is able to extend what the teacher has learned in the course by helping her apply it to the children's work. Thus the teacher in the inservice course learns from working with materials at her own learning level; later she learns more as, with the advisor's guidance, she observes the work of her students with the same materials. This continuing learning on the part of the teacher is the overriding goal of the English advisor. The development or introduction of new, highly recommended curriculum materials—such as Nuffield guides or Dienes math blocks—is secondary.

American teachers' needs for advisors

In contrast to the English teacher's experience of welcoming an advisor-teacher is the American teacher's feeling about specialists who visit her classroom, as paraphrased by Seymour Sarason: "I do not need someone to tell me what more I should or could do with the child. When I ask for help I am asking someone else *to do something.*"[5]

Sarason believes this is an expression of the average American teacher's nearly constant feeling of being "drained." She is in the position of having to give, give, give all day to children, yet she herself does not *get* from anyone.

> To sustain the giving at a high level requires that the teacher experience *getting*. The sources for getting are surprisingly infrequent and indirect. . . .
> One of the consequences of marked disparity between giving and getting is the development of a [teaching] routine that can reduce the demand for [the teacher's constant] giving.[6]

An advisor who works in Clegg's or Kallet's definition of that role is nearly unknown in American school systems. But recently American teachers who have participated in the federal Follow Through programs for educationally deprived children have received help from master teachers called "program advisors." These advisors have worked in classrooms with teachers to show them how to use new curriculum materials or instructional methods devised by the developers of the various Follow Through "models." A few American teachers thus have begun to experience and value some "getting."

The Far West Laboratory's Responsive Education Program, an innovative K-3 instructional design chosen by 11 school districts receiving Follow

Through funds, in 1972-73 surveyed 428 teachers and teacher aides who were changing their classrooms according to the Responsive design. The survey asked the teachers to rank in order 13 factors influencing their teaching and to describe them as either positive or negative. Federal funding pays for a teacher aide for each Follow Through classroom, and this factor—"the other teacher in the room"—was chosen as the most potent and the most positive influence by the teachers in the Far West Laboratory survey. Rated as the second most positive influence was the program advisor—ahead of the school principal, who was rated third. In contrast, "curriculum personnel" were rated weak in influence and only slightly positive, and the curriculum itself just barely above the midway point in influence and positive nature.[7]

Similar evidence about an advisor's value to the American teacher was established by the Ypsilanti (Michigan) Perry Preschool Project, which developed the prototype for another Follow Through model program. A study by David P. Weikart and his colleagues compared the effects of three very different preschool programs on matched groups of three- and four-year-olds from poor families in Ypsilanti. The programs were the Piaget-derived "structured cognitive program" developed by Weikart, the stimulus-response-based program developed by Bereiter and Engelmann, and a traditional nursery school program.[8]

Because all the programs served children equally well, the researchers concentrated on finding the common factors in all three programs that contributed to their success as measured by standardized tests and observations. The researchers concluded that the addition of teacher aides, the regular routines, the home teaching, the teachers' strong commitment to each program's goals and methods, and the teachers' planning were all influential. But in addition:

> There was one supervisor for all three programs who was an experienced teacher and whose duties were educational not administrative. She regarded her role in a nonauthoritarian light and spent most of her time in the classrooms and in planning and evaluation meetings. . . . [Being] free of bureaucratic duties, [this supervisor] was able to devote her energies to helping . . . each teaching team keep its particular goals clearly in focus . . . .[9]

This finding was reinforced in the Weikart group's subsequent consultations with its "High/Scope" Follow Through programs throughout the country. As Weikart put it, "It does seem clear from our experience that *the classroom supervisor must be and must function as an educator, not an administrator.*"[10]

An American advisory: EDC

Though both the Far West and the High/Scope Follow Through programs used advisors as the means to install new curriculum materials and instructional strategies designed by the developers, another Follow Through program—that of the Education Development Center in Newton, Massachusetts—viewed the advisor himself as the main instrument for change. The first EDC Follow Through director, David Armington, had observed and worked with Leicestershire advisors. He described the job of the EDC Follow Through advisor:

> Within broad areas of agreement, the advisor does not attempt to impose specific ideas; he does not try to sell ready-made programs, "packages," or methods. On the contrary his job is to respond to the demands of the situation. He does not tell people what they should do, but tries to extend what they are capable of doing. He tries to sense what can be built upon . . . . The advisor's strategy is to work in places and with individuals who are ready for change. . . . Advisors go only where they are invited, and the relationship must always be one of mutual trust.[11]

Thus the EDC advisor is not only the means for implementing open education philosophy, he is also an extension of that philosophy, observed Anne Bussis and Edward Chittenden of Educational Testing Service's

Early Education Research Group. These psychologists observed EDC advisors at work in schools and classrooms during the 1969-70 school year, in order to develop assessment procedures appropriate to open education goals. They noted the following characteristics of EDC advisors:

1. Diversity of activities and of people they work with—not just teachers.

   For example, the advisors frequently spend time with small groups of children; they talk to the principal, the custodian, the secretary; they may seek out the owner of a nearby company from which teachers might get free materials. Their work with teachers and aides may take the form of a private conversation, joining the teacher and a group of children in some project, assisting with the rearrangement of a classroom, or conducting informal workshops (for teachers and aides and perhaps parents) at the conclusion of a school day.[12]

2. Emphasis on *how* children learn rather than *what* they learn.

   The advisors tend to accept the particular instructional goals of a teacher or school, reacting less to the wisdom of those goals than to procedures a teacher might use for achieving them. . . . The advisors continually sought ways in which to build upon the teacher's present approach and to extend this approach where it seemed promising. To build or to extend necessarily means to accept much of what is there. What is often accepted are the local objectives of a particular classroom . . . what is challenged are the ways of reaching those objectives.[13]

3. Emphasis on each teacher's own specific everyday events and problems.

   The actual exchange between advisor and teacher is . . . over very specific things. . .showing a teacher how to operate an electric sabre saw for cutting tri-wall cardboard, helping her arrange an activity corner . . . . Discussions take place over what might be done when a boy is unable to settle down, what are some ways to get children started with Cuisenaire rods, how to house a turtle. To operate in this way, the advisors must be able to draw upon. . .their own teaching experience, what they have learned in visits to other classrooms, . . . what they have gained from the [EDC] advisory center . . . . Teachers relate to children over real and specific events and materials; advisors relate to teachers over real and specific issues and actions . . . .[14]

4. Viewpoint of the teacher as an experimenter and decision maker.

   Bussis and Chittenden noted that EDC advisors support the teacher when she tries new ideas, support her in daring to risk failure, and encourage her to incorporate into her teaching what she has learned from past experience, especially from failures. They do not make her decisions for her. Advisors believe they must teach this attitude to teachers so that they can continue their professional growth on their own after the advisor has gone.

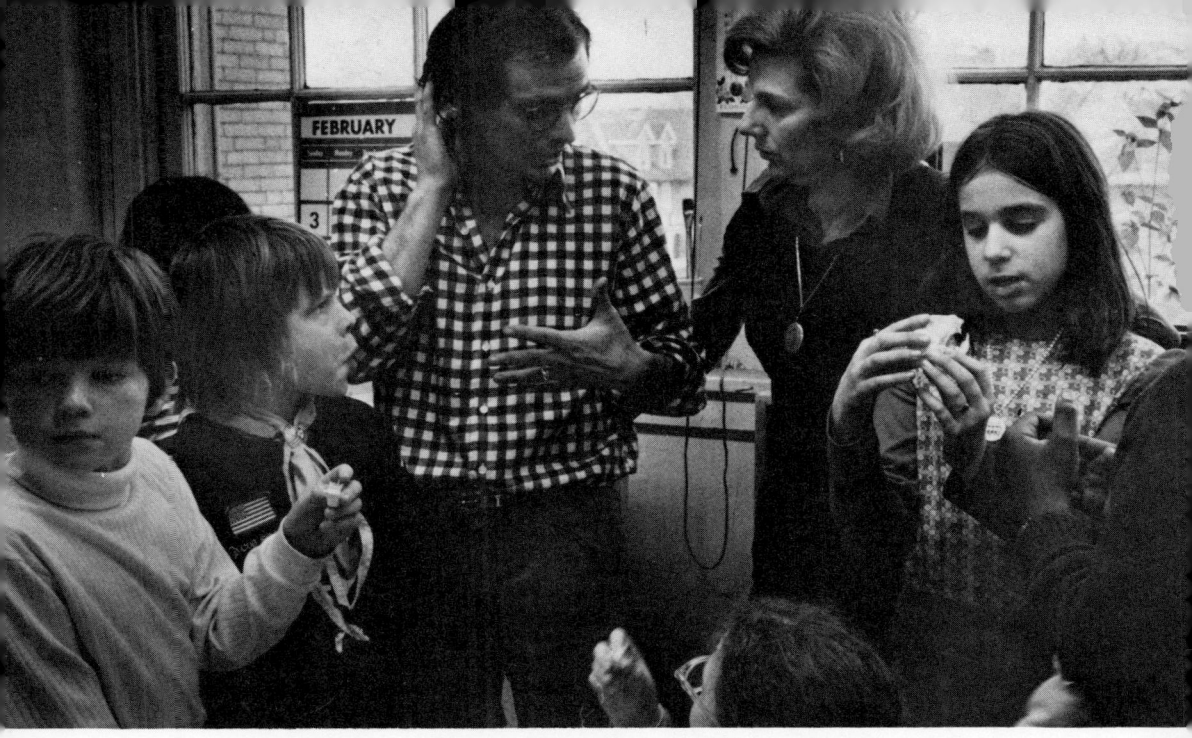

One of the EDC advisors, Norellen Stokley, sums up the advisor's work in the phrase "showing the teacher the next step."

Whether the teacher has experienced success or failure with something she has tried in the classroom, the advisor who has been in the classroom with her can help her find out what is the next step to take—whether to change the classroom environment, the materials, or the teacher's own behavior with children. American teachers as a group lack diagnostic abilities, whether they teach in formal or informal classrooms. This lack can be covered up in a traditional classroom but it becomes very striking in an open classroom.

Stokley was chosen by her fellow advisors to lead an EDC advisory group offering services on a contract basis to school districts that are not Follow Through sites and are seeking help in beginning open education.

What an advisor does

Every advisor's work is different, a function of the particular needs of the school and teachers he or she works with, but a general pattern has evolved since 1968 from the experience of EDC and several other American advisories. This pattern is that each week the advisor spends a whole day or part of two days in the school (or each month the advisor spends one full week). The advisor works with teachers and children in classrooms, shares lunch and planning periods with a group of teachers who work together, has individual conferences with teachers, gives a lunchtime or after-school workshop on curriculum materials or a seminar on learning theory, works out problems or stretches school regulations with the principal, gains cooperation from the librarian, the custodian, and other school personnel, plans and conducts educational meetings for parents, and so forth.

The most immediate resource an advisor offers is to help a teacher reorganize and refurnish the classroom—following the teacher's ideas, not the advisor's—and then to help the teacher observe diagnostically how each child functions in the new environment. This process may take several months, or the better part of a year. Throughout the whole period of work in a school, the advisor continues regular visits to each teacher's classroom, observing children, teaching them, and suggesting new curriculum materials and activities to the teacher. This is not done to ease the teacher's burden or to enrich the curriculum but to present a different model for the teacher, a different way of working with children, and to impart to the teacher the confidence and skill needed to select and improvise materials.

Martha Norris, an Open Corridor advisor working in New York public schools, describes her work as follows:

> First thing I do in the morning is to go around to each room and greet each teacher. I will have planned the night before some special things to do, but I am flexible to respond to the immediate needs I see when I am in the room saying good morning. After that I will work in all the classrooms. I do no formal demonstration lessons. I will work with a group of children or just watch. When I work with children my actions indicate what I value for children. I will discuss with the teacher how she got started on an activity that I observe, talk about how to extend it beyond what's happening now, talk about Johnny's particular problem. I'll point out the two children I see on the periphery of a group, point out to the teacher the ones she has forgotten. At lunch time we'll have a meeting of all the Corridor teachers together.
>
> When you're an advisor you get very attached to your teachers. It's a peer relationship, not supervisory. My goal is to develop the teacher's independence. Therefore I work in a way that's personal and still impersonal. For instance, in talking about their problems I try to get them not to question or doubt them*selves*; instead I say something like, "What went wrong with that *day*?" With some teachers it is important not to give a lot of curriculum ideas, but to give them time to develop their own. If it is an inexperienced teacher I will make materials for her and with her for the first two months, and then stop to see what she will do on her own. At this point, I may step in and expand her own ideas. I also ask other Corridor teachers to help, so that they may become resources as well.
>
> The point is not to get the teacher hitched on "ideas" and gimmicks. I want the teacher instead to look at what the children are doing, what questions

they're asking, and to develop their learning from that. I relate the open education philosophy to specific problems I see with children. I talk about developmental levels—Piagetian learning theory—whenever I talk about a child's learning or when I see an activity that is pitched over a child's head. I make an effort to know all the children on the Corridor by the end of November. My personal connection with them is very important.

Every advisory goes about these tasks with a slightly different style. At EDC the emphasis is not only on finding and extending "growing points" in teachers but on helping teachers gain more autonomy within the system. Thus EDC advisors work to create understandings and resources in school systems and communities that will insure programs' continuance after the Follow Through money runs out. In several Follow Through communities—among them Philadelphia, Washington, D.C., Burlington, Vermont, and Laurel, Delaware—EDC advisors have developed resource centers for teacher training and curriculum development, where teachers and parents work together. They have planned ways to keep these centers funded, both for staff and supplies, at the end of Follow Through funding.

Open Corridor communities

The unique character of the Open Corridor advisory is defined by the word "community." The role of the advisor was not adapted from the English pattern, but evolved from Lillian Weber's original work with teachers in two New York public schools in 1968-70. By the end of 1973, 20 advisors had worked under Weber's direction, reaching 117 classrooms in 13 schools. (The Ford Foundation assisted in their financial support during the apprenticeship.) Advisors do not install "a developed and perfected organizational form existing in itself," Weber says. They lay "a new floor of possibility," on which *teachers* can design learning environments more hospitable to the natural learning behavior of children than what now exists in the huge, inflexible public schools.[15]

The advisor's first task is a *social* reorganization of "a piece of a school"—four, five, or six teachers who teach different grade levels of racially mixed classes and who voluntarily choose to form a "collaborative community." They share not only the corridor on which all their classrooms open, but also an Open Corridor advisor and the experience of learning together. Yet each teacher keeps his or her own classroom as home base.

At first the job of the advisor is to help the teachers enrich their individual classrooms by providing more than the completely symbolic experiences of books, workbooks, and blackboards, and also to transform the empty space of a mere passageway into a common space for those activities that would be beyond the capacities of the single classroom and the teacher just beginning to open up. The corridor provides room for greater movement and diversity in children's school work and friendships. It expands the number of children and adults available as friends and helpers, and enables children to stay in a familiar setting for longer than one year. As Weber pointed out in her observations of the English open schools, the children are nurtured and stimulated not just by their own classroom experiences, but by their feelings of belonging and contributing to a small school community.[16]

An equally pressing reason for creating community is that the teachers need it. Although all those who participate in Open Corridors volunteer for the program, Weber points out that they begin with greater and lesser degrees of understanding about how they will have to change, differing abilities and styles, and varying levels of tolerance for the stress of change. Through lunch time discussions and weekly curriculum workshops, the Open Corridor advisor strives to create an atmosphere where the teachers learn to trust and depend on each other and unlearn habits of isolation, so that they can give each other courage, praise, rescue, and refreshment, and so they can pool planning, resources, and experience.

The Open Corridor advisor's efforts to build community extend also to parents, since children are not enrolled in open classrooms unless their parents volunteer them; parents' participation in classroom and educational decision making is central. Further, the organized political power of parents is a bulwark against threats to the program from school district policies (hiring and firing), administrative practices, and budget cuts.

The Open Corridor advisor functions as a link in still another direction—to the principal, assistant principals, district supervisors, and other consultants in the school. This link is needed not only because these people evaluate children's achievement for the school district and parents, and they have powers of hiring and tenure-granting over Corridor teachers, but because Open Corridor aims to implant its communities as normal, permanent subsystems within the larger schools. Weber observes that advisors' efforts to widen the circle of community by inviting principals, supervisors, and others into Corridor teachers' workshops, can result in the loosening of supposedly inflexible structures.[17]

Mountain View Center for Environmental Education

The distinction of this advisory, indicated by the phrase "environmental education" in its title, is its emphasis on helping the teacher use the students' own environment as learning materials. The Center is at the University of Colorado in Boulder. With University and Ford support it serves about a dozen schools and nearby Head Start centers. Its director, David Hawkins, is a professor of philosophy and science and an open education theorist. Hawkins was an early director of the Elementary Science Study, a federal science curriculum project of the 1960s, which was influenced by the English informal primary schools.

Hawkins says that the Mountain View Center is a reaction to the American curriculum development movement, "where you could go to a willing teacher with materials you had cooked up and you could write a teacher's guide, but you found out that these couldn't change schools."

Instead our advisory is a process of working with teachers and opening their eyes to things and happenings in their world that are new and different. It is a process of helping them with their mechanical problems; it is helping them scrounge, helping them deal with teachers down the hall who oppose what they're doing, helping them operate in a schoolroom that's not designed for the exploration that should go on there.

Mountain View emphasizes the similarity between the spontaneous work of children and the disciplined work of scientists and scholars: both investigating in order to explain the world. An advisor can help children (and teachers) see the similarities and can introduce the scientist's way of investigating, Hawkins says. To do this the advisor must have "both wide knowledge and wide sympathies."

Here is a teacher who has thought it worthwhile in instructing children about the clock, for example, to introduce a sundial. The adviser is one who knows a little about the central place of this instrument in the history of astronomy, and suggests an investigation of light and shadow, making shadows in the school yard through the day, working indoors with sticks, (flashlights), mirrors, pinhole images, and all the rest. Many of the phenomena are familiar to children and adults, but have never been invested with educational value for either. Yet out of just these phenomena came beginnings of cosmography, of geometry, and of that extraordinary history which leads from ancient Mesopotamia and Egypt to Athens. . .and in the end to landings on the moon and Venus. But it begins in the school yard and returns there repeatedly to catch new phenomena, new discussions, new involvements . . . .[18]

Thus a Mountain View advisor who has observed some spontaneous enthusiasm on the part of a child or a group of children will fan this spark, using as bellows a depth of scholarship and a breadth of experience unavailable—or perhaps available but unrecognized and thus unused—in the average teacher. In this act that Hawkins calls "blowing sparks into flame," the advisor uses his experience in learning to provide both a stimulus and a model for both the teacher and the students. Hawkins specifies that a "spark blower" needs to have his "second wind" as a teacher (that is, nearly intuitive familiarity with children's varied learning behaviors). The advisor also should have obvious enthusiasm for learning more himself. It is not only the advisor's pre-existing, specialized knowledge that teachers need, but also his example of intellectual curiosity and determination. A Boulder teacher describes the effect of this quality in Frances Hawkins, David Hawkins's wife and colleague: "Having seen the way Frances tackles things that she doesn't know a whole lot about, I find I myself can't say, 'I can't do music because I don't know anything about it.' I have to pitch in and try."

The open education advisor exemplifies another quality of the scientist-scholar in the interdisciplinary humanist tradition, Hawkins says, by helping teachers and children see the significance of their learning in terms of its "linkage" and "pathways" to other subject matter.[19]

Mountain View Center offers three kinds of assistance to schools or individual teachers who are dissatisfied with their present teaching and ask for advisory help: advisors can go into one or more classrooms in a school; individual teachers can take semester-long series of weekly workshops at the Center in curriculum areas such as math, music, weaving, physical science, reading, and language and invite their workshop teachers to help them in their classrooms; teachers can work with the curriculum materials the Center advisors have collected or constructed. There is a frequently changing array: a giant pinhole camera made from a washing machine carton, big enough for kids to crawl inside and see the projected image; terrariums; a spinning table; looms; collections of a dozen different kinds of beans—sprouting, fermenting, molding, arranged in a mosaic; old and new plot maps of Boulder and environs; musical instruments made from pot lids and plumbing pipe and cardboard tubes; all in all a miniature hands-on museum for inquisitive kids and adults. Nothing is there just because it is "fun"—only materials that encourage conceptual or skills investigation.

Because they believe teachers should learn to improvise learning materials from their students' surroundings, Mountain View advisors do not arrive in a school with armloads of apparatus. Instead, they offer to help teachers observe what students respond to in their own school environs. Advisor Chuck Mena spends one whole day each week in each of the four schools he works in, assisting in the classroom routine and chores and joining the teachers' planning sessions so that he gets an authentic feel for the teachers' situations and so that he is not regarded as an expert with a bag of tricks.

Mena does not persuade teachers to abandon their textbooks, but encourages them to find familiar, concrete things that will animate textbook lessons. "Until teachers feel confident in saying 'I don't know but I'll find out' to a child asking a question, there is no point in suggesting that they break away from the textbook."

Even teachers who want to break away from texts to an informal classroom, and who spend days at the start of the year making materials and bringing equipment and projects into the classroom, may be disappointed at their students' lack of response. Frances Hawkins explains:

> The trouble with most teachers' rooms even if they are "open" is they focus on projects which the teacher makes up, or that some outside consultant or curriculum project has put in, and which don't arise from observations of what the children like. The teachers don't know how to read the directives the children are giving.

A teacher can learn how to read students' directives by watching an advisor at work with them. Frances Hawkins believes,

> You earn the right to tell teachers things when you're there with their kids. Also you're not just talking about what might be nice. When they see you working with their kids they have the living proof.

A way for the advisor to model teaching behavior without taking control of the classroom away from the teacher is to set up an "outpost room" away from the classroom. There a few children can come from time to time to work with the advisor while the teacher observes. Frances Hawkins chooses materials she judges will appeal to children she has observed closely, who have trouble behaving and working.

> By my working with five or six kids in my personalized environment for an hour or so a day over a period of time I help the teacher to see that what she saw as the child's problems are the result of having his individuality squashed in a room where he has no interplay with what's around him. When the teacher sees this she can begin to change the way she looks at and provides for and acts with the child. She can use my room for short times with a few kids and get the feeling of being successful as the mediator between the child and the learning materials.

This technique is also used by Open Corridor advisors as they work with children in their corridor activity areas. A variation offered by Mountain View Center is to invite teachers to bring a few children to the Center's resource rooms and observe them working with the materials there.

In the workshops that Mountain View advisors offer teachers, they structure the learning environment with materials that invite active involvement, not just talking. Recognizing that teachers make a distinction between what they believe they need for children and what they find interesting for themselves, advisors provide materials from children's to adults' level on the subject matter of the workshop.

Hawkins experienced both the waning of the American progressive movement and the resistance to the curriculum reform movement. Thus he is convinced the changes he advocates will come about only if average American teachers understand and accept them. The requirement for depth of understanding limits the number of teachers Mountain View serves but does not limit the length of time that a teacher may continue to work with the Center. Hawkins believes that for adults to change takes a long time, especially if they work in settings which, like many American schools, actually inhibit growth. Even those teachers who are fed up and bored with old teaching methods and are eager to try something new go through a period (that may last years) when they cannot find a new style they can trust, so they do not dare let go of the old. Such teachers need time, not just for exposure to new theories and methods, but for replacing their old self-image as the dispenser of knowledge. Mountain View advisors believe this process can go faster if the teacher who is tentatively dipping toes into openness for his or her classroom can at the same time plunge into some new adult learning activity, perhaps in a personal rather than a professional interest, and with attentiveness to how learning goes forward. This personal insight may help the teacher to see that human beings, especially children, learn not only from the knowledge funneled in from teachers and books but also from self-spurred inquiries tunneling out into the world.

Creative Teaching Workshop

In a loft on the Lower East Side of Manhattan, the Creative Teaching Workshop—part of the Boston-based Advisory for Open Education—has built an open classroom for teachers in which it holds after-school and evening workshop courses for individual teachers or groups from the same school. The arrangement of and the action with a profusion of naturalistic learning materials are meant to give teachers the feeling of what an open classroom should be for children. Once a teacher catches that feeling—and usually not before—he or she is eager to have an advisor's assessment of how well the workshop experiences are being translated into children's work, and what more might be done. Thus CTW director Floyd Page in 1972 secured Carnegie Foundation support to send three pairs of staff members into three elementary schools in Brooklyn to work as advisors two days a week with groups of teachers who had been attending CTW workshops. The advisors' purposes are to provide personalized help in classrooms when teachers request it; to present the option of open education to traditional teachers as a physical reality at their doorstep; and to provide teachers, parents, and the principal with a sounding board—outsiders' candid impressions of relationships and procedures in the school that dampen children's and teachers' enthusiasm for learning. The advisors have learned not to be used as go-betweens or trouble shooters between teachers, administration, and parents but to bring all three groups together to settle problems and make decisions together.

CTW advisors conduct workshops during lunch once a week, if teachers request a particular topic, and the workshop room is open throughout the school day to any teacher who wants to work there. Near the start of the fall 1972 school term the CTW workshop at P.S. 152 was furnished with a couch and chairs and a coffee pot; cooking corner, sink and stove; woodworking tables and professional tools; recipes on the blackboard for pretzels, apple butter, elderberry-apple jelly; a map of several blocks around the school with note, "Where are the crabapple trees in the neighborhood?"; bins of buttons, styrofoam bits, colored telephone wire, bolts, tongue depressors, washers; a sand table made of triwall cardboard with two magnets and scoops and a task card ("Can you make soil from sand? Can you make sand from rocks? Can you find a paperclip in the sand with a magnet?"); Elementary Science Study teachers' guides and other teacher books; a microscope and next to it an open jelly glass with mold growing on the jelly; a balance.

This assortment was a bare beginning of the provisioning by advisors Marion Greenwood and Tony Sharkey. However, the materials in the room are not all-important, Sharkey and Greenwood explained, for the room is not meant to be just a supply depot for informal classrooms. The stuff is there to stimulate teachers' exploration of it. Still, it will not work by itself. "It takes us working with the materials," says Sharkey, "us working with the teachers, and the teachers working with the materials." The advisors do not see themselves as merely staffing a curriculum center, Greenwood makes clear.

> We are trying to teach thinking behavior. Adults in this country seldom do things any more that make them feel they are stretching their minds. Unfortunately that includes teachers. People who *think* are active, curious, interacting with people or things, mimicking. This is what we are trying to learn how to teach—interaction among the teacher, the materials, and us.
>
> We show that teachers can do carpentry with real tools with primary kids, or we start work with clay, or design storage units a teacher can build out of triwall—thereby inspiring her kids to build a spaceship with it, for instance, and write a space exploration adventure. We see our role as drawing ideas from the teacher and getting the teacher to think about those ideas.

All the teachers in the big school, many of whom continue to teach in a traditional way, are invited to use the miniworkshop. No teacher is required to consult with CTW advisors about using materials there, or about changing room arrangement or teaching style. "While my own style is informal," says Greenwood, "that's not what I think is important. I'm concerned about problem solving and independent thinking. These can occur in both settings—open or traditional."

Community Resources Institute

Another New York advisory, Community Resources Institute, has worked with teachers and principals in 12 elementary schools in the Bronx. Supported by Ford since 1970 and headed by Ann Cook and Herb Mack, CRI has developed a pattern of advising aimed at generating satellite advisories at public schools and has begun to advise secondary teachers. CRI also publishes children's work as curriculum guides for teachers of open classrooms (see Appendix 1).

CRI's advising has involved sending a staff advisor to a school about once a week to work with teachers in classrooms and consult with principals and parents, while teachers from the school take turns coming to the center for weekly workshops in math, science, arts, cooking, reading, and writing. Also teachers bring groups of students to CRI for workshops aimed at showing the teacher the individual ways her own students learn with rich and lively materials.

Over the years this pattern has evolved into one of less frequent advisor visits, in which the advisor does not assist the teacher directly in the classroom but helps the teacher define what she wants to do, why she wants to do it, and how she can accomplish her plans. Now the CRI advisor's emphasis is on developing the teacher's self-sufficiency so that all the efforts to informalize learning arise from the point of the teacher's current competency. The new advisory pattern is influenced by a cut in advisory staff and by CRI experience that teachers beginning to change need to avoid the inconsistency of teaching workshop style when the advisor is present to help, and reverting to whole-class lessons when they're on their own. Also CRI has taken on new work with groups of teachers in eight junior and five senior high schools in the Bronx.

Working with secondary teachers, CRI staff meet weekly with a small group from the same school. They focus on student inquiry and how each teacher fosters it in his or her own subject area. At a teacher's invitation a CRI advisor will observe in the classroom, both advisor and teacher will document classroom happenings, and then they will compare notes and also discuss the new approaches with students.

Preparing new elementary advisors is a gradual process starting when a new teacher or a student intern is placed in the classroom of an experienced open teacher. When the beginner gains skill the experienced teacher can leave the classroom part time and work as a resource teacher for the other opening teachers in the school. The resource teacher takes part in weekly CRI leadership seminars with resource teachers from other schools. After successful experience in that role the resource teacher may become an advisor-in-training at CRI. However, this advisory apprenticeship is only part time. The rest of the time the advisor trainee continues to work in his or her own school. The end point of the cycle—and the start of a new one—is for the new advisor to head a satellite advisory center in his or her school, reaching out to teachers in neighboring schools. The functionality of this design, says Herb Mack, is that teachers who are familiar with the character of neighborhoods and the politics of schools and districts, become the center of new programs, and are able to be realistic about how to initiate change.

However, the satellite strategy must be based in the advisor/teacher's strong mastery of his or her own classroom situation. This is the belief of Barbara Batchelor, a University of Illinois graduate fellow in open education, who during 1972-73 evaluated the efforts of open classroom teachers at Olive School in Arlington Heights who were acting as part-time advisors to teachers in other schools. Batchelor found that a teacher with only two or three years' experience in an open classroom may not be able to handle two very demanding jobs at once: extending her own students' work with materials—that is, getting beyond the stage of re-arranging the classroom into the stage where children are learning from self-initiated experiences with materials—and also supporting the beginnings of change in colleagues.

Advisor-in-residence: the resource teacher

This evolution of experienced open classroom teachers into resource teachers for their colleagues has occurred spontaneously at Grape Street School in Watts. "We are growing from within by respecting teachers as leaders, and improvising a combined teacher/advisor role," says principal Carrie Haynes. At Grape, a long-experienced open classroom teacher, the librarian, and two reading teachers are available part-time as resource teachers for the rest of the staff. Haynes comments they have been able to be more effective than outside advisors because the teachers accept them without the resentment they sometimes feel towards outsiders. Teachers' distrust is a hurdle for outside advisors to get over. Jennifer C. Andreae, an English open educator, comments on this in her report of the two years she worked as resource teacher with eight New Rochelle, New York, elementary teachers beginning open education. "They had instinctively tended to classify me as 'administration,' which meant an evaluation of their teaching."[20]

A similar reaction was met by the eight resource teachers in Hartford, Connecticut, who joined the district's elementary education director, Joseph Randazzo, in introducing informal materials and methods to all the primary teachers in the district. The changes initiated by the central administration and school board took place over a period of three years beginning in fall 1969. Teachers were given three-weeks' release-time training in open classroom settings, and they began their new style of teaching with the help of paraprofessional aides and $800 worth of new materials for every classroom. Still their anxiety about change was felt by the resource teachers as hostility. "Inner-city teachers have this tremendous conviction that they have failed," comments Ann-Marie Miller, a Hartford resource teacher. "They seemed to be thinking, 'You're going to make me throw away everything I know and the kids will go crazy!' "

The Hartford resource teachers counteracted this anxiety by being open to teachers' complaints and by providing structure, Miller points out. They did a lot of traditional teaching at the start of the training sessions because they believed traditional teachers are no more prepared to learn in a loose, choice-full, self-developmental program than are children from strict classrooms, and the first priority of resource teachers is to build teachers' self-confidence. After the three-week training period, the resource teachers were available on request throughout the year to work with teachers in their classrooms, and the training center remained open to teachers for curriculum ideas and as a workshop in which to construct their own materials.

In John Muir School, Berkeley, California—part of the National Institute of Education's Experimental Schools Project—the staff resource teacher, Judith Hayward, gains and keeps teachers' confidence by separating herself from administrative and evaluative functions. She works three days a week, spending the whole time with teachers in their classrooms and in private consultations. Hayward describes her job as doing what her principal would do if she could operate as a head teacher.

> My two guiding principles are that I do not aim teachers toward a particular model, but just try to get them to think about children and their interests instead of subject matter; and I consider that, if the teacher is in earnest, everything she says is valid, even if I don't agree with it, just the same as when I'm working with a child.
>
> I respect a teacher who opens up only a little at a time. I think that's smart: she does what she can handle and she will keep on growing. Some teachers will always be very directive but if they are good teachers it's not worth losing them as good teachers in order to put forth my ideas. You don't pull the rug out from under a good teacher.
>
> I always try to point teachers toward each other as resources, not toward me. For instance, "Liz had luck with this; would it work for you?" And then I help the teacher adapt the ideas she likes to her own situation. I try to provide any little service I can for teachers not ready for change—a listening post, a curriculum idea, a book on a subject they're doing in their class, a four-week, one-hour-a-day stint with a low or gifted child in that classroom. A principal in a school where I consulted briefly said to me, "You're not just 'open classroom,' you're good for all teachers!"

Free-lance advisors: outside consulting groups

Outside advisors do not have to work so hard as resource teachers to keep independent of school administrators, and they are less likely to have their perceptions skewed by the personal relationships within a school. Thus they may be able to see more possibilities and to confront restrictions more effectively than staff members. Pat King, a member of a consulting group —the Los Angeles based International Center for Educational Development—sees these advantages in being a free-lance advisor.

On the other hand, an advisor whom the school can afford only on an infrequent basis may be handicapped by not being able to get the feel for the ongoing problems in the school and the context of its community, and by not getting to know teachers well enough to be trusted as a confidant. Most important, the outside advisor usually cannot be in classrooms with teachers frequently enough.

In order to make themselves available to financially pressed schools ICED formed a consortium of four schools around San Francisco Bay from 1971 through 1973. Thus it could send advisors into each of the four schools once or twice a month, could hold leadership problem-sharing sessions with the four principals, and could run several workshops on curriculum and learning theory for the opening teachers in all four schools. But the main focus of the advisory service was to help staffs mobilize their own resources rather than to provide along-side-the-teacher diagnosis of children's learning needs or to model a non-directive diagnostic interaction with children and materials. ICED did coordinate a regular schedule of visits by the consortium teachers to each other's schools—a cross-fertilization valued by teachers.

Another group of open education consultants works through the Advisory for Open Education in Cambridge, Massachusetts, and in Los Angeles. Consulting on long or short-term bases, Allan Leitman and Judith Albaum in the East, and Mel Suhd and William Baker in the West have helped preschool and primary teachers design active-learning environments. But this is only the beginning of open education. If administrators do not provide advisory services beyond this stage, Suhd observes that teachers more often than not revert to more traditional ways—because they are easier and because there are so many resistances to change within the schools.

Recently Leitman has gone beyond his specialty in materials for learning environments to work as a "listening ear" in a school where some of the staff are dissatisfied with the education they are offering. He sees a few teachers, students, and the principal in regular, individual interviews. The purpose of this advising is to help the staff achieve greater self-awareness of their teaching and learning habits. He encourages them to keep journals about their day-to-day work, to be reflective, and to problem-solve rather than to react emotionally about what they experience as institutional rigidities or interpersonal hostilities. Charles Rathbone comments from his experience as a teacher receiving help from Leicestershire advisors that stimulating such personal assessment is a significant aspect of English advisors' work, but that such counseling touches on professional concerns solely; they consider teachers' deeper personal problems or strivings out of bounds in the advisory relationship.

Another open education consultant group, the Adjunct Services Department of the private Prospect School in North Bennington, Vermont, specializes in diagnostic services for schools going through the opening process. These are available on an infrequent basis and only with teachers with whom Prospect has a long-term involvement, following the teachers' participation in a summer workshop. In a visit of several days, Prospect advisors observe classrooms and the whole school environment, especially the interactions between children and teachers. Then they discuss with teachers whatever uncertainties they are feeling and conduct staff workshops and parent meetings.

The EDC Open Education Advisory—distinct from the Follow Through project—also copes with the problem of school districts not providing teachers with intensive enough advisory service. Norellen Stokley diagnoses this problem as "experiential" rather than financial.

> School systems which have no experience of how advisories work ask simply for workshops for teachers. They don't understand that what teachers need is long-term, in-depth, highly diagnostic developmental work by advisors going into classrooms where they can observe and help teachers in their interactions with children. Thus during the first year of an agreement with a district, our task is to show the administration what this kind of service can accomplish.
>
> In ensuing years we hope to work with them to figure out how they can gradually insert advisory service—performed either by district staff or by outsiders—into their ongoing budget. It need not cost additional funds. Most districts can divert money from textbook expenditures, curriculum supervisors, inservice training. We believe that if a school could experience two advisors working in the school eight days a month for ten months they would be convinced this is a service they should retain.

Gauging advisors' worth

It might be easier to convince school district administrators if they could be shown precisely what teachers actually gain from an advisor. Early, incomplete documentation is available from a project still underway at Educational Testing Service's Developmental Research Division. In 1972, ETS psychologists Edward Chittenden, Marianne Amarel, and Anne Bussis interviewed 64 teachers who were working with advisors from EDC Follow Through, Open Corridor, Community Resources Institute, and Creative Teaching Workshop. They characterized them as being "ordinary" rather than "star" teachers. Analyzing the whole set of interviews, the psychologists identified 13 different kinds of support that the teachers thought they were receiving from advisors. Different teachers were aware of different kinds of support. The psychologists set up a classification scheme ranging from advisory offerings that the teacher sees herself as "taking in," to advisor activities that require "self-investment" by the teacher. They describe the "taking in" kinds of support as follows:

"A. Service/Administrative Agent" (for instance, the advisor bringing and making materials, acting as a buffer with the administration).
"B. Extension of Teacher" (the advisor working with children, arranging the room helping in the Corridor or resource room).
"C. Stage Director/Demonstrator" (showing how to work with children, offering specific direction and criticism, giving helpful hints, showing what not to do).
"D. Diagnostician/Problem Solver" (identifying problem areas, advising on specific problems with children).

Two kinds of support are seen by teachers as emotional support:

> "E. Emotional Stabilizer/Stimulator" (reinforcing, praising, boosting morale, listening, "caring," inspiring a sense of group belonging).
>
> "F. Respecter of Individuality" (accepting where the teacher is, respecting his/her professional integrity).

A final group of support services by the advisor stimulates increasing intellectual involvement and initiative by the teacher.

> "G. Provider of Alternatives" (the advisor contributing ideas for the teacher to adapt, arranging workshops for exploring new materials).
>
> "H. Explainer/Lecturer/Theorist" (explaining reasons for specific actions in a theoretical context, providing literature on open education).
>
> "I. Modeling Agent" (providing a model of interaction with children over materials, or with teachers over issues, so that the teacher can infer patterns of new behavior).
>
> "J. Appreciative Critic/Discussant/Thoughtful Observer" (discussing matters in depth, analyzing classroom work, expanding the teacher's framework for evaluation).
>
> "K. Provocative/Reflective Agent" (asking stimulating questions, helping the teacher become aware of needs and progress, helping the teacher clarify ideas).
>
> "L. Leader/Challenger/Extender" (stimulating continuing growth, leading teachers to new insights in the teaching/learning process, acting as an "enabler" of the teacher, as the teacher is an "enabler" of children).
>
> "M. Agent of Social/Philosophical Change" (promoting new patterns of relationships among teachers, between teachers and children, between school and parents, encouraging new values in teachers for decision making, responsibility).[21]

Amarel, Bussis, and Chittenden write that an intriguing, if only tentative, finding seems to be that the kinds of assistance which teachers value in their advisors appear to be related to the teacher's "frame of reference"—that is, values and working assumptions "about how children learn, about the nature and organization of knowledge, about the purpose and goals of the curriculum."[22]

Among their interviewees the researchers found teachers whose frame of reference was basically "a method orientation"—doing new things and introducing new materials. Others had "a managerial orientation"—basically a wish to individualize instruction. Still others had "a model orientation, struggling to replicate some vague or fairly detailed image of what British Infant School classrooms look like." But a distinct group had a frame of reference based on the desire to investigate the whole teaching/learning process—to broaden their definition of what learning is, where curriculum comes from, how teachers teach, and also how they learn. In short, these teachers seem to be searching for different standards of quality in schooling than they see in traditional education.

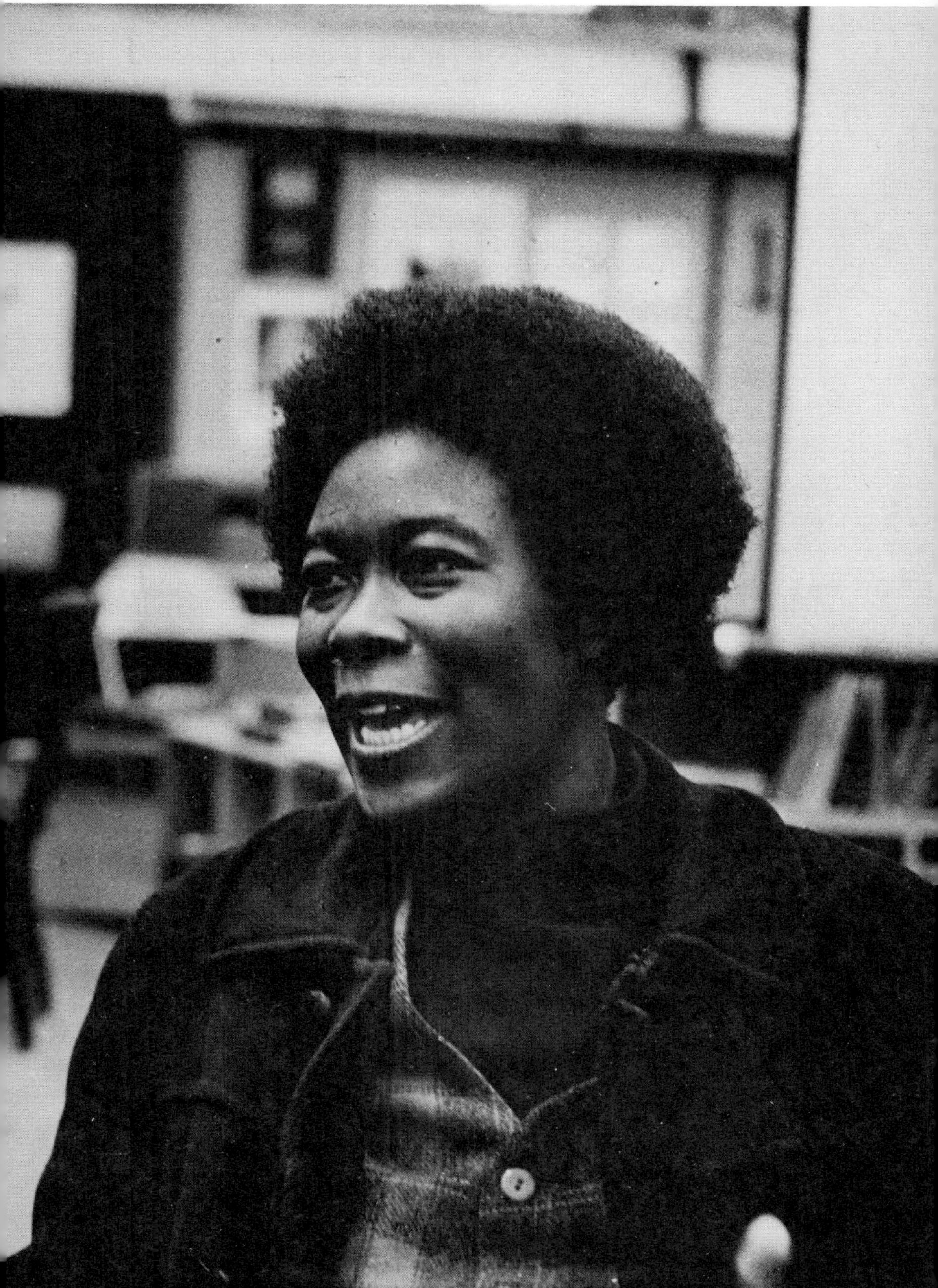

> Those teachers who seem to be operating from more of a "model" or "method" framework— those who regard open education more as an "it" which they are trying to do—are pulling almost exclusively [on the kinds of assistance labeled A through E]....In contrast, those teachers who seem to be operating from a more independent, active, "evolving standards of quality" framework are clearly drawing from the whole range of support (A through M) available to them.
>
> It should be emphasized that these are initial findings, and obviously there is more coding and integrating [of the interviews] to be done. We also intend to re-interview a small subsample of teachers [in spring 1973] and to visit their classrooms. It seems clear at this time, however, that one result of the study will be useful implications for how advisory groups might best work with teachers over time.[23]

University of Illinois professor Bernard Spodek, co-director of an advisory at Urbana serving six Illinois communities, has also identified differences in the way teachers respond to advisors. It is not just that different teachers want different supports, but that over time the same teachers seem to want different kinds of help from advisors. Spodek illustrates this with what he calls "the onion construct."

> Teachers may be viewed as being made up of various levels. The external levels might include accepted room arrangements, specific selected texts, classroom materials, etc. Closer to the core come specific instructional strategies....Within the core of the teacher are a set of professional beliefs and values, beliefs about the nature of childhood, the nature of education or schooling, the role of the teacher, and so on....
>
> Characteristics in the external layers of the teacher are more responsive to external stimuli or pressures, hence they are easier to change. (For instance, teachers seldom resist reorganizing the physical structure of the classroom or creating activity centers.) As we move to deeper layers, greater resistance to change is felt. (It is harder to affect the reading program than the science program.) And characteristics closest to the internal layers of beliefs are even more resistant to change. (It is difficult for many teachers to share real decision-making power with their children.) Understanding the depth of layering of a particular practice might help the advisor to develop more effective strategies for change as well as help him accept resistance and difficulties related to certain kinds of change.[24]

Spodek says there is need for ethnographic research—observations of several kinds of advisors in different working situations with teachers. This might be used to identify styles of advisories, from which teachers and administrators could decide which would suit them best. It could also be a beginning for formulating some guidelines about how to perform this new role in American schools.

Characteristics of advisor

For instance, though it seems obvious that there is no one way to structure an advisor's work any more than there is one way to be an open classroom teacher, the collective experience of the advisory projects described in this chapter suggests the following ideal qualities in an advisor:

• Mastery of classroom teaching—as David Hawkins says, the advisor needs to be a teacher who has gotten his "second wind."

• Experience in teaching with naturalistic, open-ended learning materials.

• Understanding of developmental learning principles and talent for clarifying and making real this approach to instruction—so that teachers gain a point of view.

• Some depth in one area of curriculum or scholarship.

• Enthusiasm to learn more, especially in a personal interest—inquisitiveness and resourcefulness that communicate naturally to teachers and children.

• Confidence and leadership in working with adults—unforced authoritativeness and assertiveness that can enable the advisor to maintain independence from the school administration and to command teachers' attention in entirely voluntary situations.

• Interpersonal communication skill.

• Preference for becoming involved in other people's growth—teachers and children—as distinguished from interest in other important elements of school management—budgets, evaluation systems, equipment—or espousal of particular instructional products or methods.

• Respect for teachers' individuality and privacy—unwillingness to prevail upon a teacher and insistence on being specifically invited before going into any teacher's classroom. Mary Stitt, Arlington Heights, Illinois, principal, comments on the need for a form of reserve in the advisor:

> Changing one's classroom to open education is an intensely personal experience. Some teachers going through this experience do not want another person watching everything they're doing. The teacher really has to get started on her own and then reach out for help.

Advisory services as graduate training

Several colleges and universities are examining both the qualities of the advisor and the varying patterns of their work as they pilot test what the advisor's role may be in the United States. These pilot enterprises center in universities not because there is some strong belief that a specific academic preparation should be required for an advisor—there are no such requirements in England—but because among master's and doctor's degree students in education there are available candidates to try out the new role.

The Open Corridor advisory program is attached to City College of New York, recruiting advisor apprentices who have a rich background of past experience in teaching and child development. Advisors are selected for maturity, flexibility, and generosity in support of another's strength—qualities that Lillian Weber sums up as "having gotten past the period of engrossment with their 'own thing.' " The two-year apprenticeship involves responsibility for a public school Corridor community. The apprentices begin with a two-week institute in theory and strategies for developing learning environments. Throughout the school year apprentices attend weekly all-day seminars and planning sessions with Weber. Regular seminars emphasize the cognitive and linguistic development of children, reading, Spanish language, and bilingual education. Several advisor trainees have come from the CCNY graduate program in open education for teachers with experience in open classrooms.

The University of Illinois School of Education for three years used its EPDA program to send doctoral fellows to public schools as in-classroom advisors and workshop leaders. The University of Connecticut in the fall of 1973 began an advisory center staffed by six doctoral fellows who form intensive, long-term relationships (as long as three years) with nearby schools. They also give workshops from their advisory center on campus, serving a growing network of open schools throughout the state.

The University of North Dakota's Center for Teaching and Learning offers graduate students the opportunity of doing their practicum work as "resource colleagues" to teacher interns who are spending their first year as open classroom teachers in schools throughout the state. Faculty members also act as advisors to interns, thus helping to train resource colleagues and supplementing their assistance to interns.

Moving into the system

Through university graduate degree programs and through federal and foundation support, the American initiators of open education have provided several exemplary American advisories. Continued experience and refinement depends on their ability to pioneer still further, integrating advisors into existing school systems and payrolls. Open Corridor has been encouraged by the appointment of one of its advisors to an assistant principalship in a New York public school and the appointment of another as a "coordinator for open education" for a subdistrict within the Board of Education.

Other hopeful signs are the examples of the Minneapolis Southeast Alternatives project, one of the Experimental Schools Projects of the National Institute of Education, and the Early Childhood Division of the North Carolina State Department of Public Instruction. In Minneapolis, 14 resource teachers making up a "teacher cadre" serve the five alternative schools, functioning not as curriculum installers but as responders to the needs of teachers working out new programs. They are supervised by a board composed of teachers, parents, and students, and are based in a teachers' workshop center. In North Carolina, eight advisors, who are called regional coordinators in early childhood education, work out of regional offices throughout the state. They are on call to teachers in schools that are changing their primary programs to a child-centered approach inspired by the open schools of England. In fact, English teachers have worked as North Carolina advisors. School participation is growing much faster than the regional advisory staffs, so the advisors' help tends to be spread thin.

David Hawkins suggests a study be done of the present role of curriculum coordinators in the offices of county superintendents of schools. Now they work generally as go-betweens from state departments to school districts, mainly concerned with administration and installation of state programs and legislative mandates. Could their function be changed so that they would relate not to whole school districts but to individual schools, go only where invited, not install programs but set up teachers' centers, do intensive classroom counseling, and teach school-site workshops?

Such explorations of means for institutionalizing the role of the advisor in public school systems now seem imperative to open educators. The situation in scores of schools which have successfully begun a few open classrooms is similar to that which Lillian Weber perceived after two years trying out Open Corridors in New York public schools.

> The need for the role of advisor and for the development of people who would be able to fulfill such roles became especially critical once it became clear . . . that *it was indeed possible to develop informal education within the structure of the public system.* Spreading the developments . . . depended on support from a person who understood what was involved in these changes. . . .[25]

American open educators have learned a basic lesson from the 40 years' growth of open education in England, from the American progressive movement, "R & D" curriculum innovations, and their own work in this country since 1965. That lesson is that the depth and lastingness of a teacher's change depends on a close, long-term relationship to "a teacher's teacher," one who projects the same approach to learning that the changing teacher is trying to practice. Since it seems predictable that for the forseeable future most American principals are not going to be able to act as headteachers, the role of the advisor is crucial to the growth and health of open education in American public schools.

Footnotes

1. Sir Alec Clegg, *Revolution in the British Primary Schools* (Washington, D.C.: Association of Elementary School Principals, 1971), p.43.
2. Sybil Marshall, *An Experiment in Education* (London: Cambridge University Press, 1966), pp. 18-19.
3. Clegg, *Revolution in the British Primary Schools,* p. 43.
4. Bill Browse and Tony Kallet, "Leicestershire: A Case History," *Educating Teachers* (New York: Citation Press, 1972), p. 50.
5. Seymour Sarason, *The Culture of School and the Problem of Change* (Boston: Allyn and Bacon, 1971), p. 157.
6. Ibid., pp. 167-168.
7. Nicholas Rayder and Glen Nimnicht, Determining Forces that Influence Teachers Through Force Field Analysis, unpublished document (Far West Laboratory, 1855 Folsom St., San Francisco, Cal., 1972).
8. David Weikart, "Open Framework Evolution of a Concept in Preschool Elementary Education," *The National Elementary Principal* 51, no. 1 (April 1972): 59-62.
9. *Ibid.,* p. 61.
10. *Ibid.*
11. David Armington, "Key Elements of Open Education," mimeographed (Educational Development Center, 55 Chapel St., Newton, Mass., 1969), p. 3.
12. Anne Bussis and Edward Chittenden, *Analysis of an Approach to Open Education* (Princeton, N.J.: Educational Testing Service, 1970), p. 51.
13. *Ibid.,* pp. 51-52.
14. *Ibid.,* pp. 52-53.
15. Lillian Weber, "Development in Open Corridor Organization: Intent and Reality," *The National Elementary Principal* 52, no 3 (1972): 65.
16. *Ibid.,* p. 63.
17. *Ibid.,* p. 64.
18. David Hawkins, "Development as Education: A Proposal for the Improvement of Elementary Education," *Science and Technology in Developing Countries,* ed. Zahlen and Nader (London, Cambridge University Press, 1968), p. 530. Reprints available from the Mountain View Center for Environmental Education, University of Colorado, 1511 University Ave., Boulder, Colo.
19. *Ibid.*
20. Jennifer Andreae, *Theresa, Theatre and Terrariums: Open Education, ESEA Title 1* (Albany, N.Y.: New York State Department of Education, Division for the Disadvantaged, 1971), p. 26. Another account by Andreae of her work in New Rochelle, invaluable for those who wish to work as advisors, can be found in Ewald Nyquist and Gene Hawes, *Open Education: A Sourcebook for Parents and Teachers* (New York: Bantam, 1972), pp. 220-250.

21. Marianne Amarel, Anne Bussis, and Edward Chittenden, *Teacher Perspective on Change to an Open Approach* March 1, 1973. (expanded version of a paper read at the annual meeting of the American Educational Research Association, New Orleans, La.)

22. *Ibid.*, p. 10.

23. *Ibid.*

24. Bernard Spodek (Paper presented at the annual meeting of the American Educational Research Association, Chicago, Ill., April 3-7, 1972), p. 126.

25. Lillian Weber, "Report to Ford Foundation on the Advisory Service to Open Corridors," mimeographed (1972), pp. 53-54.

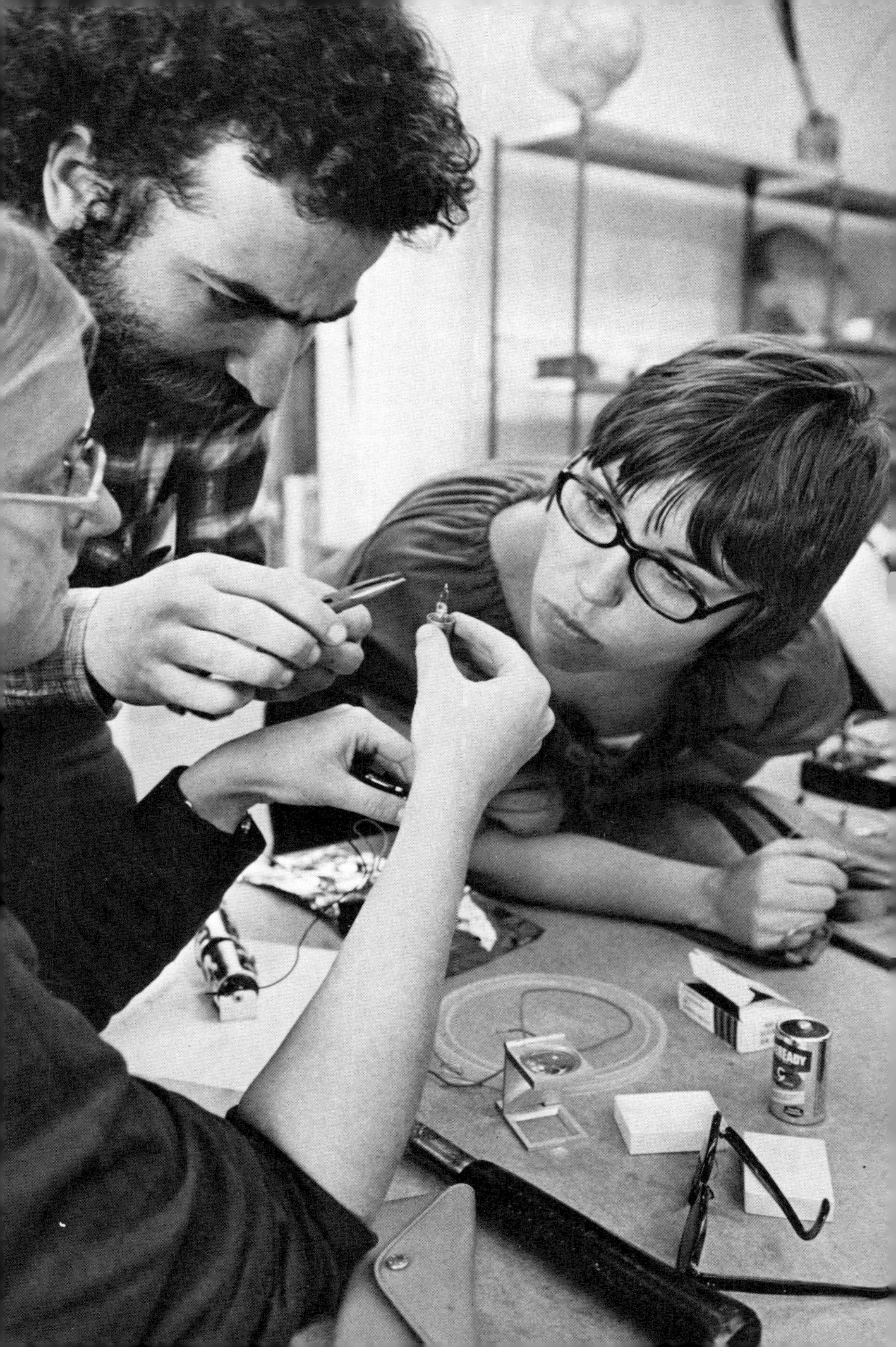

Chapter 5

The Teacher as Learner

An open classroom can hardly open—let alone survive and thrive—without decisiveness in the teacher. But making instructional decisions is a power too rarely wielded by contemporary American teachers in public elementary schools. Thus it is ironic that in the United States the teacher is seen as the key to quality education. The assumption that the American teacher controls quality is obvious in those recent American curriculum innovations which have aimed to improve instruction by reducing the influence of the teacher and introducing "teacher-proof" curriculum materials. Belief in the controlling role of the teacher is also evidenced by the American accountability movement, which would have the teacher at the start of the year guarantee a certain standard of pupil performance and would hold him responsible for achieving that standard by the end of the year. These attempted reforms assume a degree of control over the instructional process which most American teachers neither possess nor believe they possess.

The teacher's role in England

Both the image and the reality of the American teacher as decision maker contrast with the situation in English informal schools, as Bernard Spodek points out.[1] There teachers participate in the instructional planning in each school but the head teacher is held responsible for the quality of the whole educational program. With the security of the head's active, teaching supervision, teachers together exercise choice about the syllabus for the entire school and individually choose the specific materials and methods they will use in their own classrooms. They make much more broadly influential educational decisions than American teachers do, and they do not have to make them in isolation. Perhaps because English teachers do not feel alone on the barricades, good English open schools are characterized by the excellence of teachers' personal relationships with children and with other teachers, and these also have a powerful educational influence. Alec Clegg writes, "Right personal relationships will do more for education than gadgets, kits, rules. . . ."[2]

Such relationships are striking to an American visitor because they connote the teachers' deep involvement in their jobs and professional growth. Edward Chittenden comments that in some English open schools the spirited, practical, and cooperative interchange among teachers made it appear that these schools were settings for adults' as well as children's learning.[3]

101

In England the teacher's learning has just two basic elements, Clegg says; first, instruction *of* teachers is *by* teachers who exemplify successful practice, and second, they teach teachers as they would have teachers teach children.[4]

The most influential teacher of teachers is the head. Following formal college preparation, the teacher continues to be taught informally. Cook and Mack say that the teacher looks to the head for support as the child looks to the teacher. During the year of teaching required before permanent certification, young teachers experience what amounts to an apprenticeship situation, in which they work alongside the head or assistant head until they are confident about taking charge on their own. It is expected that each teacher will develop individual style and strengths within the framework set by the head. The head personally introduces new approaches and new materials to the staff, and has the teachers work through them in the same way that the children will use them.[5]

Preparation of teachers in England

The education which prepares for teaching in England may be a nationally-supported college of education course of three years, or a university one-year course, leading to the master's degree, for holders of bachelor's degrees. Prospective teachers begin part-time classroom teaching at the very start of their training. This assignment helps them gain practical understanding of the developmental learning theory they study through lectures, seminars, and readings. As one instructor put it, "I saturate students in children."[6] The second stage of preparation emphasizes a disciplinary major and elementary curriculum, paralleled by more in-classroom work at an increasing level of responsibility. Finally, teachers in training spend a full term in a responsible classroom situation.

There is no attempt to provide teachers a "once-and-for-all" preparation, write Molly Brearly and Nora Goddard, but rather to instill "understanding of principle and flexibility of mind."

> We leave our teachers as helpless as dinosaurs if we devise an education for them which purports to "equip" them in the initial stages for the rest of their teaching life.[7]

Inservice in England

A rich variety of subjects and learning styles is available for English teachers' continuing education. Courses are provided by the universities, the national Department of Education and Science, the teachers' union, county advisors coming into a school, and local education authorities' teachers' centers. The latter are well-staffed and -supplied workshops and classrooms offering afternoon, evening, and weekend or vacation-term courses. They also encourage teachers to make drop-in visits for socializing or informal discussions and information seeking. The first centers were established by the Nuffield Foundation and the National Schools Council, when Nuffield mathematics and science guides were introduced to teachers, so that they could work with each other on the practical problems of implementing the new materials and ideas. Now centers offer work in all subject areas. Fees for all courses are minimal, but most provide no credit or points toward advancement on salary schedules. Bill Browse and Tony Kallet comment that this is all to the good.

> In general, the fewer extrinsic reasons there are for attending courses, the more likely teachers are to benefit from them. There is little to recommend a course if the participants would rather be elsewhere.[8]

During his work in Leicestershire, Kallet observed that 700 of the 1500 teachers in the authority attended a no-credit course at some time during a year.

Professional status

In addition to the support received from their preparatory and continuing education and from their head teachers and colleagues, English teachers perceive community support by virtue of their professional status, which is, in Kallet's estimation, much higher than is that of American teachers. He defines the "profound difference" between the English and American school systems not in terms of differences in people but of differences in the conditions under which they work.

> English teachers have lots of complaints but morale is pretty high. There is a real sense in which teaching is a profession. The schoolmaster was traditionally a remote and powerful figure and the community did not enter into his kingdom. A lot of this is gone, thank goodness, but the public, even though it is involved in education increasingly, still feels that teachers are people who have training and knowledge which ought to be listened to.

In contrast to the "authority" accorded to English teachers, Kallet and others see the ordinary American teacher as ill prepared for the realities of the classroom, vulnerable to community criticism and pressure, unable to contribute effectively to the educational goals of their schools or to choose curriculum materials, isolated from other teachers, unstimulated by continuing education courses, and bored.

From his British perspective, Peter Raggatt observed that American teachers' professional judgments frequently succumb to community pressure groups or that controversial matters are avoided entirely, because of tenure anxieties.

> Closely related to the teacher's readiness to make decisions is his occupational security. In England, the first year of teaching is termed a probationary

year, and the teacher's competence and professional growth are evaluated at the end of that period. If successful . . ., the teacher is then qualified and gains tenure. This tenure is recognized by every authority in England and lasts until retirement. . . . Firing a teacher, except for proved incompetence, is unknown. . . .

In America concern about tenure may often become central to a teacher's objectives. Not only is the period of probation longer, but with the high rate of geographical mobility in the United States, tenure is a recurring problem. Few teachers are prepared to be contentious in the selection of materials and in the thrust of their teaching while they are seeking tenure. By the time they have tenure, . . . [it may be] impossible to recapture their independence or to change their institutionalized employee role.[9]

Seymour Sarason's interviews with both experienced and new teachers convinced him that the average teacher "is alone with her problems and dilemmas,"[10] and finds neither social nor intellectual stimulation in teaching. Although older teachers routinely took advanced courses in education, "they did not, or could not, see the relevance of these courses to their daily work in the classroom . . ."[11] Nor did young teachers look forward to professional growth and change. *"In fact, some explicitly pointed to some older teachers in the school as examples of what they feared they might become."*[12]

. . . If my observations have merit, they force one to raise a most serious question: *if teaching becomes neither terribly interesting nor exciting to many teachers, can one expect them to make learning interesting or exciting to children?*[13]

Teachers' attitudes toward innovation

The elementary principals' survey in 1968 shows that most principals look for new ideas to come from higher up in the school bureaucracy rather than inviting or welcoming ideas from teachers. (See Chapter 2.) Thus teachers tend not to volunteer ideas. They also tend to depreciate the ideas of other teachers. This situation has been documented from studies of teachers' attitudes toward innovation. A 1969 survey about teacher attitudes toward open education showed that the respondents believed that other teachers—especially older teachers—as well as their principals would disapprove of open classrooms.[14]

The belief that teachers are inherently resistant to change is widespread. There is a general assumption that the curriculum reform movement bent its pick on the rocks of teacher apathy or conservatism. A more thoughtful analysis shows that teachers have been conditioned against innovation. Lillian Weber writes:

It is standardization of administration that perpetuates the organizational modes of the "usual" school. Change goes through the bureaucracy—not through the teacher. The prescribed syllabus, prescribed standard, teacher lessons, produce a lesser freedom for teachers and a lesser involvement in "idea".... The teacher is *not* the experimenter . . . [but] has adapted to the systematization of the school and feels helpless to produce change.[15]

Many teachers themselves believe they are incapable of making judgments about what children need: They trust in the tests and the "teacher-proof" curriculum.

We'll probably go with one of those fancy new reading systems next year because our teachers feel very strongly they need something to help them. They have test data to show that kids are below grade level in reading.[16]

Concerned, uncynical teachers often read such data to mean that they, the teachers, have failed and that if left to their own devices they will inevitably fail. A first-grade teacher in an open classroom in an inner-city school described her former feeling of failure as a sense that she, the teacher, had nothing to give to children.

Mis-education of teachers

Open educators do not believe that the teachers have failed, but that the educational system has failed both the children and the teachers. Teachers, after all, are even more products of the system than are children; they have been in it longer. The educational system has distorted the natural learning system with which teachers were born, says J. Richard Suchman, a teacher educator and curriculum developer at Human Resources Research Organization, Monterey, California. Thus he believes "you cannot persuade the teacher to change unless you liberate him as a learner. The top must be spinning on its own before you can change its direction by touching it."

Such views both precede and transcend the open education movement. A recent incication of dissatisfaction with teacher education can be found in the "Value Statement" of the National Study Commission on Undergraduate Education and the Education of Teachers at the University of Nebraska, funded by the National Center for the Improvement of Educational Systems in the Office of Education. In 1972 the commission sent to more than 1,000 institutions of higher education a "Value Statement," urging the following reforms in the way they educate prospective teachers.

 1. Liberal arts and science faculties should interest themselves in teacher education and create undergraduate programs "more attuned to career needs and less oriented to research."

 2. Professors who teach theory and schools which provide practicum experiences should interweave their efforts so teachers are prepared to meet classroom realities.

 3. Colleges must do a better job of selecting prospective teachers.

4. School boards and parents should be involved in setting policy for teacher education programs.[17]

North Dakota's Center for Teaching and Learning

Several of these reforms have been underway at the University of North Dakota since 1968, when the New School of Behavioral Studies in Education was begun as an experimental program within the College of Education. In order to fulfill a state mandate to re-educate practicing teachers not holding bachelor's degrees, as well as to prepare new teachers, the New School chose to apply the ideas of open education—both in the classrooms the student teachers would prepare for children and in the organization and conduct of the college program itself. Thus George Frein, one of the humanities professors who joined with educationists to form the faculty of the New School, came to think of his teaching as "improvisation on themes composed by students."[18]

Vito Perrone, director of the New School and now dean of its successor, the Center for Teaching and Learning, described what he considered to be the unique qualities of the New School:

> We select faculty who have backgrounds that will be useful to schoolchildren as well as to college students, and who have varied talents rather than narrow academic interests.
>
> Every faculty member needs to be involved every semester in the field—in touch with advisees interning or practice teaching in the schools; in touch with children.
>
> A student here can study almost anything that he feels is really essential to working with children. A faculty member can put up a notice that says, "I feel these things are important and would like to discuss them for the next few weeks. These are things you might read. You can sign up here." This is a way for a course to be organized. Students can do this, too. People here have to establish their own structure, and they do. This means they have to break their habit of depending on knowledge givers. A lot of students do express, early in our program, considerable frustration. Later they begin to believe they can establish a direction of their own, and they have resources in themselves, and they can use faculty as resources rather than as experts.
>
> Goals are established and progress is evaluated by the student and his faculty advisor together, meeting in conference every week. The experienced North Dakota teachers who come to us for our internship master's program all are at different points of professional growth. Each is struggling in her own way, working in different school circumstances. So we don't make judgments about them either while they are here or when they return to their schools. We evaluate teachers to see how we can improve the quality of our program and to assist individual teachers to improve.

With the merger of the New School faculty and the rest of the college of education into the Center for Teaching and Learning, the open approach is being applied in a much larger setting—1,400 undergraduate and graduate students, including prospective school administrators. But the cornerstones are still the convictions that students should "assume greater initiative and independence in their own learning;" that the full-time faculty should be a combination of educators and science and liberal arts professors; that students should have "first-hand ongoing contacts with children and youth [to] fuse their academic background, knowledge of child and adolescent growth and development, and educational and learning theory;" and that the governing bodies of the Center should not be composed of professors only but of students, faculty, practicing teachers, local school board members, state and local district officials, and parents.[19] This last point emerges from increasing involvement with communities, especially parents' groups. Perrone and other faculty members have generated parent and community support systems to sustain fledgling open teachers, who are frequently isolated in their schools.

The New School approach is also projected in the Center's Follow Through program in Fort Yates, N.D., Zuni, N.M. (both Indian communities), Great Falls, Mont., and three communities near Seattle—Burlington-Edison, Ferndale, and Sedro Wooley, Wash.

Selecting and training new teachers

One major problem in teacher education named by the Study Commission—how to select prospective teachers—has caused debate within the North Dakota faculty. The New School gained a national reputation for open education that attracted students from outside the state—not only highly qualified people but also some with no commitment to intellectual work either for themselves or for children. Such students are familiar elsewhere. A British open educator who has taught at the University of California, Berkeley, describes the American student who should be discouraged from enrolling in teacher preparation programs:

> He has a low valuing of expertise, a fear of playing an adult role, and a fear of imposing something on children. This is expressed in his relatively inarticulate, self-effacing, childlike speech and rejection of any structuring. He seems to believe, "If you tell children at any time what to learn you're telling them how to live."
>
> Isn't it ironic that people who convey and apparently feel so little sense of their own competency should attempt to give children an experience that will lead them to competency? It seems that their ideas flow out of their experiences as students rather than out of experiences as teachers. The sense of their being students results in immature, shallow concepts of learning; heavy emphasis on children's choices but almost none on their responsibilities.[20]

On the other hand, open education's concept of curriculum and teacher role is so different from the conventional idea of the elementary school teacher that it attracts young people with talent and background in science and liberal arts who see open classroom teaching as a challenging, experimental, and intellectual activity.

English advisors and heads who have met young American teachers interested in open education are impressed by greater eagerness to learn and more enthusiasm than they are used to seeing in average British teachers.

However, American open educators believe that, in the long run, patience and other coping and learning traits are more valuable than enthusiasm. For example, the University of California Cooperative Teacher Preparation Project (in Berkeley) uses a set of tasks instead of personal interviews when selecting participants for their three-year graduate-level program. These tasks "test" for patience and other "enabling behaviors" deemed essential to open teaching.

Among these behaviors are accepting, listening, tolerating periods of silence, questioning, provisioning environments for learning, assessing, and modeling the self-directed, inquiring behavior desired of children in an open classroom. Project director Lawrence F. Lowery says that he does not expect entering graduate students (30 each year) to be highly accomplished in all these behaviors, since these are the skills the program expects to develop. However, Lowery does want to enroll people already tending in these directions rather than to put time and effort into students whose main recommendation is enthusiastic embrace of open education.

An example of one of the Project's screening tasks is as follows:

> Two candidates, separated by a screen, are seated at tables. Each has materials with which he can build a tower or other structure. One of the candidates is instructed to build whatever he pleases. The challenge is for the two to work together, staying on separate sides of the screen and talking with each other, so that the second candidate is able to build a copy of the first candidate's structure. The task probes listening and questioning behavior, consideration and assessment of the other person's point of view, sense of mutuality, and diagnosing. It reveals egocentricity, authoritarian, interrupting behavior, passivity, etc.

The project piloted several such tasks with sets of the candidates they interviewed in each of the first two years of the program (1971-73). Other candidates were screened using conventional scholastic and personal references and personal interviews. By the end of each school year differences in the teaching performance of the student teachers had convinced the project staff that the tasks were far more predictive of success in open teaching than were staff judgments in interviews. They now use these tasks for all screening.

This program also demonstrates the kind of close cooperation between a university and a school district (Mt. Diablo district in Walnut Creek, California) called for by the study commission on the preparation of teachers. The student placements and subsequent hirings by the district (100 percent of graduates have teaching jobs) make it possible for project advisors to work with young teachers during the student placement year and two subsequent years when they are regular teachers. Thus they have three years in which to integrate teachers' learning of Piagetian theory—the foundation and focus of the academic program—with classroom practice in assessing children's stages of development. District teachers and principals are eligible to receive the same theoretical and practical training.

There are now teacher education programs in all parts of the country specializing in the preparation of teachers for open classrooms. Most of them are designed to "saturate" the student in experiences with children. This can be a mixed blessing to the teachers whose classes they are assigned to. In some schools the student teacher adds to the classroom teacher's already considerable supervisory load. (Teachers not yet well-experienced in open teaching, with a paraprofessional aide, several parent volunteers, and one or more student teachers all on board at once, have been known to complain that these helpers are an embarrassment of riches.) The practicing teacher may also regard the student teacher as a potential competitor for scarce teaching jobs.

It is not automatic that college programs in open education allow or require students to practice self-directed learning, so they can begin to develop the independent judgment and decisiveness which open educators consider a prerequisite in the classroom teacher. Yet this is a particularly difficult trait for many competent and idealistic American students to learn, observes teacher educator William E. Baker. Many students most philosophically committed to open education "have to struggle through their ambivalence about choice, because they have been very well rewarded for years for being docile and obedient. Thus their unconscious choice is to be directed, while their conscious, intellectual choice is to reject authority." They need many opportunities for self-directed decision making while they are still in college.

"Seasoning" the young teacher

Beginning teachers who want to teach in an open way also need a substantial apprenticeship, writes Edward Yeomans, director of the Greater Boston Teacher Center. Since 1968 Yeomans has been directing workshops in open education for American public and private school teachers. From this experience he observes:

> Young teachers, full of idealism and rebellion at the formulations of graduate schools and teachers colleges, need time to become integrated as people before taking responsibility for an integrated environment. . . . [T]hey should intern as active and involved apprentices under a secure and skillful teacher, to allow time for their energies to focus. . . . Practice teaching for a term is not apprenticeship. A full year is not too long a period for the beginning of that seasoning process which is indispensable. . . . [21]

It is this seasoning which is indispensable, not the academic degree, says David Hawkins:

> But who is the skilled teacher? I think of two Kikuyu teachers, in the Ngong forest of Kenya, with primary schooling plus two years of secondary; one would not trade them for very many B.A.'s. To be a skilled teacher in primary school is to satisfy criteria which higher education seldom aims to bestow: to be easy and attentive with children, to find them fascinating bundles of capability and potential; to love the world around, and to wish to induct children into the exploration of its marvels and mysteries; to know enough of the disciplines to be able to learn sometimes with children rather than ahead of them. . . . [22]

Hawkins believes teachers should learn the way children learn, and learn from children, "rather than getting bookish knowledge."

> The learning we need in teaching is not what you get in college—it's more fundamental, more basic, much richer. Preparing teachers should spend more time with the really elementary things because they are the really difficult things—like number. Education is not for a pre-assigned task. It's to be able to become your own teacher.

Yet Vincent Rogers, observing accomplished English open teachers for a year, came to think that their superior performance might arise from their "broadness of educational background," their "varied" and "provocative . . . intellectual and cultural *repertoire*."[23] On the face of it these seem far different qualifications from those Hawkins observed in the Kikuyu teachers. However, from their American admirers' descriptions it is clear that both the English and the African teachers have in common a breadth of personal interest and a depth of intellectual involvement, each in their own culture, that enables them to become their own teachers.

Ann Cook and Herb Mack, who supervise a group of Queens College students in open classroom placements in New York public schools, observe that in nonwhite communities there are adults who meet Hawkins' qualifications, who could and should be full teachers in open classrooms, not just assistants. Mack believes that the teacher preparation and credentialling system should be changed to bring into the profession such seasoned, personally integrated but, by academic standards, unsophisticated people.

If such opinions were to become common practice in teacher education programs and school hiring policies, as a result of open education becoming a significant alternative in American public education, educational values would change substantially. School systems with long-term plans for open education would reward teachers for qualities of decisiveness, capacity for continuing learning, cooperation, willingness to change and take risks, and commitment to children, instead of seniority or curriculum specialization. Over years, this change would result in the recruitment of a different kind of person into teaching, and it would change some of the teachers already long established in the profession.

Changing the "seasoned" teacher

But that last statement would be more prophetic if it were turned around: Only if open education *does* change some of the present teaching establishment will it be a significant movement in American public education. As Yeomans says:

> [R]eform in education rides upon the backs of teachers. However compelling may be the theory . . . its ultimate impact upon the experience of children will be proportional to its impact upon the experience of teachers. Moreover, change in education will not take place if its only advocates are beginning teachers . . . . Change must take place in the minds and hearts of at least some of the highly experienced, much respected teachers in a school, who then will welcome the energy and enthusiasm of younger teachers as aids to their commitment rather than as threats to their security.[24]

For change to take place, Yeomans says, the experienced teacher has to replace much of what has stood her in good stead over the years with a new set of beliefs about how children learn, a new stock of materials, and a new repertory of teacher behaviors. In short, the teacher must learn.

That traditional American teachers *can* learn a new style is proven by the experience of teachers in widely differing settings. They are not all "Super Teachers working in super conditions," as ETS researchers Amarel, Bussis, and Chittenden point out in their 1973 analysis of their interviews with teachers in open education projects. But they do have certain characteristics in common.[25]

These are not commonalities in age or length of experience but in beliefs, behaviors with children, and professional style. They include beliefs about how children learn; attitudes about themselves (responsibility, decisiveness, and continual personal learning); honesty, warmth, and respect toward children; provisioning the classroom; continually assessing children's cognitive development; and "guiding and extending" rather than directing children's learning.[26] The ETS researchers suggest that "changing the teacher's image of herself [may be] more difficult than changing her image of children;" in other words, shouldering greater responsibility herself may be a "more central and radical change" than giving more responsibility to children.[27]

Among traditional teachers there are many whose shoulders have been broadened and strengthened by classroom and life experience. Thus, if they begin to accept the learning principles on which open education is based, and when they feel support for change from their administrations, they may be able to effect radical changes in their teaching. Probably such teachers will not have to change their basic personal and professional resources so much as the focus and technique with which they deploy them.

Predictors of success in open teaching

Traditional teachers' rapid, successful change toward open education is documented in a study conducted by an ESEA Title III project (Project COD) in New Bedford, Massachusetts. This project provided advisory services from January to June 1971 to 21 teachers in fourth through eighth grades in several schools. The project goal was to create "a classroom in which the teacher is a supportive resource for students who are extensively self-directed in both what and how they learn."[28] Evaluation of the amount of teacher change was accomplished through an observation instrument focusing on teacher and student behaviors, through analysis of journals kept by teachers, and through questionnaires given to the teachers and their students. Project evaluators concluded that eight teachers' classrooms exhibited a high degree of openness along 36 dimensions, and they all had the following personal characteristics in common:

1. Had five or more years of teaching experience.
2. Was quite directive in previous teaching and was considered successful by peers and supervisors.
3. Tended to be firm and had clearly understood rules.
4. Was considered demanding by students.
5. Considered self as "generalist" rather than subject matter "specialist."
6. Was liked and respected by other staff members and administrators.
7. Showed obvious concern when listening to others.
8. Was very open in relationships with others.
9. Conversed easily with students.
10. Worked cooperatively with the staff members when appropriate.
11. Responded *in action* to the needs of others.
12. Appeared to be confident of themselves.
13. Not easily rattled in a demanding situation.
14. Rarely reacted in extremes.
15. Behaved consistently in varying situations.
16. Was slow to change, but became firmly committed to successes.[29]

What Project COD calls the teacher's commitment to successes, Amarel, Bussis, and Chittenden might term a change in the teacher's frame of reference, a deepening understanding, and firmer acceptance of open education theory and values.[30]

Steven Wlodarczyk, of the University of Illinois open education advisory, considers that belief in the truth and practicability of open education theory is "the crucial factor in a move toward open teaching." He believes a teacher attempting to open her classroom may first have to learn "to trust beliefs and values that may be alien to her own beliefs," acquired during a lifetime career as a student and teacher.[31]

The integrated teacher: "idea" infuses action

It is vital that the teacher's classroom actions match her beliefs; that is, that she not attempt to practice what she has not yet begun to believe. Conversely, Wlodarczyk observes that she should not assume that because she believes in open education theory she is automatically applying it.[32] The teacher beginning to open her classroom needs an advisor or a teaching principal to provide an outsider's objective perspective, over time. The knowledgeable observer helps her compare activities in her classroom with the learning goals she has established for students. The advisor or principal also reassures and teaches her when she falls short of her own standards and helps her clarify new standards and design new practices as she gradually forms her personal idea of open education.

Several open education projects assist the teacher and fulfill their own requirements for self-evaluation by providing descriptions of behaviors of teachers and students common to open classrooms. These are not meant to be copied faithfully but to stimulate the beginner's own ideas.[33]

Mary Collins, advisor at the San Francisco public schools' Teacher Learning Center, tells the beginning teacher that his or her own beliefs about children and about education must form the structure of the open classroom.

> I have them decide what purposes they want to structure for. For instance, I structure for children to make choices about what they read, where they want to be in the classroom, how they learn spelling. *My* structure is for children to take more and more responsibility. Other purposes are for intellectual growth—so you provide a lot of materials for kids to manipulate and have questions about; for social interaction; for privacy; for movement; for building language.
>
> Framing purposes tells the beginning teacher what he wants the classroom to *do* for children. This helps allay anxiety about change because once he has his own guidelines, he sees where he will start and also sees the future in it. He begins to satisfy the purposes he urgently feels, and learns to live with those areas he knows are still unfulfilled.
>
> The awful burden the teacher has—for *environment, climate, relationships, and learning*—makes teachers look for panaceas. So right from the start I say *there is not one right way,* and make them look to themselves for a few decisions. With those decisions made, we look at child groupings and teacher role, and try out several alternative ways of organizing materials, space, and time. Because of so many decisions to be made, that must be based in the teacher's own purposes, it is best for him to think of a time line of two or three years to open a classroom.

Kathleen Raoul, a teacher at Shady Hill School in Cambridge, Massachusetts, adds that this amount of time is also necessary for the children to change.

> Until children feel entirely comfortable in their room with their teacher and with each other, little high-quality work will take place. Nor will it occur without a lot of fumbling and wrong choices and blind alleys.[34]

Inservice first priorities: practical ideas for coping

Both children and teachers need familiar patterns to hang onto during the period of change. English advisors recognize that teachers need "specific ideas for coping with the demands they will face on Monday morning. Most people will sample the unfamiliar, if they are secure in the familiar."[35]

The inservice program that lays out specific materials and suggests room organization may not seem innovative, but it may be indispensable if teachers are not yet prepared to choose from a wide range of possibilities, to make decisions on several aspects of the classroom at once, and to improvise curriculum on the spur of the moment.

> Many of the situations teachers face in their classrooms require specific action at a particular moment. It is important that they be able to draw on a store of techniques and materials which have worked for others and will probably work for them.[36]

There is no requirement that everything done by the open classroom teacher be original; rather that it be thoughtfully prescribed for individual students. The teacher should select materials by working through them and thoroughly understanding the concepts and skills the student can learn from them. Kallet explains:

> It may be useful to think of a dialogue between a child and material, accompanied by a monologue . . . which the child carries on in his mind. . . . In order to join a child-material dialogue, [the teacher] must know what it feels like to work with material. . . . [37]

It is usually harder for an adult teacher to engage with concrete learning materials than to stimulate young students' involvement with the same materials. Thus the instructor of the inservice workshop for teachers may need to suggest a place to begin. Browse and Kallet recommend:

> During a period of rapid educational change, when many teachers are making the transition from formal to more flexible learning situations, a combination of both information and starting points [open-ended explorations of materials] may be more valuable than either alone. From the secure base of help with existing problems teachers can begin to explore new paths . . .[38]

An example of giving information and encouraging exploration was a lunchtime workshop for a small group of teachers at P.S. 152 in Brooklyn, during which Creative Teaching Workshop's advisor Tony Sharkey showed women teachers how to use crosscut, backsaw, and coping saws and hammer and nails, while he answered their questions—first of all, questions about the dangers of tools for children.

Tony: Safety is a function of calmness. Have just a few kids working at one time and they won't be fighting over the materials.

Teacher: What is a knot in a board?

Tony: Where a branch grew. There are many extensions from carpentry; for instance, to learning about trees, learning about paper, and uses of paper, learning to measure and compute. But for young children it's mainly to give them an experience of tools and the physics of hammering, of pulling out a nail, of sawing.

Another teacher: How do you cut down the noise?

Tony: Put the woodshop in the corner of the room and put carpet on the inside of the room divider . . .

This place is available whenever you want to work by yourself, if you don't have familiarity with hand tools. Come and work so you can get familiarity before you work with your kids.

Inservice as the teacher's own learning

When open education instructors set teachers to work with open-ended raw materials, they do not ask them to *pretend* they are children. On the contrary, they challenge them to acknowledge honestly that they are adults whose academic training fails them when approaching basic intellectual tasks that children are confronted with. Pamela McKeown, an advisor in

Bristol, England, who was a consultant at the University of Illinois advisory, gave teachers the simplest materials (water, clay, sand, wood) because most adults have no preconceived ways of how to explain their properties. McKeown believes that an adult faced with materials that do not have a "right" answer or a set of rules will be in the same mental place a child is, and will begin to understand how a child thinks. McKeown gives teachers in a workshop basins of water and plastic drinking glasses and says:

> Estimate how deep in the water this will float. If you put in one handful of wet sand, what will happen? If you put in a half-dozen chestnuts, what will happen?[39]

She takes away rulers, scales, and other standardized measuring instruments and directs teachers to estimate, test, and graph results. For every result she asks, "How do you know?" At the end of a session she and the teachers discuss together the different ways in which each person has worked and thought. Besides the experience of thinking and the knowledge gained of subject matter, teachers gain another essential insight, McKeown believes: understanding the diversity of children's thinking.

How can you say that there is one right way for each child to learn to read or do math or anything?[40]

Once an "opening" teacher gets his feet on the ground, he should have the experience of investigating by himself some non-bookish form of learning he has never done before. Open educators believe such an original learning experience conveys two benefits: 1) If he is paying attention to the progress and the manner of his own self-directed learning, the teacher can compare his problems and satisfactions with his students'. 2) The new learning experience gives him needed practice in making choices and helps him break out of old patterns of being dependent on a knowledge giver.

This form of inservice was developed by the English open educators in residential institutes lasting several weeks. Charles Rathbone, assessing what he gained at such an institute in Leicestershire, wrote that it made him face up to the failures in learning he had avoided before; it also changed his old submissive student habits—looking to the professor, or the lesson, or memory, for the posing of problems and directions for solving them. Most of all, Rathbone realized, the experience revealed to him talents and energies that he hadn't dreamed he had. Rathbone believes that awareness of new-found personal resources is a prerequisite for taking the professional risks that are involved in change to open classrooms.[41]

In this country the National Association of Independent Schools has sponsored such institutes for public and private school teachers in all parts of the country since 1968. City College of New York offers a three-week institute for teachers and principals every summer. Miriam Dorn, CCNY education professor, writes that during the 1972 summer institute teachers selected projects on which they would do "a serious and sustained piece of work. . . ."

> If they have never experienced sustained learning this way (and most have not), it is probably impossible to understand, plan for, and believe in this kind of learning for children.
>
> Students were also informed about what goals they were not to pursue; they were not to stockpile materials for use with children in the fall, they were not to accumulate art objects, they were not to try to approach the materials as they thought a child might. The work was to be adults' work, on an adult level. . . .
>
> Most of the students . . . found themselves out of the kind of learning situation in which they had spent most of their lives . . . The difficulties are innumerable . . . First of all there is great fear of exposing the very elementary level of their understanding. There is also an inability to question. . . . And there is the old fear of "not meeting expectations."
>
> After considerable anxiety and random exploration for the first few days, breakthroughs became evident. One student spent at least four hours trying to wire a bell so that it would ring. She finally got it to do so, and was ecstatic.

. . . Her attitude was, "I'm amazed. I knew all the applicable laws of physics and I didn't have a clue as to how the damn thing really worked. I'm terribly excited because I see how important this kind of thing is for understanding. I really see the difference between verbal, rote understanding and genuine 'how it works' understanding."[42]

Extending and integrating

There is a further stage in the continuing education of teachers that a few open educators have reached. It involves helping experienced open classroom teachers extend a child's initial investigation of a topic into sustained inquiry, and encouraging his branching into other related studies. "Extending" requires first experiencing this kind of learning oneself, in order to perceive what an instructor contributes to inquiry. The teacher also must be able to assess a student's learning from his activities and open his eyes to new possibilities for using his learning. Floyd Page of Creative Teaching Workshop and Lillian Weber of Open Corridor, knowing teachers who have achieved success in organizing their classrooms and using materials with children, now try to provide inservice education which can take them beyond collecting "nifty curriculum ideas" and help them to map out a continuum of learning that a child can pursue with a given material. For instance, says Page,

> If blocks have the power to fascinate children from ages three through eight, they can be used as a starting point for some isolated pieces of learning, but we also have to help teachers see what a child can learn from his use of blocks at all those ages—and how blocks relate to science, math, language, affect.

Teachers' involvement in inservice planning

Open educators have found that some teachers need more structure than others and that many teachers seem to go back and forth between wanting more choices of their own and wanting someone else's guidance. This variation is probably related both to the responses of children in their classrooms and to the uneven development of their teaching technique and understanding of how children learn.

This back-and-forthness can be accommodated if teachers help design their own inservice program around their own problems. Norellen Stokley of the EDC advisory describes the variety that results:

> Workshops we hold for teachers may be related to classroom curriculum or to extending teachers' learning and experience as adults. Thus we have held workshops in the arts; in literature as demonstration of how language develops; in how to keep individual children's records; how to design math and reading games; how to use wood as a medium for interdisciplinary work. We give workshops teachers need because we have advisors in the schools. And the advisors are there after the workshop helping teachers in their classrooms to adapt new curriculum ideas to particular kids.

This manner of offering continuing education to teachers is typical of open education projects but strikingly different from the prevailing American practice, as James F. Collins points out:

> Typically we send teachers away from their teaching environment . . . to take courses at the university or to participate in a regional workshop. The involvement of the teacher in the planning and directing of these experiences is minimal and frequently the interest, enthusiasm and perceived benefit is likewise marginal.[43]

Teachers' centers

The teachers' centers of England have inspired American teachers' centers, now found in most major cities of the United States. They constitute a new, non-establishment form of teacher education, since they evidence varying degrees of teacher participation in program decisions, a minimum of bookish learning, and a maximum of teacher voluntarism. Because academic credit is seldom offered and attendance at particular courses is never mandated by school districts, teachers come to centers to fulfill their own needs and interests. Typically, afternoon and evening courses involve teachers in active learning—math, science, drama, crafts, guitar, dance, photography, and the like. Courses are more often at beginning than at advanced levels. They are given in an atmosphere of no pressure, maximum social interaction, and application to classrooms.

Many centers provide a work space with staff, tools, and construction supplies where teachers can build classroom equipment and learning apparatus. Many centers function also as supply depots where teachers can pick up "stuff" for their classrooms (such things as bolts, rubber washers, wallpaper sample books, parachutes, bleach bottles, cardboard tubes, outdated blank diaries, wood scraps, batteries, refrigerator cartons, paint). Most centers invite parents to participate with the teachers. Many centers serve as headquarters for advisors, who teach in the centers and also help teachers in their classrooms.

A teachers' center need not offer courses at all, if it provides raw materials and workshop facilities. The beginning open classroom teacher first of all needs "a great slew of stuff," Bill Baker says, "and the amount of energy he has to put out to gather it is fantastic." Giving the teacher a place to build is basic, not only because it provides a way to make equipment and storage units the teacher cannot afford to buy, but also because it gives the teacher the experience of imposing his own ideas on materials. Thus the tried-and-true cardboard carpentry workshops pioneered by the Workshop for Learning Things in Watertown, Massachusetts, can hardly be improved on, in Baker's view, as a beginning experience for "opening" teachers.

Teachers well along in their development continue to use centers such as the Workshop Center for Open Education, associated with Open Corridor at City College of New York. The workshop extends the Open Corridor advisory service, providing a place for experienced teachers to extend and integrate curriculum for their students and to teach beginning teachers and CCNY students.

Don Rasmussen, director of the pioneering teachers' center at the Durham Child Development Center of the Philadelphia public schools, describes the way that a workshop creates not only curriculum materials but curriculum itself:

> One second-floor third-grade classroom had a balcony outside one window, and I suggested the construction of a bird feeding station. . . . The teacher liked the idea, and we gathered branches, made feeders, and set up the station. The children observed the kinds of birds that came by, the numbers of each, the times they came, what the birds liked best to eat. They drew pictures, made graphs, and wrote essays. . . .[44]

> We always have hot coffee or tea available at the workshop and explain to people that drinking a cup gives one permission to ask anyone else what he is making and why. It also requires a drinker to explain, when asked, what he is making and why. We try to facilitate as much conversation and exchange of ideas as possible because the best teachers of teachers are other teachers.[45]

The indispensable quality of an open education teachers' center is that the teacher himself decides "what he is making and why," or what he has come to learn and why. Hence, centers must keep themselves open to programming influence by teachers themselves. Some "opening" teachers distrust school district sponsorship of teachers' centers. Even though such sponsorship might solve the budget problem, they fear central administration control of programming.

But there are school-district-sponsored teachers' centers where teachers administer the programs. In San Francisco, the Park South Teacher Center is sponsored by the school district to serve ten public schools in the same attendance zone. Director Doug Haner believes the center's great asset is its emphasis on neighborhood among teachers.

> Teachers' centers need to foster the idea of teachers being committed to a community and to a school. Teachers want something they can be committed to. Once they've been going a few years they will fight to keep the center.

Haner says the teachers' sense of commitment to the Park South Center comes from their being in control by means of the all-teacher advisory council which has one representative from each school. They not only manage the programming to reflect the needs they see in their own schools and to stimulate teacher participation, they also take responsibility for maintaining the relationship with parents and with district administration which are necessary to keep the center funded.

In Minneapolis, the teachers' center for the five schools in Southeast Alternatives project was begun with federal Experimental Schools money. In fall 1973, it began a cooperative relationship with the University of

Minnesota so that it will provide both preservice, inservice, and parent education functions. The inservice activities and expenditures are directed by a committee in which teachers predominate but students, parents, and administrators are also represented.

Parents participate in several teachers' centers. In Philadelphia the District 6 Advisory Center was started by EDC Follow Through, and is now more than half supported by the school district. "Sometimes it gives you the feeling of a settlement house," says Ernestine Rouse, former director. Parents and paraprofessionals take part in curriculum materials workshops and in seminars on learning theory. Their learning has practical results for teachers, Rouse points out.

> Our Philly parents have been instrumental in changing the form of report cards. As they took part in our Center workshops they could begin to judge their children's growth through their conversations and observations at home. They realized that schools have done a disservice to parents by training them to ask only for test scores.

The EDC center participants benefit not only from the mix of parents and teachers but also from the mix of city and suburban teachers, Rouse believes.

> Teachers' centers can break down the wall between inner-city and suburban schools. You can't put your finger on what's communicated in a workshop. But they see that they have the same problems and needs. The suburban teachers learn that inner-city teachers need more support.

What open teachers should be and become

A teacher preparation program for open education starts by enrolling warm people who are committed to children (rather than to a curriculum specialty) and who are unusually energetic, intellectually curious, practical, and flexible.

It should provide these people with the following:
- developmental learning theory,
- immediately useful curriculum materials and classroom organization plans,
- basic concrete experiences with and conceptual understanding of elementary school subject matter,
- adult-level learning experiences requiring sustained inquiry and self-direction,
- ways of assessing children's learning levels, and
- in-classroom modeling and feedback by advisor teachers.

All these components of an inservice program have the objective of helping the teacher develop a personal style of teaching that subtly but firmly supports a child's structuring of knowledge without *pre*-structuring it. In keeping with this objective, teacher educators encourage each teacher

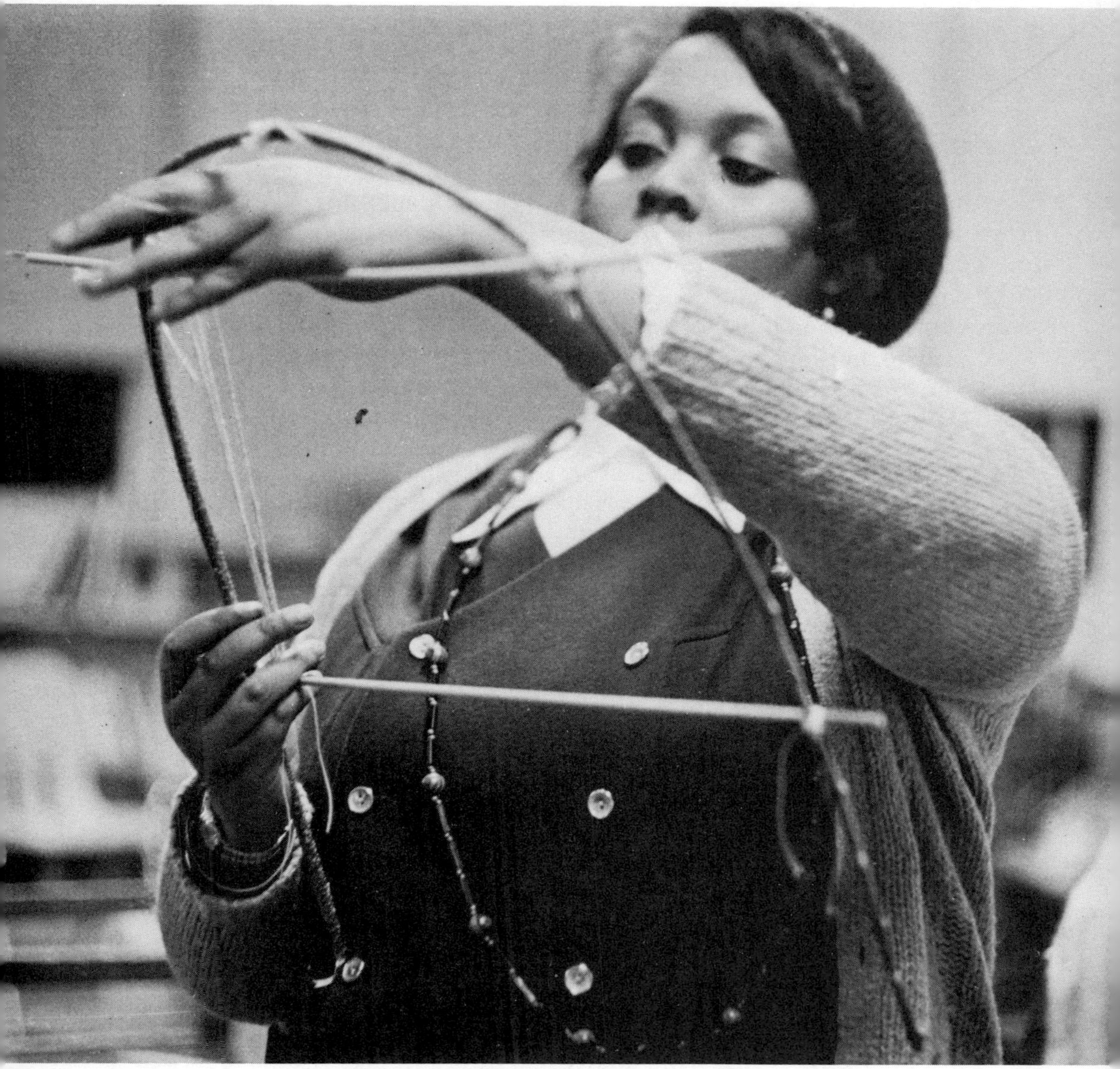

to decide what kind of learning experience he or she needs when. However, as a general rule they place enthusiastic young teachers in practical long-term apprenticeship situations to give them intensive experience with many children, and they steer successful older teachers toward experiences that will encourage them to be curious and creative.

Authority and community

Almost everything American open educators do to prepare teachers is aimed at developing and reinforcing the teacher's decision making, which grows out of purposefulness, self-confidence, authority. But, as Tony Kallet observes, Americans are "very conflicted" on the issue of authority. We do not define an authority as one who knows something and therefore one to whom people voluntarily give their attention, but rather as someone who demands or enforces attention. Open teachers in England have few such conflicts, Kallet says, because they assume that they will receive respect without having to act in authoritarian ways. They do not strive for perfect control, but set firm limits against behavior that will interfere with learning. They have a blend of what Lilian Katz calls "nurturance" and "demandingness."

> [T]he child's feelings and ideas are treated by the adult as valid, but . . . the adult exercises control and sets limits. The adult also makes decisions where his greater experience and maturity can be counted on to lead to better ones than the child alone would make. . . . [T]he quality of authoritativeness is applied to the children's work, as well as to their conduct. . . .[46]

George Hein notes that the whole level of expectation about children's behavior is different in England than in the United States. "Control, discipline, noise, crime, affection, all are expressed at a different level in England, a less intense one."[47] Thus English teachers changing from traditional to open teaching do not imagine that some children are going to create chaos, as many American teachers do. As one American said:

> I saw slides of the English schools and got turned on and wanted to try it, but the reality is that there are always going to be those goofballs. I'm scared to try it. A few lulus are going to screw things up.[48]

Many American teachers feel this way because they have often experienced their administrations not backing up teachers' disciplinary actions. But the ability to project authority with children is also related to the teacher's decisiveness and ability and desire to take responsibility in relationships with other adults. A teacher cannot create a successful open classroom unless he or she has, or gains, confidence in making and carrying out decisions. These decisions almost inevitably involve not just the teacher's own classroom but others in the school. So the price of making individual decisions is to participate in group decisions and to invest the time required to make sound decisions. Many American teachers feel ambivalent about this amount of responsibility. They express the desire to make educational policy but resist involvement in the preparation necessary for policy decisions. Says a resource teacher in an "opening" school:

> We are wanting to involve the teachers in a lot of decisions but we find they don't want to give the time.[49]

And an advisor in a school where parents are working with teachers to plan gradual change toward open education comments:

> The parents are frustrated because the teachers resist making decisions. They keep looking for decisions from the parents. They can't get themselves into a functioning, decision-making body. They can't even get together on a yard program. Teachers' meetings are mindless. The first suggestion that's made gets accepted as the group's decision.[50]

If teachers feel they lack authority and are unwilling to shoulder responsibility, these attitudes frequently arise from experiencing that they are only cogs in the system. Open educators believe these feelings also result from teachers being physically and intellectually isolated and emotionally drained. Ordinary American teachers' mind-sets are toward individual classrooms, where they must work out problems by themselves. Perceiving no significant support coming *in* from the school at large, they are unable to put effort *out*. Being alone all day with 30 children in a classroom drains all their resources.

This is the reason that teacher preparation programs for open education emphasize establishing a sense of community among teachers and parents and administrators within a single school. This community not only can facilitate a wider, richer learning environment for children but also can break the physical, intellectual, and emotional isolation of teachers and provide the outside energy a teacher needs for growth in personal authority and individual teaching style.

Many American admirers of open education have expressed doubt that it can be brought about by "ordinary" teachers. Nevertheless, the experience of American practitioners of open education says quite clearly that if relationships with the central administration, with the principal, with parents, and with other teachers are attended to with the same seriousness, urgency, and energy that the teacher invests in the classroom, then ordinary teachers can create open classrooms. Ann Cook and Herb Mack observed in England:

> [T]he total school environment makes possible the maximum use of the teacher's abilities as well as those of the child. In this way, quite ordinary individuals become what appear to be extraordinary teachers when compared to those functioning in more traditional settings.[51]

Footnotes

1. Bernard Spodek, *Extending Open Education in the United States* (Paper presented at the conference of the National Association for the Educators of Young Children, Denver, Colo., March 5-7, 1970), ERIC ED 038 182, p. 12.
2. Sir Alec Clegg, *Revolution in the British Primary Schools* (Washington, D.C.: National Association of Elementary School Principals, 1971), p. 43.
3. Edward Chittenden, "Open Education—There and Here," *Learning* 1, no. 6 (April 1973): 7.
4. Clegg, *Revolution in the British Primary Schools,* p. 4.
5. Ann Cook and Herb Mack, *The Headteacher's Role* (New York: Citation Press, 1971), p. 44.
6. Jennifer Nias, Lecturer on education at the School of Education, University of Liverpool, personal communication.
7. Molly Brearly and Nora Goddard, "Educating Teachers," *Educating Teachers* (New York: Citation Press, 1972), p. 10.
8. Bill Browse and Tony Kallet, "Leicestershire: A Case History," *Educating Teachers* (New York: Citation Press, 1972), p. 46.
9. Peter Raggatt, "Administration in British Primary Schools," *National Elementary Principal* 52, no. 3 (November 1972): 28.
10. Seymour Sarason, *The Culture of School and the Problem of Change* (Boston: Allyn and Bacon, 1971), p. 162.
11. *Ibid.,* pp 163-164.
12. *Ibid.,* p. 165.
13. *Ibid.,* pp. 166-167.
14. Edward Nussel and Mildred Johnson, "Who Obstructs Innovation?" *Journal of Secondary Education* 44, no. 1 (January 1969): 3-11.
15. Lillian Weber, *The English Infant School and Informal Education* (Englewood Cliffs, N.J.: Prentice-Hall, 1971), p. 235.
16. Personal communication with a teacher who did not wish to be quoted.
17. *Newsletter* of the Study Commission on Undergraduate Education and the Education of Teachers, Andrews Hall, University of Nebraska, Lincoln, Nb., March 1973, p. 1.
18. George Frein, "Teaching as a Form of Improvisation," *Insights* 4, no. 7 (April 1972): 4. Published by the New School Behavioral Studies in Education, University of North Dakota, Grand Forks, N.D.
19. Vito Perrone, "The Center for Teaching and Learning," *UND, Undergraduate Catalog 1972-1974* (Grand Forks, N.D.: University of North Dakota), pp. 73-75.
20. Jennifer Nias, University of Liverpool.
21. Edward Yeomans, *Preparing Teachers for the Integrated Day* (National Association of Independent Schools, 4 Liberty Square, Boston, Mass., 1972), p. 11.
22. David Hawkins, "Development as Education: A Proposal for the Improvement of Elementary Education," *Science and Technology in Developing Countries,* ed. Zahlen and Nader (London: Cambridge University Press, 1968), p. 529.
23. Vincent Rogers, *Teaching in the British Primary School* (New York: Macmillan, 1972), pp. 285-286.
24. Yeomans, *Preparing Teachers for the Integrated Day,* p. 11.
25. Marianne Amarel, Anne Bussis, and Edward Chittenden, "Teacher Perspective on Change to an Open Approach," (Paper presented at the annual meeting of the American Educational Research Association, New Orleans, La., March 1, 1973), p. 5.
26. Anne Bussis and Edward Chittenden, *Analysis of an Approach to Open Education* (Princeton, N.J.: Educational Testing Service, 1970), pp. 30-31.
27. Amarel et al., "Teacher Perspective on Change to an Open Approach," pp. 1, 78.

28. Gerald Johnson and William Page, "Selected Classroom Project: Helping Traditional Teachers to Plan and Implement Student-Centered Classrooms," *Project Cod,* ESEA Title III (Final Report, 52 Ash St., New Bedford, Mass., June 1971), ERIC ED 055 962, p. 3.

29. *Ibid.,* p. 28.

30. Amarel et al., "Teacher Perspective on Change to an Open Approach," p. 6.

31. Steven Wlodarczyk, *Teacher Beliefs and Open Education* (Paper presented at AERA Conference, Chicago, Ill., April 3-7, 1972).

32. *Ibid.*

33. The definitions on pages 3, 4, and 5 in Chapter 1 include several such statements. (See Chapter 1—Notes, footnote 3 for sources.) The dimensions of openness defined by Project Cod are another example of such objectifications. (See pages 34-36 of the ERIC reference previously cited.)

34. Kathleen Raoul, "The Quest for Quality," *Schools Talk to Parents About the Integrated Day,* ed. Edward Yeomans, previously cited, p. 66. (See footnote 21.)

35. Browse and Kallet, "Leicestershire: A Case History," p. 61.

36. *Ibid.,* pp. 60-61.

37. Anthony Kallet, "Some Thoughts on Children and Materials," *Open Education: The Informal Classroom,* ed. Charles Rathbone (New York: Citation Press, 1971), p. 79.

38. Browse and Kallet, "Leicestershire: A Case History," p. 61.

39. Pamela McKeown, "No One Right Way of Learning," excerpts from a meeting with McKeown adapted by Helene Rose, *Open Line* 2, no. 3, EPDA Open Education Project, University of Illinois, Armory Building, Champaign, Ill. (January 1973): 2.

40. *Ibid.*

41. Charles Rathbone, "On Preparing the Teacher: A Lesson from Loughborough," *Open Eudcation: The Informal Classroom* (New York: Citation Press, 1971), pp. 164-167.

42. Miriam Dorn, "Summer Institute as a Prototype," *Notes from Workshop Center for Open Education* 1, no. 3, City College, N.Y. (October 1972): 4-6.

43. James Collins, Teacher Centers and Teacher Renewal (Paper prepared for the National Association of State Boards of Education, Syracuse University School of Education, Syracuse, N.Y., March 1972), pp. 15-16.

44. Don Rasmussen, The Philadelphia Teacher Center: A View from the Shop (Paper prepared for the SURC Policy Institute, Syracuse University School of Education, Syracuse, N.Y., April 13-14, 1972), p.1.

45. *Ibid.,* p. 3.

46. Lilian Katz, *Open–Informal Education: Recommendations for Research and Development* (Final report submitted to National Institute of Education Planning Unit, University of Illinois College of Education, Urbana, Ill., 1971), ERIC ED 058 944, p. 9.

47. George Hein, *Visit to England: February 26- March 17, 1972* (Unpublished paper written with the support of a Ford Foundation Travel Study grant, 1972).

48. Personal communication with a teacher who did not wish to be quoted.

49. Personal communication with a teacher who did not wish to be quoted.

50. Personal communication with an advisor who did not wish to be quoted.

51. Ann Cook and Herb Mack, *The Teacher's Role* (New York: Citation Press, 1971), p. 11.

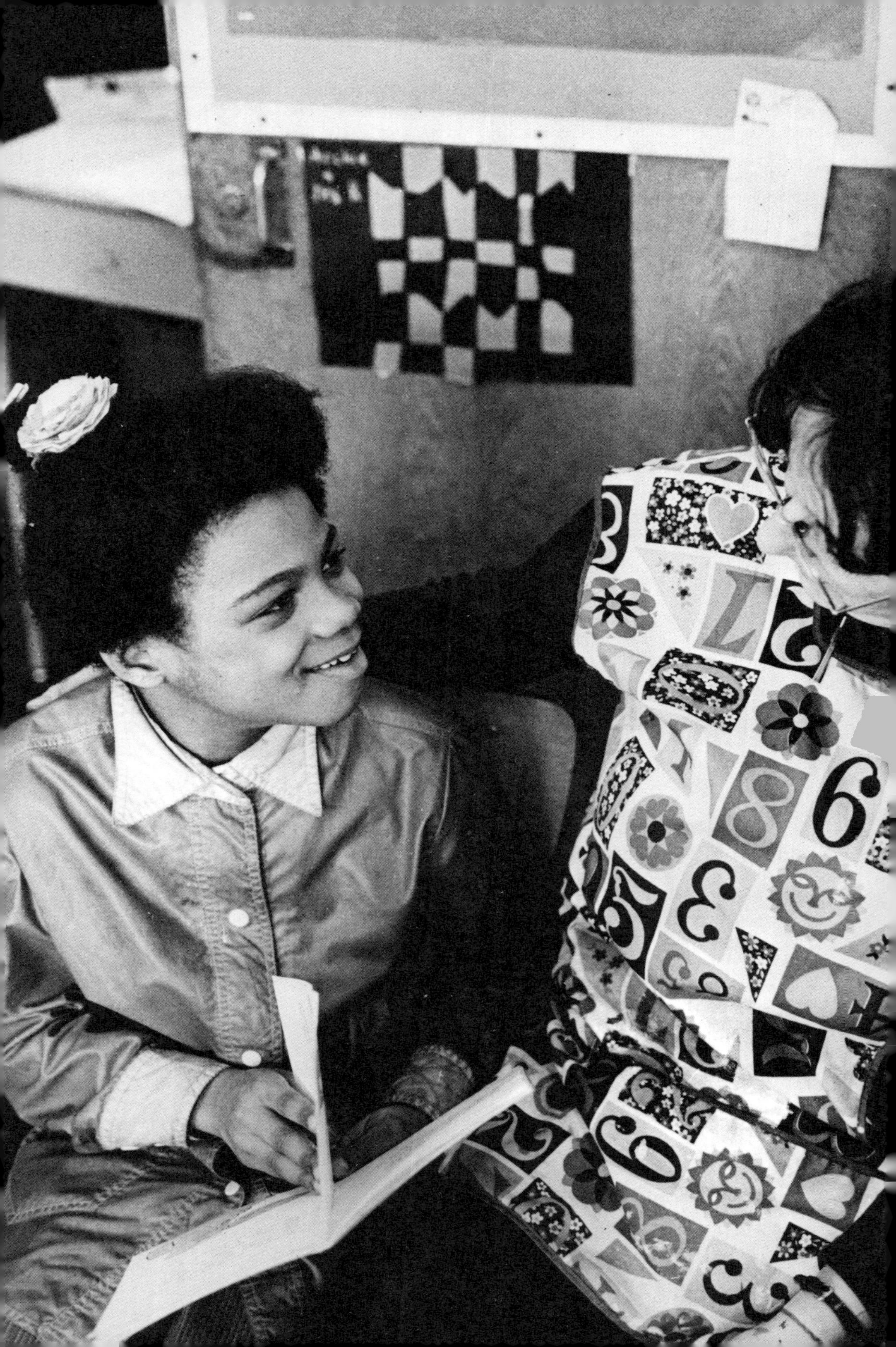

Chapter 6

Relationships with Parents

The ordinary teacher's view of the school in which he or she works is typically short-range and close-up: one year's personal effort poured into a single classroom of 30 children, more or less. The parent's perspective is likely to be diametrically opposite, envisioning one child's (or several children's) educational journey through all the grades of the whole school. Thus, even between parents and teachers who share an equal commitment to open education, there is a fundamental difference in aim: the teacher concentrates on producing one high-quality open classroom teacher, namely herself or himself. But the parent perceives a big difference in a child's life between having one or two excellent teachers and having a good school for six years. The parent is not satisfied with one able teacher; he or she wants a good *whole school*.

Open educators thus place a high priority on enabling parents and teachers in American schools to find a common focus so they can work together to change a school. In England it was not necessary, nor would it have been deemed appropriate, to mount such a lay-professional movement because the power to enact change was easily available to head teachers. This power has been used by some of them over the past 40 years to develop a quality in open classroom teaching that has had influence far beyond the numbers of schools involved. As Maurice Kogan puts it,

> [S]omething remarkable has been pulled off. Within a generation, humane attitudes have taken hold of a powerful cohort of primary schools, and they set the pace so that a majority are affected by the mood, even if they do not fully participate in it.[1]

English parents' role in schools

Although Mark Heyman notes that in the flood of literature describing the infant schools "few reports . . . have been concerned with the nature of the parent-child relationship,"[2] there is abundant evidence of parents being welcomed in the open infant schools and of heads and teachers having warm relationships with families. Jennifer Nias points out that many of the best open schools developed in villages, where schools are very small and parents share a common value system. Some English open educators now speak deliberately to the issue of parent involvement in schools. John Coe, senior advisor for primary education in Oxfordshire, said in an interview that he regards parents' participation in the open schools as one of the important reasons for the increasingly rapid spread of the movement.

> I would think now that in three out of four primary schools I might walk into in the course of a day I will find parents inside the school in some capacity or other. Not just observing, or assessing what is going on, or being informed about it, but being *active participants* in the act of learning. Perhaps setting up a discovery area, perhaps setting up a cooking area, or helping with rebinding books, doing some paperwork associated with the next school sale, or very often helping with school journeys. . . . We want, then, to create schools which will be . . . community schools, so that we can educate the children through and with their families.[3]

However, open education in England does have its detractors. There are pressures not only from traditional educators but from traditionalist parents for more standardized curriculum—especially reading—and standardized measures of children's learning.

Alec Clegg writes,

> Such pressures are fierce. Interestingly enough, their impact varies from one segment of society to another. In England at the present time . . . change in the schools is most likely to succeed in areas where parents . . . seek change, . . . and in areas where parents don't care enough to ask questions about change. It is in the middle area of suburban social aspiration that change is resisted and that schools are pressured to groom and train traditionally for the great rat race of life.[4]

However, the source of pressure on schools is not entirely middle-class social aspiration. Kogan points out that there are disadvantages in a system that places so much authority in the hands of head teachers and so little in the national education department, or in local parents' councils (which exist but have little influence). British infant schools are not uniformly excellent, creative, humane. "If creativity finds lush pastures," he writes, "mediocrity has many secure bolt holes."[5]

When mediocrity is secure it does not deal with emergent problems such as England's recent, pressing need to educate large numbers of immigrant, minority group children. Leonard Marsh, an English writer and teacher educator, acknowledges that there are problems with children's reading, but he opposes calls for government standardization of reading programs and tests. He believes the solution will be found by heads and teachers in open schools holding fast to their philosophy and methods and extending these to include parents.

> I think the task is to make parents as much at home in the education of their child as at present the children are at home in the school. . . . You must not feel that you have to exclude a parent because he is an amateur. He is professional with his child's education; why shouldn't he be in school?[6]

Nevertheless, few open educators in England are prepared for parents to participate in decisions about the learning program, and by American open educators' standards many seem patronizing to parents, especially to poor parents. The British class system seems by and large intact even in open schools.[7]

People like Kogan are aware of such blind spots and inadequacies in the English open movement, but point out that English schools like American schools are part of the larger culture and must deal with their problems within that context. Thus Kogan writes:

> Ways of reconciling [head teachers'] power and authority with the growing and legitimate demands of parents and others need yet to be found. Participation is indeed the largest single issue facing the British Welfare State in the 1970s.[8]

Thus a comparison of the English and the American educational systems shows that both are facing the issue of greater parent participation. The difference is that in England this question is barely emerging after 40 years of development of open education, during which head teachers had wide latitude to create a profoundly different educational approach; whereas in many places in the United States the open education movement must take its first steps in tandem with a community control movement, which often projects different goals—reflecting political as well as educational facts of life—and is suspicious of innovation.

Americans' disagreement on educational goals?

American open educators entirely endorse the movement for greater parent participation in schools—including educational decision making—even though they acknowledge new sets of problems occur when teachers and parents work together. They know that the parents who have frequently expressed opposition to open education often have been justified. Some of what passes for open education is no more than "do-your-own-thing." Some teachers have attempted to open their classrooms without sufficient help from their administrations or adequate preparation for themselves or their students, with predictably chaotic results. Some schools have begun open programs without consulting parents or explaining how the new program can fulfill parents' educational goals for their children.

The fourth annual Gallup poll of public attitudes toward education in September 1972 showed that public (not just parents') priorities for the elementary school were reading, writing, and arithmetic first, and "teaching students how to solve problems and think for themselves" second. In third place was "teaching students to respect law and authority;" in fourth was "how to get along with others."[9] Gallup respondents' long-range goals for schooling were as follows:[10]

1. To get better jobs	44%
2. To get along better with people at all levels of society	43%

3. To make more money - achieve financial success   38%
4. To attain self-satisfaction   21%
5. To stimulate their minds   15%
6. Miscellaneous reasons   11%

Although some may hold different priorities, most open educators do not see themselves either in an adversary or missionary relationship vis-a-vis the American public about these goals. However, to the 3R's open educators add social studies (which the Gallup respondents ranked far down in eighth priority, after vocational skills and health and physical education) and the arts and sciences (which were not even mentioned in the poll).

The area of disagreement is that open educators project fundamentally different *ways* for children to encounter these subjects than those the average American endorses. This difference is apparent from the portion of the Gallup poll that shows that respondents think the *existing* curriculum and teaching are the strongest features of their schools. As Roland Barth points out,

> [T]he fact of the matter is that *most* parents' concepts of quality education are along the lines of the traditional, rigorous, transmission of knowledge model. . . . When confronted with a kind of education which . . . differs so completely from the established path toward these goals, most parents fear for the success of their children. Many inner-city parents see informal classrooms as appropriate only for middle-class children who already "have it made"; many middle-class . . . parents see informal classrooms as appropriate only for working-class children, who aren't going to college anyway and thus have little to lose.[11]

Although there are instances in which large and effectively coalesced groups of parents have rejected traditional educational goals so thoroughly that they have organized alternative schools within the public system—the St. Paul (Minnesota) Open School[12] is an outstanding example—the more common pattern is that parents as a group do not understand how open education can produce competence. Their own experience of school was "defined things to learn and defined times to learn them," as Mel Suhd says. He points out that if adults cherish the memory of their own school days and live by old-school values, they may consider that a different educational philosophy demeans their concept of self and poses a challenge to their authority over their children, as well as being a waste of children's time.

Nevertheless, the disparity between parents' past school experience and their children's present need not be a fundamental issue. Parents with traditional expectations of schools can be favorably impressed by the purposeful work of children in open classrooms if they are invited to spend extended time there. Some find remarkable their children's enthusiasm for school, remembering their own and their children's boredom in traditional classrooms. Vito Perrone writes that doubting parents in the small towns and rural communities of North Dakota have taken heart from their

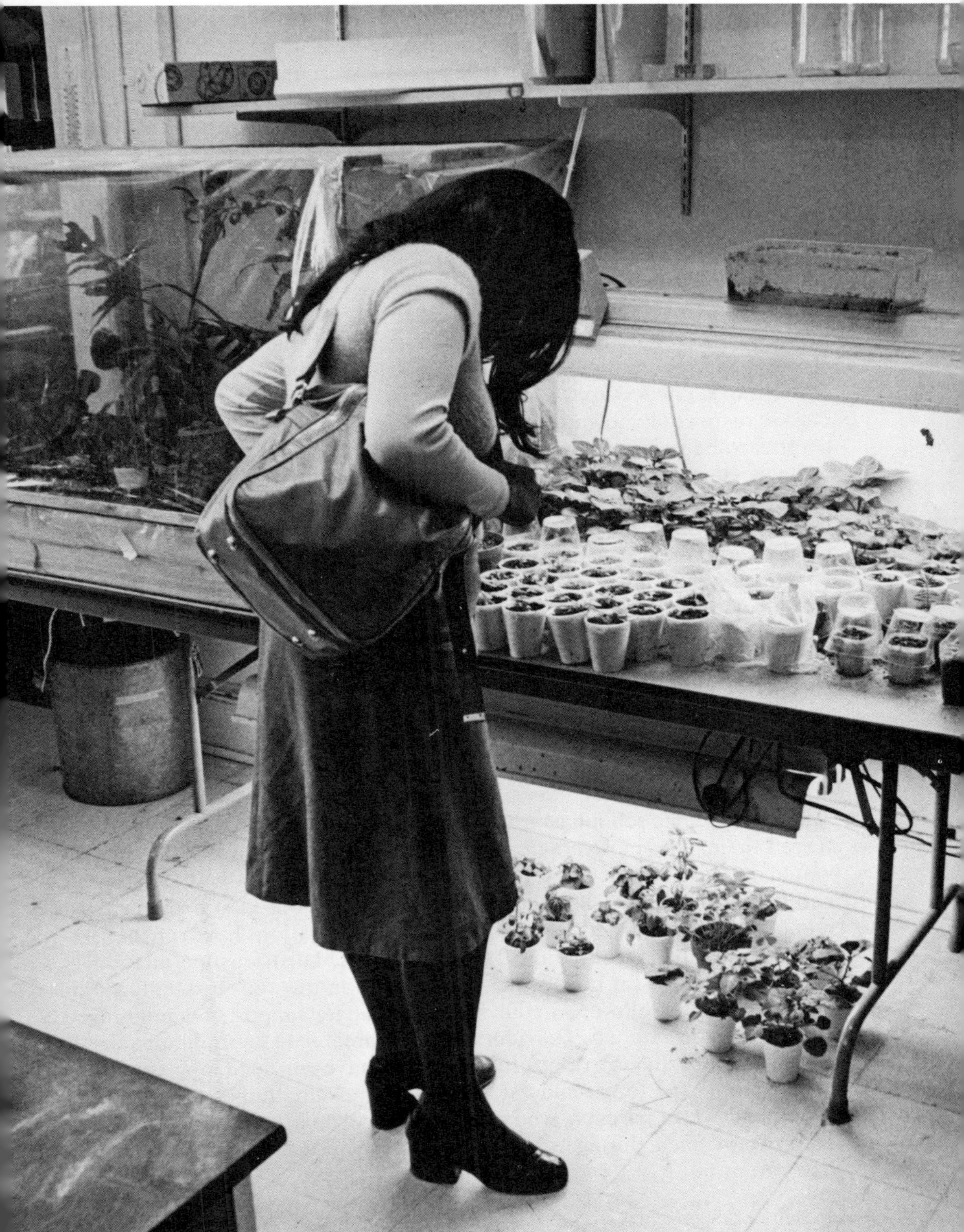

children's improved school work and their own visits to classrooms. Volunteer work in classrooms, parent workshops stressing no-textbook learning materials, and discussions with teachers and with university faculty about educational goals have helped parents re-examine their traditional assumptions about schools.[13] It also has been amply demonstrated that when inner-city Black parents participate in setting goals and ongoing policies for a school, and/or become familiar with classroom activities by visiting and working with competent open teachers in classrooms, these parents solidly endorse open education.[14]

The key, says Perrone, is to bring the parents into the schools. Parents cannot be expected to take on faith alone the open educators' promise to enhance children's natural desire to learn, build self-motivation and self-reliance. In addition, besides these character traits, parents of all races and classes want schools to teach children to delay present satisfaction for later reward; to do necessary tasks even if they're not fun; and to respect and behave respectfully toward adults. To see a good open classroom is for most parents to be reassured on all these points.

Open educators recognize that some parents will continue to prefer traditional schooling and that some children seem to do better in highly teacher-controlled classrooms. It is very important that parents who cannot be reassured are not coerced into accepting an education for their children which they cannot endorse. An open program cannot thrive in the face of parent apathy or resistance, because of teachers' need for parents' support. Thus most open educators recommend that schools give parents options of open or traditional classes at all grades, or if a whole school is open that parents be able to place their children in other schools in the district.

Parents' power

Open Corridor, which exists side by side with traditional classrooms in Manhattan public schools, enrolls only children whose parents have volunteered them. The most pragmatic reason for voluntarism is that teachers would not have time to work out their new teaching styles without consent and help from parents. Parents contribute much more than patience. In a number of Open Corridor schools, parents' organizations have run interference for the Corridor program. They have lobbied district superintendents and school boards for racially integrated and non-tracked classes, for principals sympathetic to open education, for budget support, for multi-aged classes, and for retaining Corridor teachers threatened by staff cutbacks. It is doubtful that the Corridor program could have survived long enough to grow without the tough-minded and tireless resourcefulness of organized Black and white parents, who used decentralization and the community control movement during its beginnings in 1968 to start open classrooms. As one parent put it,

Before decentralization we had a failure of an educational system in New

York City. The time has passed in major cities when the professionals can change the system by themselves, along the line of their own ideas. What community control has meant to Open Corridor is that the actual changes were made by the teachers and advisors because we parents demanded that the schools be answerable to the local community. We picked the principal. He supports the right of parents to have a choice in the kind of education they want for their kids.[15]

Parents collectively can be powerful, individually can be patient. Open Corridor advisors also value the parent as the child's first teacher. Parents are sought as volunteers and visitors in classrooms and the corridor in order to widen children's adult acquaintances, enrich the curriculum, and make the school contiguous with the child's community.

Finally, Lillian Weber seeks an educational partnership between teachers and parents in planning and evaluating the learning program, even though she knows this is hard for "opening" teachers, who feel the need for "private soul-searching rather than the goldfish bowl of shared consideration of obviously inadequate implementation." If teachers do not plan *with* parents, Weber says, they become vulnerable to evaluation *by* parents who feel like outsiders judging others rather than like participants evaluating themselves.[16]

A Corridor parent, who understands this dilemma of teachers through trying to form a joint parents-teachers educational policy committee in a Corridor school, says that the school district bureaucracy and the teachers union both enforce teachers' view of themselves as subordinates rather than as decision makers. In addition, since teachers feel vulnerable to the system, they inevitably feel vulnerable to parents who demonstrate power to pressure the system. Parent-teacher antagonisms can arise when both parties feel manipulated by the central administration.[17]

Planning with parents

When teachers and parents feel united together against external pressures, and they start out planning together, they can evolve a partnership in which parents give teachers influence, money, supplies, volunteer time, and emotional support. This has been the case at Crocker Highlands School in Oakland, California, which has a 40 percent Black, 50 percent white, and 10 percent Asian pupil population in a mainly middle-socioeconomic class neighborhood. An open education program has been evolving there since 1968, carried on in classrooms with enrollments ranging from 32 to 38 children per class, even though they have had no teacher aides, no advisor or resource teacher, no supplementary district funding, and no vice principal.

The program began when the passage of a 1968 California law allowed schools to depart from strict time scheduling for every subject, and the Crocker principal, Caroline Murphy, encouraged several teachers to experiment with flexible schedule and curriculum. After a year of experimenting, the whole staff on a Back to School Night asked parents for ideas for further changes. There followed six months of joint parent and teacher study, sparked by townhall meetings about educational innovations and spearheaded by the principal and a newly-formed school-community planning council. This activity culminated in a comprehensive plan for change toward openness and a $20,000 budget request. A delegation of 100 parents presented it to the school board, which turned them down flat. The council then raised $10,000 by door-to-door solicitation in the neighborhood. They spent the money for inservice training for teachers, materials for children, carpeting (for noise-proofing), and remodeling the school. Most of the work was done by parents.

The school now has 100 parent volunteers, half of them working weekly in classrooms, the others making curriculum materials, running the media center, and conducting minicourses for children in topics children choose—care of pets, cooking, crafts, and the like.

Murphy comments that this cooperation has come about only after a great change on the part of teachers.

> It used to be if a parent walked into the teachers' lunchroom the teachers had a stroke. Now you can't tell parents from teachers. Everybody assumes they have a part in this—that includes the custodian and the secretary.

It is notable that this partnership with parents was initiated and is maintained by the principal, in contrast to the situation of some of the Open Corridor schools, where the parents hold the initiative through their influence on the hiring of principals. The teachers' welcoming of parents in their classrooms is a function of the unflagging support they receive from the principal, while the parents' active participation in the school is stimulated by the principal's offering each parent the choice of his child's classroom —at every grade level a choice of traditional as well as open settings.

Parents as loudspeakers in the community

In some communities there is no need to convince parents of the need for change, and thus the issue is not participation in planning for change, but frequent and frank communication with parents as they form their impressions of new programs. This was the case in Hartford, where everybody believed that traditional primary education was failing, and where a successful, small, open education program begun in 1968 was gradually expanded into a citywide implementation in kindergarten through second grade. The major instruments of change were teacher aides for every classroom plus inservice preparation and advisory services for teachers and aides. By hiring the new paraprofessionals from the community, assigning them to schools in their own neighborhoods, and training them as members of a teaching team, not as menial helpers, program directors built into the schools a grassroots parent relations network. One teacher said these aides were like loudspeakers interpreting the classroom innovations to neighborhood parents. The program administrator invited PTA members to participate in the teachers' inservice workshops and instituted the policy of having teachers send home frequent reports and examples of children's daily work, emphasizing skills and neatness. Parents were welcomed in schools and classrooms. The Hartford district's school population is 67 percent nonwhite, of whom 17 percent are Spanish-speaking. Among the whites are Italian, French, Portuguese, and Greeks, each group retaining its ethnic identity. An "opinionnaire" to parents in 1972, seeking their reactions to the new K-2 program, showed 80 to 90 percent agreement among this diverse constituency of parents on such items as "My child is learning self-discipline," ". . . learning to read," ". . . learning responsibility."[18]

Parents as the constituency

Whether or not they feel that something is desperately wrong with their children's school, it is now common for parents to seek more than routine information about schools. Less and less can educators rely on the truism that parents' ignorance is bliss. Parents' criticism of schools can arise not only from evidence of outright failure but from no evidence at all. Vito Perrone points out that although most school administrators claim that educational programs reflect parental wishes, in fact they do not know what is important to parents because they rarely consult them.[19] North Dakota open education graduates are urged to seek out parents at the start of the school year, explain to them how their children will be working and learning in school, and scour local communities for ideas for curriculum themes and projects. The North Dakota faculty is available to facilitate teacher-parents-administrator dialogues in any community in the state, and to conduct teacher-parent workshops with curriculum materials, so that they experience how children learn.

North Dakota's Center for Teaching and Learning also consults parents formally, as evaluators of the teacher preparation program in open education annually conduct interviews of parents throughout the state. From a February 1972 survey of 277 parents of children in open classrooms in 15 North Dakota communities, the Center research team found that 76 percent of the respondents were favorably impressed with their children's classroom—40 percent of them "very favorably."[20]

Parents participate in the North Dakota Center's policy-making committees, and in seminars on campus with undergraduate students so that they have some input into the university's preparation of teachers. Says Perrone:

> In the past, parents got whatever we sent out, whether the teacher had any understanding of life in a particular community or experience with its children. Now we are asking parents to give us some sense of what they really cherish and value, what kinds of people they think teachers should be, what experiences and background they should have.

This policy has particular import in relation to North Dakota's Sioux communities. The Center sends intern teachers to reservation schools and has a four-year teacher preparation program for youth and adults from four North Dakota reservations.

Parents as community

All open educators know that parents heavily influence children's learning—intellectual, affective, and social—and thus must be closely involved in their schooling. Going beyond that, EDC open educators believe that parents have a fundamental right and responsibility to be involved in decisions about children's learning. Parent decision making is a tenet of their program. The commitment to parents' rights developed partly out of the experience of EDC's Pilot Communities Project in Black community schools in Boston and Washington, D.C., but mostly out of Follow Through advisors' learning from teachers and parents they worked with. The idea is, of course, not new in American education. This tradition conceives of the school as the instrument for poor children to learn how to gain the control over their lives that their parents so obviously lack. Such a social goal for children's learning may well imply helping parents to gain more control—or at least influence—in the governance of the school.

As expressed in EDC open education projects, this social theory of education strongly encourages parent participation in the life of the school—through classroom teaching and preparation of curriculum materials, as well as in decision making. In some EDC projects parents observe and document children's performance on specific tasks or behaviors in school and at home. EDC advisors bear a responsibility to inform, respond to, and work with parents as well as to educate teachers. EDC resource and training centers typically put parents alongside teachers in workshops and seminars, and encourage parents' renewed interest in learning.

As Mary Stitt of Arlington Heights, Illinois, comments, the gradual growth of "a learning community" of teachers with parents can be as remarkable and satisfying a feature of open education as is the growth of children.

However, this cannot happen unless parents feel on equal footing with teachers. Babette Edwards, co-chairman of the Harlem Parents' Union, a 300-member organization of Black parents in school district 5 of New York City, points out that parents cannot effectively dialogue and plan with teachers and participate in decision making with administrators unless they have information.

> Principals give lip service to the notion of parent participation but parents feel silly and stupid participating when they don't have any information on which to base decisions. So they just agree with the principal. What information they do get is second-hand accounts of new programs, and accounts which usually look at administrative considerations rather than what's good for the child. Parents need machinery so they can take care of business about the schools. They need first-hand information about new programs like open education. Low-income Black parents believe they want traditional education because they understand traditional math and reading. They have to see alternative methods first-hand or else they are suspicious of them. We suggest that parents go into schools and observe what's going on. Getting information about schools is not being "militant," as inquiring parents are usually labeled. It is just parents as citizens asking questions of their public servants.

The Harlem Parents Union therefore sponsors semester-long, free, college-credited seminars series for parents on topics such as curriculum, history of public education, parents' and students' rights in suspensions, pupil records, teachers' unions, paraprofessionals' duties and qualifications, ESEA Title I program requirements—anything that affects a child going to school. Student teachers at Fordham, Marymount, College of Mount St. Vincent, and Malcolm-King in New York City also take part in these seminars.[21]

Many open classroom teachers go out of their way to encourage parents' feeling on equal footing with them because of the educational importance they ascribe to family and community setting. Some teachers hold regular meetings with class parents, write newsletters, or walk children home from school in order to talk with parents in their homes. In schools where some children live in extreme poverty, isolation, and sometimes fear, some teachers feel the greatest value of the open classroom, and a major responsibility of the teacher, is to make the classroom fill some of the roles of families—to provide cooperation, responsibility, trust, companionship, affection, relaxation, fun.

The prerequisite parent

The school's openness to parents can produce several kinds of parent participation in educational matters: (1) Increasing children's achievement through supportive, cooperative attitudes toward the school; (2) volunteering as teacher aides in the classroom; (3) providing curriculum materials and personal experiences or talents as lessons for children; (4) influencing administrators and school boards and other parents; and (5) setting educational goals along with staff.

If a school is in trouble and change is imperative, open educators believe that parent involvement is equally imperative—even though school people on the one hand, and parents themselves on the other, may regard it as onerous or downright painful. In our system parents are the middlemen between the school and the society at large.

As Lilian Katz points out:

> There are no problems in education which are not also problems in the rest of our society: mistrust as well as demandingness, abuses of power as well as abdication of authority, doubts about values as well as passivity, ad infinitum.[22]

In open education parent involvements are prerequisites, not options.

Footnotes

1. Maurice Kogan, *The Government of Education* (New York: Citation Press, 1971), p.39.
2. Mark Heyman, "Learning from the British Primary Schools," *The Elementary School Journal* 72, no. 7 (April 1972): 342.
3. Vincent Rogers, "Primary Education in England: An Interview with John Coe," *Phi Delta Kappan* 52, no. 9 (May 1971): 534-535.
4. Sir Alec Clegg, *Revolution in the British Primary Schools* (Washington, D.C.: National Association of Elementary School Principals, 1971), p. 45.
5. Kogan, *The Government of Education,* p. 40.
6. Leonard Marsh, quoted in *The London Times Educational Supplement,* January 9, 1972.
7. George Hein, "Visit to England," unpublished manuscript, p. 5. Edward Chittenden, "What Makes the British Bandwagon Roll?" *Learning–The Magazine for Creative Teaching* 1, no. 6 (April 1973): 9.
8. Kogan, *The Government of Education,* p. 40.
9. George Gallup, "Fourth Annual Gallup Poll of Public Attitudes Toward Education," *Phi Delta Kappan,* September 1972, pp. 33-35.

10. *Ibid.*, p. 35.

11. Roland Barth, *Open Education and the American School* (New York: Agathon Press, 1971), pp. 205-206.

12. *See* Nancy Pirsig, "Bumpy Road to the Open School," *American Education* 8, no. 8 (October 1972): 17-23. *Also* Joe Nathan, "Report from an Open School," *K-Eight* 2, no. 3 (January-February 1973): 19-25.

13. Vito Perrone, "Parents as Partners," *Opening New Schools,* ed. R.W. Saxe (Berkeley, Ca.: McCutchan Publishing Co., 1972), p. 385.

14. EDC Follow Through and Pilot Communities Programs, Open Corridor, Hartford, Grape Street School, for examples.

15. Lenore Engle, personal communication.

16. Lillian Weber, "Development in Open Corridor Organization: Intent and Reality," *The National Elementary Principal* 52, no. 3 (1972): 67.

17. Barbara Rosen, personal communication.

18. *Hartford Follow Through Report 1* (Fort Lauderdale, Fla.: Nova University Behavioral Sciences Center, November 1972), pp. 48-57. An independent survey conducted for the Hartford Board of Education by James Browne of the National Program for Educational Leadership, commented on the remarkable contrast between Hartford parents and parents nationwide, in that Hartford parents rated their schools' "up-to-date teaching methods" as the number-one asset of the school system. Parents polled by Gallup's national survey put this item in fifth place.

19. Vito Perrone, "Parents as Partners," p. 394.

20. Michael Patton, *Structural Dimensions of Open Education and Parental Reaction to Open Classrooms in North Dakota: A Sociological View of the Diffusion of Open Education as an Innovation in Organizational Structure and Processes* (Grand Forks, N.D.: University of North Dakota Center for Teaching and Learning, Spring 1973), pp. 191-192.

21 Harlem Parents Union, 514 N. 126 St., New York, N.Y. 10027.

22. Lilian Katz, *Open-Informal Education: Recommendations for Research and Development,* Final Report (Urbana, Ill.: University of Illinois College of Education, 1971), ERIC ED 058 944, p. 36.

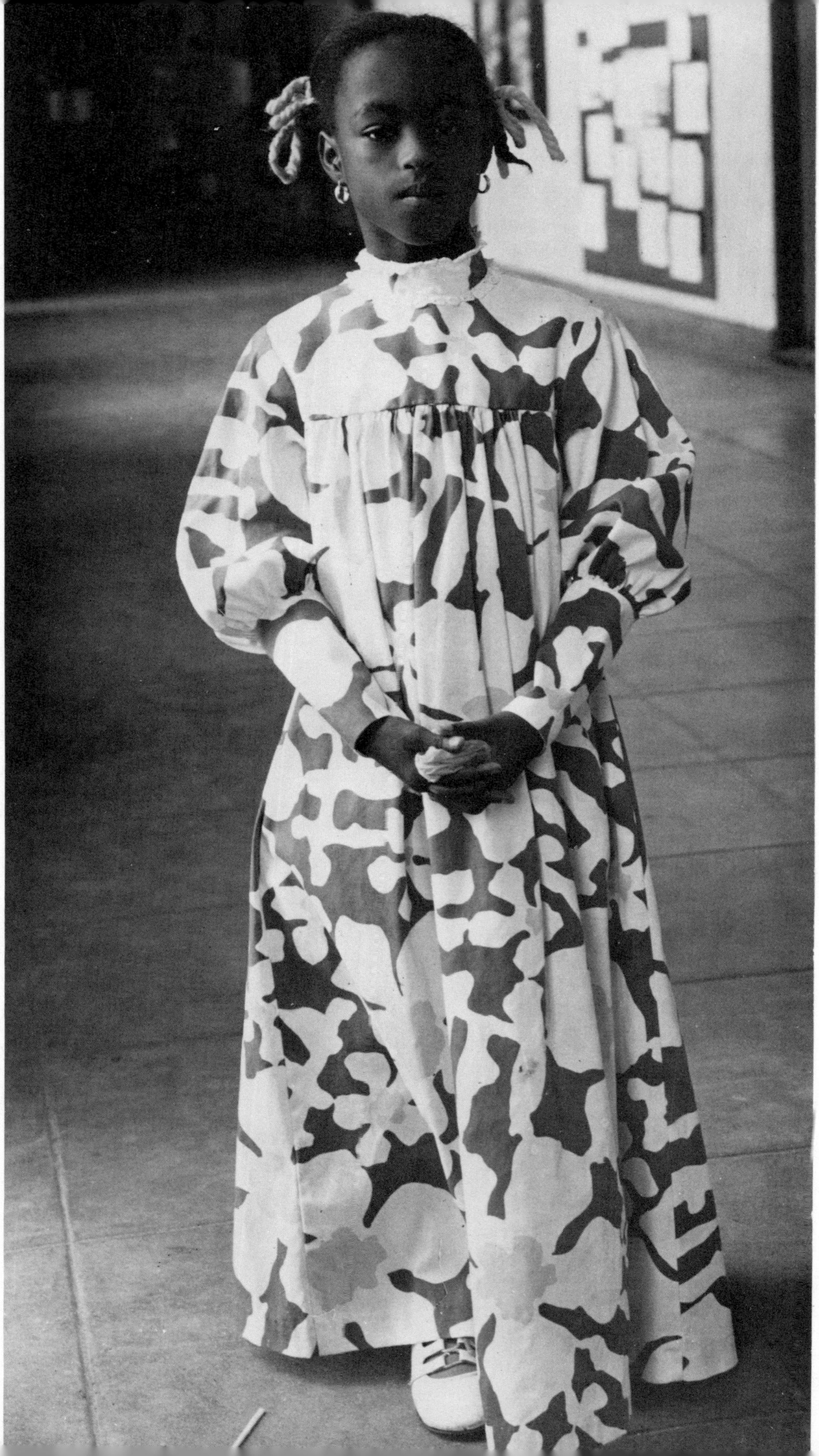

Chapter 7

Evaluating Children's Growth

In December 1972 Philadelphia's School District Six reported that third-grade children who had been in the EDC Follow Through open classrooms since kindergarten significantly exceeded the achievements of comparable children in traditional classrooms on vocabulary, reading, and arithmetic skills, as tested by the Iowa Tests of Basic Skills. The open classroom children made greater gains in reading during the foregoing two-year period when the District had made this a priority than were made by other children throughout the District.[1] The response of EDC open educators to these results was neither surprise nor glee. Said George Hein, EDC Follow Through director:

> Of course our children do well! They get care and attention! But these results do not tell us much. Standardized achievement tests do not measure anything but a low level of cognitive learning. The important things—like the children's growth in critical intelligence—are not measured.

The incident illustrates the disparity between open educators' view of evaluation and that of many parents. Roland Barth notes:

> The prevailing conception in this country of good education is education which provides and displays evidence of students' immediate, assured, measurable, cognitive achievement. This expectation is embedded in mortar no less enduring than a parent's love and concern for his progeny and for himself. Neither open education nor any alternative which would tamper with these ends, or with commonly accepted means toward these ends, is likely to be easily accepted.[2]

While the ends of an open classroom include cognitive achievement, the means are drastically different. They specify that learning is different for each child, not only in pace, but in style and content. So learning should not be measured by instruments which count how many separate, standard concepts and skills the child can demonstrate. It should be assessed by procedures which sense how each child is gathering intellectual power. This is the difference, says Thomas C. O'Brien, between looking at memory and looking at mind.[3]

Evaluation in England

In England, open educators have been conscious of this difference and have conceived evaluation as instruments for assessing and directing teacher-child learning interactions rather than as standardized instruments for reporting performance. This is because of the lesser pressures on individual schools from parents and from central authorities, and also probably because the English educators' 100 years' past experience with national standardized testing procedures convinced open teachers why, how, and when not to use them. John Blackie sketches this history:

> From 1863 to 1898, children in English elementary schools had to take an annual examination in the three R's. The examination was held by Her Majesty's Inspectors of Schools, and the size of the teacher's salary depended, in part, on the results. This appalling system was believed to ensure continuous effort on the part of the teachers, and thus, the best possible education for the children.[4]

After it was abandoned in 1898, the English schools adopted a grading system, frequently administered by standardized tests, until 1926, when head teachers were given discretion over pupil placement and curriculum. "Streaming," which Americans call "tracking," was an innovation of the 1940s and still prevails in many junior schools (grades three to six). Only recently have the British begun to provide comprehensive secondary schools and to phase out still another form of standardized evaluation, the 11-plus examination, which selects students for the academic secondary schools.

The English open educators' rejection of formal standardized testing is not a rejection of *standards* but of norms. Alec Clegg quotes an open teacher on how he maintains standards without standardized examinations:

> It seems to us that high standards of academic achievement were obtained of old for just the same reason they are obtained today—somebody was determined on getting them. Yesterday it was a matter of command; today it is much more a matter of influence. But there would not be high quality results in either situation *unless objectives had been clearly defined*.[5] (Emphasis added.)

With objectives clearly in mind from the local decisions made by the head teacher and the staff, the English open teacher concentrates on forming a thoroughly rounded impression of each child. English teachers design their own systems of observing and recording children's growth. These may include the results of quizzes following lessons, diagnostic procedures such as the Piaget-derived "check-ups" in Nuffield math, checklists of skills mastered in reading and math, lists of books read, logs of assignments completed, narrative commentaries about individual children, the children's diaries of their school work with the teacher's running commentaries, the teacher's own journal of the class progress and problems, and sampler collections of each child's drawing and painting, writing, mathematics, science projects, etc. The teacher seeks other teachers' observations of a particular child at work if she is puzzled or worried about him, and backing up all her own assessments she has the critical, experienced judgment of the head teacher and/or an advisor from the county education authority. These records form the basis of personal conferences with parents or written reports which take the place of conventional report cards. Such records follow a child through the school.[6] They can be extraordinarily rich and illuminating, as Joseph Featherstone observes:

> If American parents could ever see some of the detailed histories kept of each child's separate path, including his art work, they would feel, quite rightly, that a report card is a swindle.[7]

Nevertheless, English open educators are beginning to hear demands for more systematic evaluation of their work. The pressures come not only from traditional educators and parents. Some open educators themselves express a need for more precise explanations for successes as well as for failures, and for studies of large numbers of children—especially problem learners—which could reveal patterns of needs and suggest patterns for solutions. The American educator Vincent Rogers expresses this need:

> [Visitors can] recognize almost intuitively that what we are seeing is mostly right, mostly effective, mostly sound. On the other hand, many educators have a way of asking questions that cannot be answered adequately by referring to one's personal observations. How, in fact, do children in such schools perform on various objective measures when compared to children who have had quite a different sort of school experience? . . . How does the [open education] experience affect their approach to learning, their problem-solving strategies . . . their persistence, their curiosity? . . .
>
> The nondisciple deserves answers to these questions and many more. . . . [8]

In 1967 the Plowden Report, the national study describing and endorsing open methods, called for national surveys of attainment in primary schools but not for one standard of attainment. It recommended long-term comparisons of open schools with traditional schools.[9]

Since then the national reading comprehension surveys of pupils at age 11 show that children from open schools do as well as children from formal schools.[10] In 1966 the late D.E.M. Gardner published the third of her longitudinal studies on children in open schools, this one comparing ten-year-olds who had spent all their schooling in open classrooms with ten-year-olds in traditional schools. She assessed a great many more performances than reading and found that children in open classrooms "are undoubtedly superior" in writing, somewhat less ahead but still measurably superior in reading and handwriting and "general information," and less able in arithmetic. Gardner also assessed other cognitive traits, social and moral attitudes; she found that the open classroom children excelled in ingenuity, drawing and painting, "neatness, care, and skill," listening and remembering, and "interests." These children were equal to or a little bit ahead of traditionally schooled pupils in concentration, moral judgment and conduct, and social behavior.[11]

Gardner's findings are regarded with some reservation by both English and American evaluators because of they way in which she selected the student populations to compare and the way in which she analyzed scores.[12] Douglas A. Pidgeon, deputy director of the National Foundation for Educational Research in England and Wales, says that studies of the effectiveness of open schools should be done by comparing both good and poor open schools and both good and poor traditional schools. (Gardner compared only superior schools, according to her judgment— good open *vs.* good traditional schools.) Pidgeon also says that the objectives tested should be not only those valued by open educators like Gardner but also those valued by traditionalists.[13] Nevertheless, Gardner's book, which includes her tests of attainments and attitudes and her comments on problems in designing and administering the study, as well as on her results, is a provocative resource for American evaluators.

As British evaluators plan for systematic comparisons of open schools with traditional schools (or children *before* open classrooms and *after* open classrooms), they must be aware, Pidgeon emphasizes, that the critical factor to be assessed is not simply student outcomes. Teacher inputs—their beliefs and their classroom behaviors—also must be measured or the evaluation will prove nothing, Pidgeon writes.[14] This point is made by American researchers as well.[15] Clegg also emphasizes the importance of measuring the teacher's influence. He believes that if children's achievement drops when a teacher opens the classroom, it is probably the result of the teacher lowering his or her standards or substituting "wooly thinking" such as "do your own thing" for the teacher's responsibility to inspire, influence, and clarify children's choices.[16]

The failure of the standardized tests

While open educators in England are just beginning to plan for systematic testing on their own terms and for their own purposes, American open classroom teachers frequently have to prove their effectiveness in terms of normative tests whose design and purposes they do not accept. They are not alone in their view of standardized achievement tests as a hindrance to educational innovation. The 1970 Rand review of American educational research lays the deficiency of recent educational research in large measure to these tests. The review cites their three signal failures: (1) They provide only "crude measures" of ability because of the difficulty of interpreting their scores. (2) They measure a narrow range of cognitive skills without tapping higher cognitive processes or social, affective, aesthestic, humanistic, moral, or other kinds of learning. (3) They do not relate achievement to teacher inputs and "what actually goes on in the classroom."[17]

In addition, open educators and many others in and out of the profession believe that the sorting and ranking function of these tests is now inappropriate in American education. Many American open educators' vision of good schooling is much wider and deeper than plans for the organization of informal classrooms. It extends to a view of how schools ought to fit all children for adult life in an open society, one which requires "open access to knowledge for all individuals at any stage of life."[18] Lauren B. Resnick and Robert Glaser, University of Pittsburgh learning psychologists, are not members of the open education movement, but they comment that it is inappropriate for any educational theory which emphasizes human potential and individuality to use a testing system which was designed to select a few for the academic track of life and to sort others out.[19] Furthermore, the tests are based on a rather sparse bunch of competencies taken from curricula of the most conventional American schools, and they define "intelligence," "achievement," and "success" in terms of an earlier social era and outdated psychology. As Glaser writes:

> Our penchant for a fixed educational mode arises in part from an old-fashioned psychology, from the . . . tendency to think in terms of fixed categories of human beings with consistent drives and dispositions . . . rather than in terms of human beings who are highly responsive to the conditions around them . . . [and] show great subtlety in adapting their competencies to different situations. . . . The traditional measures of general ability and aptitudes err on the side of assuming too much consistency. . . .[20]

As we realize that human beings are marvelously inconsistent with each other, and even with themselves, and as schools and society break out of fixed systems into adaptive environments, we will have to broaden our definitions of ability and achievement. Benjamin Bloom, the University of Chicago learning psychologist, has written that intelligence has so many facets that if enough different tests were used it is likely that "almost all children would be found to be superior in at least some area measured by the tests." Thus each student should be searched by the teacher for his unique talents instead of a few students being selected out for their high generalized ability.[21]

In spite of the evidence of their inadequacies, school system administrators cling to standardized achievement tests because they are convenient and little else is yet available. A frequent result, described by Henry S. Dyer of Educational Testing Service, is that the system puts children into slots very early and then "the whole academic establishment can rest on its oars and let the inevitable stream of academic routine do its work."[22]

Besides being socially and theoretically inappropriate for measuring learning in open classrooms, standardized tests have the additional disadvantage of interfering with day-to-day instruction. Dyer calls attention to the distortion of both the tests and the instruction if teachers coach children in order to help them do well—"teach to the test"—or if children try to outsmart the tests.[23]

Barth points out that conventional tests give children the idea that they must not make mistakes, while open educators want children to learn to *use* mistakes for future learning.[24]

Bussis and Chittenden write that standardized tests coerce the teacher to derive the curriculum from the tests rather than from children's individual needs and resources, and that since tests are designed to rank children they teach teachers to look at children's differences as deficiencies rather than as uniqueness.[25]

Elliot W. Eisner comments that conventional tests do not tell the teacher the difference between "what students will do and what they can do"—the artificial tasks they present and the artificial settings in which they are given do not indicate how children will perform in real-life situations or with materials that are naturally interesting to them.[26] Related to this point is Bussis and Chittenden's analysis of why standardized tests may pick up little difference between open classroom students and traditional classroom students.

> [M]ost existing achievement and ability tests attempt to assess the extent to which . . . components of the curriculum have been mastered. As such, they may answer the question of whether the child has learned a particular fact or idea, but they do not reveal what else he may have learned about the idea or *what it really means to him*.[27] (Emphasis added.)

An eloquent and detailed discussion of many of these points in relation to tests of beginning reading—the most crucial tests of all—has been written by Deborah Meier, an open education advisor in New York City District 2 schools and an Open Corridor consultant. Meier claims that the standardized reading test makes it harder to teach poor Black and Puerto Rican children because the test treats reading as a set of separate mechanical skills and pressures teachers into drilling these. Meier is convinced that children do not learn to read this way. If sufficiently drilled they may, to be sure, learn "shallow" skills, but these are only a "mimic show" of reading. Real reading is produced, Meier maintains, by the teacher carefully observing what the child *can* do and fitting reading instruction to his strengths.

The other glaring facet of most standardized tests, Meier writes, is that they are biased against poor children and those from minority group backgrounds. She analyzes and illustrates with examples from her own teaching experience, seven aspects of the Metropolitan Achievement Test which assume white, middle-socioeconomic class background and thus confound poor children who *do* know how to read.

In addition, the normative scoring system of the test, which induces teachers, administrators, and parents to strive to "get children at grade level," makes fools of everyone, Meier writes.

> [E]ven if all second grades in our nation were able to fluently read *The New York Times*, half would still be below grade level. That is simply the name of the game—half above, half below.

All in all, standardized tests might be considered quite laughable, Meier concludes, if one were able to overlook the perniciousness of wasting teachers' time teaching trivial skills and labeling poor Black children as failures.[28]

Another discussion of the damage standardized reading tests do to children with reading problems emphasizes the mistake of thinking that early performance of separate, drilled skills such as phonics, word recognition, and decoding, predicts later reading. Margaret deRivera, research director of the EDC Follow Through program in Philadelphia, writes:

> In Philadelphia and other large American cities, children's achievement scores, on the average, go down from the third grade on relative to their grade level.... [There is] massive evidence that early success in reading and arithmetic has not prevented later failure.... For many children ... these academic skills are very much in the formative stage until about the third or fourth grade. When the child becomes an independent reader, he will go on to use this skill with enthusiasm and enjoyment in learning, consolidating the skill *as he uses it for his own interest*. This developmental progression is not apt to happen in a program which emphasizes early skill learning to the neglect of other opportunities for growth.[29] (Emphasis added.)

Learning for learning's own sake is the best guarantee of later learning, deRivera writes, but if tests are mandated, children get the idea that they learn in order to pass the test. One of the most significant supports an administrator can provide open classroom teachers is to arrange that there be no standardized testing of reading for first and second graders—that such tests be postponed at least until the level of third grade.

Chittenden and Bussis recommended that the time to assess reading is in the period of "consolidating" skills—perhaps fourth, fifth, and sixth grades—not in the years of skills acquisition. And "measures should not just assess whether children *can* read, but whether they *do* read and with what understandings."[30]

Developing new forms of evaluation

It's obvious that new forms of evaluation must be developed by open educators because the conventional instruments do not fit open classrooms. Standardized tests cannot sense what open educators believe are the virtues of their methods nor provide the teacher with vital feedback on *how* the child is learning. Conventional evaluation instruments bend teachers' and children's efforts toward what open educators regard as unworthy, trivial, and outdated purposes. Thus administrators who are serious about implementing open ideas must place priority on evaluation and take initiative in bringing together researchers and classroom teachers to design new forms of evaluation. Whether, as David Hawkins recommends, the evaluator apprentices himself to the open classroom teacher, or the other way around, there is urgent need for cross fertilization between research and teaching in natural school settings. Evaluation is just as intrinsic a part of the open classroom teacher's job as is invention, Eleanor Duckworth says.

> There are two major aspects to [the] complex job [of teaching]. One is the inventive aspect—having ideas about possible ways to do it. The other is the

evaluative aspect—being able to tell how these ideas are working, which ones to keep, which ones to discard, and which ones to change.[31]

Bussis and Chittenden in 1970 suggested four kinds of assessment activities for evaluators and teachers in open classrooms.

1. Development of techniques for evaluating *child outcomes* in an open educational setting;

2. development of *materials to assess the individual child's learning level*;

3. development of *comprehensive assessment programs*; and

4. development of procedures for appraising the *extent to which open education is implemented*.[32]

Specifying and evaluating "child outcomes"

Clearly the first evaluation task for the school implementing open education is not the choice of the tests to measure outcomes but the definitions of outcomes sought for particular children by particular teachers. The first test of an administration's commitment to open education is its willingness to include teachers in the specification of such outcomes, and the first test of the teachers' commitment is their willingness to look searchingly at children's needs, parents' desires, and their own capabilities. (This is the "structuring" or "purposing" point which Mary Collins recommends as the best way to get beginning teachers started in opening their classrooms [see Chapter 5, p. 114].) From such honest and pragmatic consideration can come definitive rather than rhetorical statements about aims, standards, and methods. Conventional skills learning goals are restated to incorporate broader definitions of the intellectual activity desired, and free-floating wishes about children's affective learning are anchored to concrete expectations.

These goals statements should represent the open educator's conviction that abilities (that is, cognitive learning objectives) and attitudes (that is, affective objectives) are not separated in real children and in real life; just as the content of a subject, and the process by which it is learned, are not naturally separable. Teachers' statements of learning objectives should indicate their commitment to fostering this interaction of intellect with attitude, Bussis and Chittenden recommend. They call for assessments of the following major kinds of "outcomes:"

Resourcefulness—Evidence that the child is deploying his unique capabilities (which include cognitive skills but not at any prescribed level), under the teacher's direction, to derive meaning from his experience. Tests for skills should be given in contexts which show the use of the skills in activities which have some *purpose* for the child. In tests of problem solving, evaluators should not just value logical analysis but also associative and intuitive ways of organizing experience.

Self-perception—Such assessments would provide evidence that children view themselves as "active organizers in their own learning and contributing participants in the classroom."

Personal and cognitive styles—Evidence that individual children are flexible in their working and social traits, not behaving in ways that are easily stereotyped as "neat," "impulsive," "withdrawn," etc.

Self-others frame of reference—Evidence that children are learning from each other but that the individual child relies on himself in matters of judgment and opinion.

Use of language as a form of thought—Evidence of such qualities as diversity and complexity of sentence structure, richness of vocabulary, questioning behavior, "interest in 'playing' with language—e.g., enjoyment of puns," individual style or "flavor" in writing.[33]

Most American open classroom teachers have been making assessments of such desired outcomes not from formally stated objectives and criterion-referenced tests (which do not yet exist) but from intuitive and improvised judgments. Such judgments are informed by their theoretical understanding of open education, their advisors' or principal's advice, and the kind of evidence that English open teachers keep: checklists in reading and math, lists of books children have read, documentations of special talents or problems, and collections of work—math, art, science projects, writing, and the like. Open classroom teachers rely heavily on evaluation techniques provided with commercial curriculum materials based in developmental theory, such as Elementary Science Study, Nuffield math, Bank Street or Scholastic readers, etc.

Bussis, Chittenden, and Amarel at ETS have developed a number of assessments for resourcefulness using the concept of quantitativeness, which includes skills in arithmetic. These have been pilot-tested with children in both formal and open classrooms, showing open classroom children's better grasp of the meaning and uses of skills, but the researchers have not had funding to validate these assessments and publish them. Their work has been extensive enough to convince them that it is a mistake to assess "achievement" separately from "self-concept" and "creativity," as if these qualities could be compartmentalized.

[A]ny definition of achievement which is appropriate to a modern, informal program must include the self and creative effort within that definition. We should investigate thoroughly the areas of traditional concern: language, arts, mathematics, sciences, and should assess whether children's accomplishments in these areas are marked by mindless application of poorly assimilated rules or by judgment and creative effort.[34]

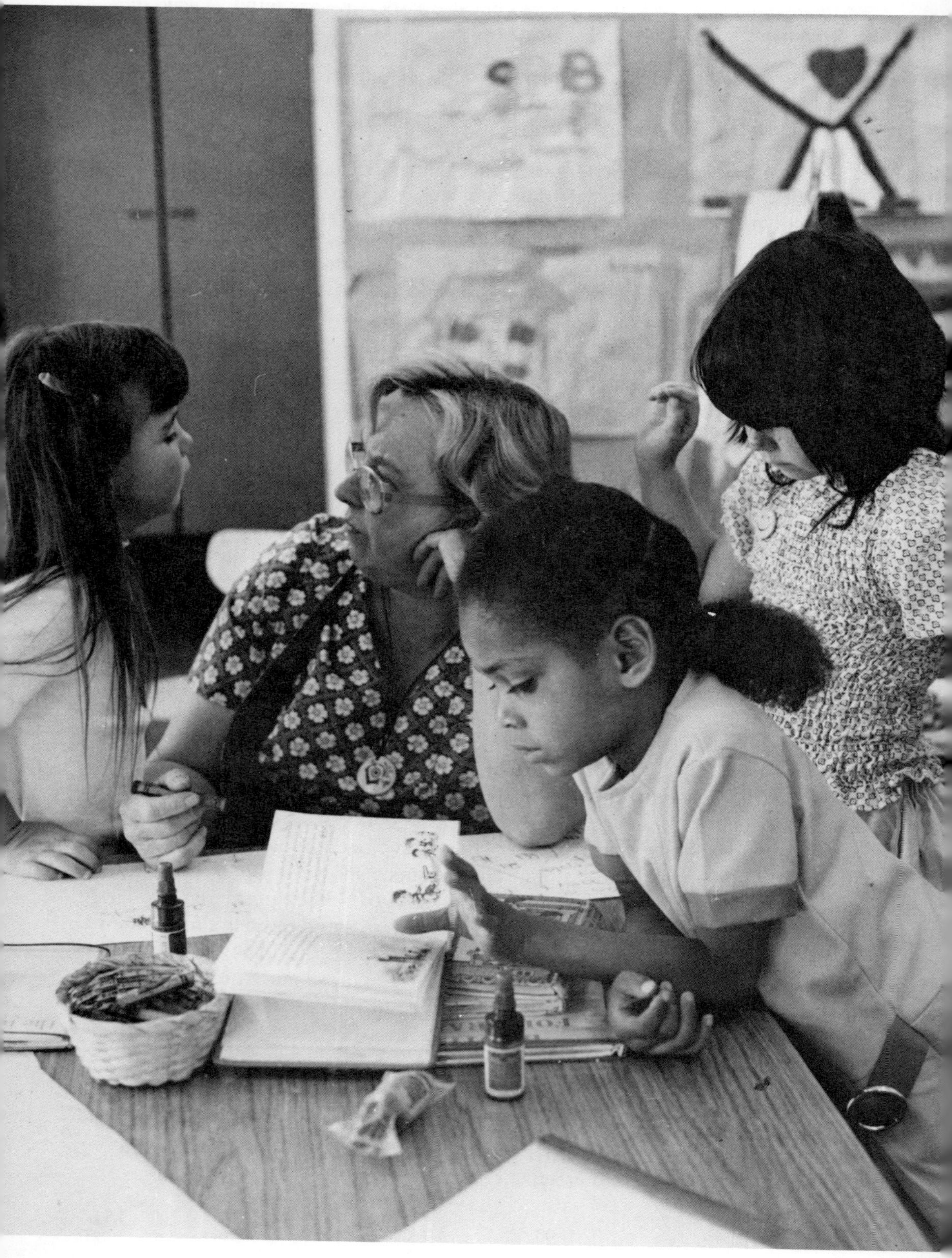

At best, progress along the emotional growth and values dimensions of open education is difficult to measure, and such outcomes will remain impossible to assess if teachers do not crystallize clear personal, local intentions out of the clouds of rhetoric surrounding open education. Charles Rathbone suggests statements of some ideal "affective, psychological and attitudinal expectations of the open classroom," which should be viewed as an integral part of the student's performance of his intellectual tasks.

The child will have the ability and desire to set his own goals.

The child will take responsibility for his own decisions and actions [having made decisions independently].

The child will possess self-discipline and will not need externally applied discipline.

The child will have a capacity for long-term involvement at learning tasks of his own choosing.

The child will possess a willingness to experiment; he will demonstrate an ability to seek new solutions and new problems.

The child will feel free; he will be socially and intellectually adaptable.

The child will exhibit trust in himself and others.

The child will be in touch with his own inner impulses; he will not fear fantasy or feeling.[35]

Will such expectations apply to all children or to particular children? How long will it take to see evidence? How will these outcomes be manifested? When such goals are written down, teachers and parents can consider their appropriateness for their students and for themselves and whether they should be immediate or distant aims. Rathbone suggests the kinds of questions which should precede a teacher's specification of such outcomes.

Perhaps [some] children have a special need for clear and consistent—even inflexible—time schedules, rules for behavior, subject-matter distinctions, etc. Perhaps, too, there are stages when even the average, normal child needs discipline from without to shore up his developing discipline from within.

Aren't there times (and subjects) when the quickest, most efficient, and most thorough way to learn something is simply to be told? . . . Aren't there some children who, naturally verbal and basically people-oriented, tend to become frustrated when faced with a constant barrage of strictly manual manipulative tasks?[36]

It is a broad jump from the teacher's preparing his or her classroom by specifying clear purposes in terms of child outcomes, to a district's evaluating that teacher's performance on the basis of tests of achievement of those outcomes. Open educators have expressed their distrust for such "accountability" systems, even when teachers themselves write the instructional goals, because the evaluation instruments that exist to measure child outcomes are typically so narrow in the scope of achievement assessed. Usually such instruments are restricted to cognitive skills. Vito Perrone and Warren Strandberg of the University of North Dakota express their distrust of "accountability."

> It has been argued that to be accountable, goals and objectives must be translated into specific behaviors that can be observed and measured. But in doing this, an essential quality of human action, as distinguished from behavior, is lost. It is the intentional or purposeful nature of human action that distinguishes it and makes it intelligible. . . . Achievement tests, typically used to measure accountability, simply are not sensitive to the intelligible quality of human action. . . .[37]

Children can learn responsibility only if they have practice in forming and carrying out their own purposes, Perrone and Strandberg write. Defining human action as "separate and isolatable behaviors . . . introduced by the teacher" deprives children of practice in responsibility because their school actions are continually evaluated on the basis of someone else's atomistic purposes.[38]

The fact that curriculum-imposed statements of objectives have been trivial and arbitrary does not ordain that teacher-written objectives must be so.[39] But open classroom teachers working under "accountability" requirements need substantial technical help if they are to be able to write outcome statements expressing the full richness of the child behaviors they want to foster—decision-making, problem-solving behaviors, diversity of ideas, ingenuity, language facility and richness, as well as social, moral, aesthetic, and self-valuing behaviors.

In an accountability system such broad purposes of the teacher must be set forth in terms of specific child behaviors. But the behaviors which an open classroom teacher cites as formal goals (and which thus structure curriculum) must appear to the child as natural and purposeful. The teacher's goals will harmonize with the child's inclination if the teacher writes objectives which challenge the student to cope with important (to the child) real-life problems without prescribing one solution or manner of solution. Allowing for the child's own purposiveness and choice about the *context* in which skills are demonstrated makes it possible for behavioral objectives to be humane, write Ashael Woodruff and Philip Kapfer. They suggest that teachers write objectives in which competencies such as vocabulary and arithmetic are mastered in the context of the two major kinds of activities which children, like all human beings, undertake of their own free will: exploring their world and fulfilling their wants.[40]

Elliott Eisner suggests that teachers use three types of objectives: Type I—directed skill learning; Type II—"expressive objectives" calling for "creative personalistic use of skills;" and Type III—prescribed problem, open solution. In the case of expressive objectives the student both envisions the problem—in art, science, language, math, whatever—and works out the solution with whatever material the teacher provides.[41] Eleanor Duckworth evaluated the African Primary Science Program on the basis of its expressive objectives—"diversity of ideas and depth to which they were pursued"—"the capacity to have wonderful ideas." She found that children who had participated in this open-ended, "messing-about" science program were far ahead of the control group on such objectives.[42] D.E.M. Gardner's book also contains examples of tests for such objectives. The USMES project (page 66) is an example of curriculum design following Type III objectives.

Assessing the individual child's learning level

Open classroom teachers individualize by assessing not only the facts and skills a child possesses but also the way he's using all he knows for further learning. This assessment is comparable in purpose to the diagnostic-prescriptive task in individualized learning systems, but open educators dislike the connotation of deficit or misfunctioning that is implied in the word "diagnosis." What is called for in open education is a close-up look at the child to see what *strength* he has. Strength is not single skills but the entire intellectual foundation on which the child builds separate learnings like letter recognition or subtraction.

The theoretical example for the teacher making such observations is Piaget's clinical observation/interview with an individual child. Lawrence Lowery and his colleagues at the University of California Cooperative Teacher Preparation Project in Berkeley have produced several self-instructional "personal workshops" presented as a series of booklets called *Learning about Learning*.[43] Student interns and experienced teachers use these to assess their students' cognitive development.

At the Educational Testing Service, Princeton, the Early Education Group, with support from the Carnegie Foundation, produced a prototype program of written exercises with accompanying toys and games. The program is for preservice and inservice teachers to learn what behaviors are associated with certain stages of learning, and what tasks and questions can help to reveal these behaviors. The theoretical base for these ETS materials is both Piagetian and psycholinguistic theory. Called *Let's Look at Children*, they are for teachers of children from four to eight.[44] They are meant to give the teacher an impression of the rich variety of ordinary classroom activities that can reveal cognitive and language levels of development. They are not meant to stimulate cognitive development but to give teachers practice in recognizing it.

Masako Tanaka, a developer of the ETS series, now director of Early Childhood programs at the Far West Laboratory, comments on the difference between Piaget-derived assessments and diagnoses in individualized instruction systems:

> The power of the developmental approach in assessment is that there are no wrong answers. Every answer the child gives, gives the teacher information. Once she understands the stages of development and can identify them in different children and activities, the teacher does not need to be limited to a set of standardized questions or procedures or equipment. By watching the child's involvement with whatever materials and activities he is interested in, and by asking appropriate questions, the teacher can make assessments about how the child is processing and constructing new knowledge and fitting it into his general body of knowledge.

The Piagetian stages and substages provide the standard the teacher works from. This is the scheme of progressively developing logical processes which Piaget found to be common in all children: the basic mental processes on which more specific learning depends. In the child beginning school, the teacher looks for the processes of sorting and classifying objects; gaining notions of number and space; putting things in serial order; realizing that quantity and length are properties that stay the same (are "conserved") even though their form is changed; and the notion of perspective or position in space—differences that different vantage points make in appearances of things. The point of Piagetian assessments is not to push children to achieve stages faster but to observe the natural attainment of the stage in order to know what can challenge him next. Another purpose is for the teacher to stretch the *range* of the child's use of a skill, so that, in Duckworth's phrase, he can have "wonderful ideas" about a large store of subject matter.

For all the power and innovation of Piaget's theory, it needs to be adapted for use in schools by ordinary teachers, and this is the subject of much needed research. An example of this is the longitudinal research project which Patricia Carini began in 1965 with Office of Education sponsorship at the Prospect School.[45] After observing children's spontaneous work in open classrooms and comparing this with their performance on researcher-designed experimental tasks, the Prospect researchers can identify aspects of the classroom learning environment which seem most useful for a child in achieving specific learning stages. The experimental tasks, the classroom observation schedules from which the Prospect evaluators and teachers work, and the theory from which they proceed are explained to visiting teachers, administrators, and evaluators who attend Prospect workshops in assessment and evaluation.

Open Corridor advisors have developed a guide for reading assessment in grades one and two, based in the advisors' belief that children have many different ways of learning to read, and the teacher's task is to discover a particular child's strengths, not drill isolated skills. The checklist has categories on the child's use of language, his physical health, and his symbolic development, all of which lead into reading, as well as on visual and auditory reading development, language comprehension, and attitudes toward reading.[46]

Comprehensive assessment programs

The nub of the problem for evaluators constructing comprehensive assessment programs—which assess the progress of the whole open education program rather than that of individual children—is to preserve the standard of the wholeness of the child's growth. Without the dimensions of the *meaning* which achievement has for a child, and the *uses* to which it is put, comprehensive testing cannot assess open classroom teachers' whole accomplishment; nor can it differentiate very helpfully between children from traditional classrooms and those from open classrooms, in which meaning and exploration are stressed, Bussis and Chittenden write.[47] Similarly, they add, comparisons of growth in problem solving, in creativity, in values and attitudes, and other broader-than-skills aspects of learning, must be made in test situations that have authenticity and interest for the child, and in which the child has to judge and marshal his own capabilities against the requirements of the test situation.[48]

Until such evaluation programs are designed, open classroom teachers must be prepared to have their progress measured by conventional district-wide or state-mandated achievement tests. This is a matter of some anxiety to many open classroom teachers, but David Hawkins believes it need not be, once the teacher's open classroom practice is well established.

> If open classroom teachers are getting anywhere in the progress toward their own goals, they don't have anything to fear from standardized tests. For instance, any child who's *involved* in reading will crack the reading tests.

Evidence that this is so is available elsewhere. Philadelphia EDC Follow Through testing was cited above. In North Dakota, children in the classrooms of New School teachers do as well as their peers in traditional classrooms on standardized achievement tests (Iowa Test of Basic Skills), and the New School Follow Through classrooms in Burlington, Washington, also show that "disadvantaged" third graders do as well on the Iowa test as do children in the regular program. At Grape Street Elementary School in Los Angeles at the end of the 1972-73 school year, the state-mandated tests showed that almost all the children in grades one through four were on and above grade level in reading. Teachers could show that all but four of the children below grade level had (a) entered school late, (b) had excessive absences, (c) had been identified as a slow learner or EMR. The significance of these results for the staff, according to the principal, Carrie Haynes, was that they had achieved the best-ever results even though they had not been "teaching for the test" but rather "to build reading vocabulary and thinking skills, and to have children read for information, pleasure, and directions."[49] They had used the "key word" reading approach—in which children begin to learn to read and spell words they want to use—as a major method.

The results at Grape have other implications for evaluation of open education. After three years of an open education program throughout the school, the fourth-graders were doing significantly better in reading than the fifth- and sixth-graders, who had not received their beginning reading instruction in open classrooms. Comprehensive evaluation in the next few years can show whether the 1972-73 achievement persists into the fifth and sixth grades, and if that proves to be the case can add documentation to Haynes's belief that the reading achievement of the fourth-graders is attributable to the children's open education reading foundation. Such evaluation results would bulwark a major tenet of many open educators: their focus on building *communities* of open education practice within a school rather than converting individual teachers to open up isolated classrooms. Comprehensive evaluation almost everywhere shows the importance of consistency of treatment over the child's long-term school experience. It emphasizes that a teacher's performance, if measured by his or her pupils' test scores, is strongly influenced by the other teachers in the school, and thus underlines Seymour Sarason's contention that the results of innovation are controlled by the dynamics of the whole school organization, not by individual talent or zeal.

Appraising the extent to which open education is implemented

In constructing such comprehensive testing programs, evaluators must attend to the point emphasized by the English evaluator, Douglas Pidgeon; that is, to interpret student outcomes in the context of what teachers commit themselves to do—their beliefs—and what they actually do—their behaviors. In determining the extent to which classrooms are actually open, evaluators can be guided by the observation instrument for primary classrooms (ages five through eight) developed and validated in the United States and England by Judith T. Evans of the Education Development Center's Pilot Communities Program.[50] This is a 50-item classroom observation rating scale, with a parallel teacher questionnaire, constructed along dimensions which reflect the characteristics of open classroom teachers identified by Herbert Walberg and Susan Christie Thomas and by Bussis and Chittenden. These teacher characteristics are provisioning for learning, humaneness (respect, warmth), assessment of child's learning level, teaching by means of guiding and extending children's choices, individual rather than standardized evaluation of children's growth, teacher's own search for learning activities, teacher's belief about learning and about children, teacher's self-perception.

Evans's validation study for the Office of Education showed that when the activities of teachers and children in open classrooms in the United

States and in England were compared along her dimensions with traditional classrooms, a very marked difference could be statistically verified. "This general finding tends to refute the common assertion that open education is vague and imprecise," Evans writes.[51] The observation scale can be used before any evaluation testing is done to make sure that children being tested as representatives of open classroom practice actually have experienced openness in teaching and learning. Evans says the scale is not intended as a diagnostic model for teachers to use on themselves. An experienced advisor observing a single classroom over a period of time is a better critic of the teacher's practice. However, Evans suggests that teachers can check their own intentions and self-perceptions by comparing their scores on her questionnaire with the scores of observers who rate their classrooms.

An instrument for teachers themselves, "Self-Evaluation of Openness," is being developed by Hermine H. Marshall of the University of California School of Education. This is a chart on which the teacher can mark his or her "points of growth" (from "not ready to move," "just beginning," "progressing well" to "feel satisfied most days") on 57 items, grouped as "Atmosphere, Feelings, Interpersonal Behavior," "Teacher's and Student's Role in Learning," and "Curriculum and Learning Environment."[52]

Chittenden and Bussis emphasize their belief that it is better to know, in depth, what teachers *intend* than to observe what their classrooms look like, for outside observers are likely to miss subtle but critical teacher behaviors.

> [O]bserving behavior by whatever currently available technique, is no substitute for understanding behavior. At least much of the data we know from studies in which teachers have been observed and rated (who interacted with whom over what and for how long) remain largely uninterpretable to the very people who gathered it.[53]

The study of open teachers' belief systems which Bussis and Chittenden carried out through interviews (see pages 92 and 93) exemplifies their belief—comparable to Pidgeon's and to Alec Clegg's—that what teachers truly believe they *will* carry out.

> [O]ur framework depends mainly on the assumption that a teacher's perception of the working environment and of the teaching task, together with characteristic beliefs about children and about learning, have pervasive effects on behavior—which, in turn, critically influence the learning environment. . . .[54]

Instead of using a classroom observation instrument to assess the extent, quality, and persistence of open classroom practice, the University of North Dakota Center for Teaching and Learning uses in-depth interviews with teachers who have done internships in its open education preparation program. The interviews assess openness along seven dimensions: *peer interaction* among students; *diversification* of learning materials and activities; *informality* of relationships between students and teacher; *individualization* of lessons according to learning level, interests, and style; decentralization of *decision making* (both teacher and students contributing to choices about school work); *integration* of subject matter; and use of the *community as a resource* for learning.

The teachers' descriptions of classroom organization, activities, and relationships are compared with descriptions given in interviews of children in their own classes. Parents are interviewed too. The first evaluation study (1972) was done of interns midway through their first year of open classroom teaching. A National Institute of Education project begun in 1973 will trace the development of these teachers over a period of five years.

The results of the first series of interviews have been compared with findings from a lengthy questionnaire of teachers in the state who were not involved in the University's open program. These comparisons indicate that not only were the University graduates significantly more open in their practice, they also expressed different conceptions of how children learn and of what activities foster learning. These differences were clear even though the open teachers perceived no more decision making power and no more support from administrators than did traditional teachers.

The University graduates have made more progress along some dimensions of openness than along others. Their strongest points are the liveliness and diversity of classroom materials, the informality of relationships between the teacher and the students, and the interactions among children themselves. They are gaining skill in individualizing learning. As a group, the North Dakota open teachers are most traditional in the dimensions relating to decision making (the teacher still tends to make them rather than the teacher and children together); subject integration (there is relatively little cross fertilization among reading and math, social science and science, etc.); and using the community and the environment as a source of lessons.[55]

The latter are aspects of the classroom which evaluators of other projects also have observed as slow to change. It appears that these aspects are interrelated and that to change in these ways teachers need more power to make their own curriculum decisions, help from administrators, and understanding and cooperation from other teachers and from parents.

These dimensions of openness also develop out of several years' experience and reflection on experience by the teachers themselves, Vito Perrone believes. North Dakota evaluation is done by interviews in order to stimulate teacher observation and evaluations of their children's learning. Interview results are discussed with teachers as a way of adding outsiders' evaluations to their own, considering other ways to achieve their objectives, and setting new objectives.

The North Dakota evaluation incorporates basic themes common to almost all the open education projects reported here. (1) The teachers should start innovation from their own point of skill and belief and form their own goals for their classroom. (2) The teachers should be partners in evaluation with objective, but supportive, observers who help them use results as a means for self-assessment and stimulus for new change.

Forging the link between theory and practice

Open educators believe that evaluation which is meaningful to school administrators and parents and useful to teachers needs to involve not only evaluation specialists but also teachers, advisors, principals, parents, and the students themselves. Principals and advisors and teachers have to join efforts to supplement standardized achievement tests with broader measurements. Parents have to learn to value reports which reveal more than children's academic accomplishments. All adult parties to the children's education have to help students learn new standards by which to evaluate their own learning.

Open classroom teachers tend to view school district demands for evaluation as narrow and short-sighted requirements which restrict and distort teachers' vision of whole-child learning and mislead everyone—teachers, parents, and the students themselves—with results which may be mere fleeting appearances. As Judith Hayward comments:

> Educational systems are hooked on evaluation, but the truth is that "results" or the influences of education most often show up in the web of a person's life years later. It's all part of the fabric, and you won't know till all the threads are in. Children are not samplers!

Even so, leaders of open education projects in public schools are acutely aware that the failure of the American progressive movement to develop new forms of evaluation caused its stagnation in upper middleclass, laboratory, and private school education. As William P. Hull writes:

> One of the main reasons Progressive Education failed, I believe, is that there was no honest way of evaluating children's intellectual activity. If we continue to shape what is done in schools so that it will produce good results on standardized achievement tests, without developing more enlightened criteria, open education is likely to take the same route.[56]

The American developmentalists of Dewey's era never "forged [the] essential, inextricable link between theory and practice," Lillian Weber writes. They never challenged the standardized organizational and evaluative methods of the public school system. In turn, they never gained the experience in realistic school situations which could have taught them to modify their practice.[57]

Looking back, Lawrence Kohlberg and Rochelle Mayer observe:

> [I]f a broad concept of development . . . is still vague as a definer of educational ends, it is not due to the inherent narrowness or vagueness of the concept. Rather, it is due to the fact that researchers have only recently begun the kind of longitudinal and educational research needed to make the concept

precise and usable. When Dewey advocated education as development at the turn of the century, most American educational psychologists turned instead to industrial psychology or to the mental health bag of virtues.[58]

As a result of this lack of research, Lillian Weber points out, it appeared that developmental theory, on which open education is based, was unsuited for mass public education and especially for educationally deprived, poor children. During the recent curriculum reform movement it has been imagined that developmental theory was an old idea that had failed in application in American public schools, when actually, by standards of proper research, it has never even been tried.[59]

Now the beginnings of proper research are refuting the critics who said progressivism ignored excellence, Kohlberg and Mayer write. Results also suggest that there need be no separation between academic and career education.[60] Open classrooms, first in England and now in the United States, are beginning to show that all kinds of students can learn when the knowledge source is not just textbooks and teacher but also personal interest, which propels the student down interconnecting paths of exploration, scholarship, work, and human relationship. To confirm such indications requires a kind of evaluation not yet performed or even designed. Open education's self-evaluation task is to substantiate what open classroom teachers believe—that academically, practically, and socially, *all kinds of children* will succeed when schools nurture children's natural urge to create order and meaning in their lives.

Footnotes

1. Joseph Gavin, *Analysis of Achievement on Standardized Tests by Follow Through Pupils in District Six* (Office of the District Superintendent, District Six, School District of Philadelphia, December 1972).

2. Roland Barth, *Open Education and the American School* (New York: Agathon Press, 1971), p. 206.

3. Thomas O'Brien, "Why Teach Mathematics?" *The Elementary School Journal* 73, no. 5 (February 1973): 263.

4. John Blackie, "Introduction," *Space, Time and Grouping,* ed. Richard Palmer (New York: Citation Press, 1971), p. 7.

5. Sir Alec Clegg, *Revolution in the British Primary Schools* (Washington, D.C.: National Association of Elementary School Principals, 1971), p. 45.

6. A detailed description of some of the ways English teachers keep records on children's progress is included in Joan Dean, *Recording Children's Progress* (New York: Citation Press, 1972).

7. Joseph Featherstone, "A New Kind of Schooling," *The New Republic* 158, no. 9 (March 2, 1968): 6.

8. Vincent Rogers, *Teaching in the British Primary School* (New York: Macmillan Co., 1972), p. 297.

9. Department of Education and Science, *Children and Their Primary Schools, A Report of the Central Advisory Council for Education (England)*, vol. 1 (London: Her Majesty's Stationary Office, 1967), pp. 201-202.

10. Douglas A. Pidgeon, *Evaluation of Achievement* (New York: Citation Press, 1972), pp. 20-29.

11. D.E.M. Gardner, *Experiment and Tradition in Primary Schools* (London: Methuen & Co., 1966), p. 199.

12. Barth, *Open Education and the American School,* pp. 15-16.

13. Pidgeon, *Evaluation of Achievement,* pp. 19-20.

14. *Ibid.,* pp. 11-12, 32-38.

15. Harvey A. Averch et al., *How Effective Is Schooling? A Critical Review and Synthesis of Research Findings* (Santa Monica, Ca.: The Rand Corporation, 1972), pp. 52-60.

16. Clegg, *Revolution in the British Primary Schools,* p. 45.

17. Averch, *How Effective Is Schooling?,* pp. ix-x, 153.

18. Lauren B. Resnick, "Open Education: Some Tasks for Technology," *Educational Technology* 12, no. 1 (January 1972): 70.

19. *Ibid.,* p. 75.

20. Robert Glaser, "Individuals and Learning: The New Aptitudes," *Educational Researcher* 1, no. 6 (June 1972): 11.

21. Benjamin Bloom, "Testing Cognitive Ability and Achievement," *Handbook of Research on Teaching,* ed. N.L. Gage (Chicago: Rand McNally & Co., 1963), p. 384.

22. Henry S. Dyer, "Testing Little Children—Some Old Problems in New Settings," (Technical Institute Paper of National Leadership Institute, Teacher Education/Early Childhood, University of Connecticut, Storrs, Conn., December 1971).

23. *Ibid.*

24. Barth, *Open Education in the American School,* p. 42.

25. Anne Bussis and Edward Chittenden, *Analysis of an Approach to Open Education* (Princeton, N.J.: Educational Testing Service, 1970), p. 16.

26. Elliot W. Eisner, "Emerging Models for Educational Evaluation," *School Review* 80, no. 4 (August 1972): 578.

27. Bussis and Chittenden, *Analysis of an Approach,* p. 69.

28. Deborah Meier, *Reading Failure and the Tests,* an occasional paper of the Workshop Center for Open Education, City College of New York, Convent Ave. and 140 St., New York, February 1973. Meier has also written a leaflet for parents on the same topic: "Reading Tests: Do They Help or Hinder Your Child?" (Community Resources Institute, 270 West 96 St., New York, N.Y., 1973).

29. Margaret de Rivera, "Academic Achievement Tests and the Survival of Open Education," mimeographed (Philadelphia, Pa.: Education Development Center Follow Through Program, April 1972), p. 5.

30. Edward Chittenden and Anne Bussis, "Open Education: Research and Assessment Strategies," *Open Education: A Sourcebook for Parents and Teachers,* ed. E.B. Nyquist and G.R. Hawes (New York: Bantam, 1972), p. 370.

31. Eleanor Duckworth, "Evaluating African Science: Case in Point," *Evaluation Reconsidered,* ed. Arthur Tobier (New York: Workshop Center for Open Education, City College of New York, May 1973), p. 27.

32. Bussis and Chittenden, *Analysis of an Approach,* p. 60.

33. *Ibid.,* pp. 66-71.

34. Chittenden and Bussis, "Open Education: Research and Assessment Strategies," p. 369.

35. Charles Rathbone, "Examining the Open Education Classroom," *School Review* 80, no. 4 (August 1972): 537-538.

36. *Ibid.,* p. 540.

37. Vito Perrone and Warren Strandberg, "A Perspective on Accountability," *Teachers College Record* 73, no. 3 (February 1972): 351.

38. *Ibid.*, p. 352.
39. Henry H. Walbesser, "Behavioral Objectives, a Cause Cèlèbre," *The Arithmetic Teacher* 19, no. 6 (October 1972): 437.
40. Ashael Woodruff and Philip Kapfer, "Behavioral Objectives and Humanism in Education: A Question of Specificity," *Educational Technology* 12, no. 1 (January 1972): 51-55.
41. Eisner, "Emerging Models for Educational Evaluation," pp. 581-583.
42. Eleanor Duckworth, "The Having of Wonderful Ideas," *Harvard Educational Review* 42, no. 2 (May 1972): 228-229.
43. Lawrence Lowery, *Learning About Learning Series* (Berkeley, Ca.: The University of California Cooperative Teacher Preparation Project, 1973).
44. *Let's Look at Children* (Princeton, N.J.: Educational Testing Service, forthcoming).
45. Patricia F. Carini, *Outline of Research and Evaluation Design: The Project School* (North Bennington, Vt.: The Prospect School, 1972).
46. City College Advisory Service to Open Corridors, "A Guide for Reading Assessment: Grades 1 and 2," *Evaluation Reconsidered*, ed. Arthur Tobier, pp. 31-34.
47. Bussis and Chittenden, *Analysis of an Approach*, p. 70.
48. Chittenden and Bussis, *Open Education: A Sourcebook for Parents and Teachers*, pp. 368-369.
49. The Cooperative Primary Tests were used in grades one, two, and three; Comprehensive Tests of Basic Skills in grades four through six.
50. Judith T. Evans, *Characteristics of Open Education: Results from a Classroom Observation Rating Scale and a Teacher Questionnaire* (Pilot Communities Program, Education Development Center, Newton, Mass., August 1971), ERIC ED 058 160, p. 6. The findings are also reported in Herbert J. Walberg and Susan Christie Thomas, "Open Education: An Operational Definition and Validation in Great Britain and United States," *American Educational Research Journal* 9, no. 2 (Spring 1972): 197-207.
51. Evans, *Characteristics of Open Education*, p. 24.
52. Hermine H. Marshall, "Self-Evaluation of Openness, Exploratory Version II" (Berkeley, Ca.: University of California School of Education, 1973).
53. Chittenden and Bussis, *Open Education: A Sourcebook for Parents and Teachers*, pp. 365-366.
54. *Ibid.*, p. 365.
55. Vito Perrone, "Report from North Dakota," *Evaluation Reconsidered*, ed. Arthur Tobier, p. 30. Michael Patton, *Structural Dimensions of Open Education and Parental Reaction to Open Classrooms in North Dakota: A Sociological View of the Diffusion of Open Education as an Innovation in Organizational Structure and Processes* (Grand Forks, N.D.: University of North Dakota Center for Teaching and Learning, Spring 1973). A 1973 doctoral dissertation by Sister Karen Craig, C.S.J., at North Dakota was a survey of all graduates of the open master's degree program from 1968 to 1972. Craig found the same over-all pattern of progress and lack of progress along the seven dimensions of openness, observed that a remarkable 85 to 90 percent of the graduates are still in teaching, and that they still persist in the ideas and methods projected during their University preparation.
56. William P. Hull, "The Case for the Experimental School," *Insights* 4, no. 1 (September 1971): 8.
57. Lillian Weber, *The English Infant School and Informal Education* (Englewood Cliffs, N.J.: Prentice-Hall, 1971), p. 241.
58. Lawrence Kohlberg and Rochelle Mayer, "Development as the Aim of Education," *Harvard Educational Review* 42, no. 4 (November 1972): 492-493.
59. Weber, *The English Infant School and Informal Education*, pp. 242-247.
60. Kohlberg and Mayer, "Development as the Aim of Education," p. 494.

Appendix 1

A Short Bibliography of References and Curriculum Materials

The following are sources of information, theory, ideas for classroom implementation (including curriculum materials), and writing (or film) which imparts the flavor of English and American open classrooms. These references have been selected by Kathleen Devaney and Gretchen Thomas, staff members of the Far West Laboratory project which produced this book, and Judith Hayward, who served as a consultant.

Section A is a minimal rather than comprehensive listing of works about the background and theory of open education.

Section B is a listing of the books which convey most satisfyingly to us the atmosphere and benefits of open classrooms and thus may serve to persuade and inspire parents and school people to work toward open education. (This persuasive task was specifically omitted as an objective of the book itself because many evocative and inspiring portrayals of the open classroom are already available.) A few films are listed in this section. Our criterion was that the films suggested should capture and hold the interest of laymen and teachers with no background in open education and, without minimizing the complexity of the task for teachers, should convey open education's potential for success in *ordinary American public schools*, not just privileged settings.

Section C includes books to help teachers organize the space, materials, and time scheduling of the open classroom. More aids of this kind are becoming available. Some imply that if the teacher simply follows the directions in the book the classroom will be open. But there is no foolproof blueprint, plan, set of apparatus, or strategy for organizing an open classroom. Each teacher needs a plan, to be sure, but it should be her own uniquely designed and continually redesigned scheme for stimulating and responding to her own students' learning interests. The author's emphasis on this point is our criterion for materials on classroom organization.

Section D lists sources of curriculum *ideas* for teachers and suggestions of learning *materials* for students. The latter should not be regarded as recommendations, since we think every teacher should make his or her own curriculum decisions from knowledge of self and students and subject matter. Those listed here have been endorsed by teachers interviewed during the course of our study. The list is admittedly partial and somewhat random, as our study did not survey all the open classrooms in the United States.

There are many other materials worth investigating on the American commercial market, including a few new textbook series in math, science, reading and social studies which, although conventional in format, project an active-learning approach. If used in the manner intended (that is, not as texts plus exercise books), these could become a bridge from traditional to open teaching. Such programs can be sized up by means of critical study of the teacher's manual: Does it recommend that the teacher supply a rich variety of manipulative materials—mainly inexpensive, natural, everyday objects? Can the teacher skip around in the book, change the order of lessons as needed? Does the text call for open-ended, playful investigation of materials and discussion of experiences *preceding* concept/skills learning and practice? Does the manual emphasize personalized pace and *manner* of learning? Does the bibliography list references to open education theory and practice?

Section A—Background and Theory

Barth, Roland S., *Open Education and the American School*. New York: Agathon Press, 1972. $7.95.
> The introduction and Chapters 1 and 2 explain the basic beliefs open educators hold about learning and knowledge and describe the essential changes which these beliefs necessitate in teacher and student activity in the classroom. Bibliography.

Beard, Ruth. *An Outline of Piaget's Developmental Psychology for Students and Teachers*. New York: New American Library, 1972. $1.50.

Blackie, John. *Inside the Primary School* (American Edition). New York: Schocken Books, 1971. $4.95.
> History, theory, and practice of open education in England (including innovations in curriculum in English, math, science, etc.) by the former chief inspector for primary schools and secretary to the Plowden Committee. Written for parents in England.

Clegg, Sir Alec, *Revolution in the British Primary Schools*. Washington, D.C.: National Association of Elementary School Principals, National Education Association, 1971. $2.50
> Why and how the English changes came about and descriptions of changes in the role of the principal, the curriculum, the advisor. By the chief education officer (similary to American county superintendent) for the West Riding of Yorkshire. Color reproductions of children's work.

Elkind, David, *Children and Adolescents: Interpretive Essays on Jean Piaget*. New York: Oxford University Press, 1970. $4.95.
> Readable essays for teachers, on such topics as Piaget himself, his concept of how the mind develops, implications for teaching, the difference between Piaget's approach to intelligence and the I.Q. approach, implications of Piaget's work for reading and remedial education by a foremost American Piagetian psychologist.

Featherstone, Joseph. *Schools Where Children Learn.* New York: Liveright, 1971.
  A compilation of *The New Republic* articles which sparked widespread American interest in the British infant schools.

Ginsburg, Herbert. *The Myth of the Deprived Child: Poor Children's Intellect and Education.* Englewood Cliffs, N.J.: Prentice-Hall, 1972. $3.95
  Readable and provocative survey of the research on "deprived" urban children's cognitive functioning, which concludes that there is no such thing as a cognitive "deficit." Useful to teachers and parents who are questioning the appropriateness of open approaches for urban Black children.

Nyquist, Ewald B., and Hawes, Gene R., eds. *Open Education: A Sourcebook for Parents and Teachers.* New York: Bantam, 1972. $1.95.
  A wide-ranging collection of articles, essays, interviews, research papers, and other writings which describe open classrooms, report teachers' and principals' experiences, discuss problems of evaluation, explain learning theory and open teaching technique. Includes Jenny Andreae on advising in New Rochelle; Mary Stitt and staff on innovating in Arlington Heights; Edward Chittenden and Anne Bussis on defining the teacher's role and new instruments for evaluation; Edward Yeomans on a British-style workshop for teachers; Bernard Spodek, Lillian Weber, and Vito Perrone on American teachers' problems in developing open education; excerpts from Dewey and Piaget. Bibliography.

Rathbone, Charles, ed. *Open Education: The Informal Classroom.* New York: Citation Press, 1971. $2.85.
  The fundamentals of open education, as explained in writings by William P. Hull ("Leicestershire Revisited"), David Hawkins ("Messing About in Science" and "I-Thou-It"), Tony Kallet, excerpts from the Plowden Report; also basic materials for outfitting an open classroom suggested by Allen Leitman and Edith Churchill, and Rathbone's essay, "On Preparing the Teacher: A Lesson from Loughborough." Introduction by John Holt.

Silberman, Charles, ed. *The Open Classroom Reader.* New York: Vintage, 1973. $10.95 ($2.95 paper).
  A very large collection of writings on the "why" and the "how to" of open education, more recent and more comprehensive than Nyquist or Rathbone, including much of the material found in both those anthologies, plus additional selections chosen by the man who wrote *Crisis in the Classroom.*

Weber, Lillian. *The English Infant School and Informal Education.* Englewood Cliffs, N.J.: Prentice-Hall, 1971. $4.95.
  Weber's analysis of theory and practice in English open schools after her 18-months study in England, and her contrasting analysis of American practice in early childhood education, revealing the problems faced by Americans who wish to develop their own, native version of open education.

Yardley, Alice. *Reaching Out* and *Young Children Thinking.* New York: Citation Press, 1973; $2.25 each.
  An English teacher explains the rationale behind the informal classroom in *Reaching Out.* The second book explains young children's modes of thinking

and tells practical ways for teachers to help children use their full powers of thought.

Section B—Flavor of Open Classroom Teaching and Learning

Ashton-Warner, Sylvia. *Teacher*. New York: Simon and Schuster, 1963.
    The New Zealand novelist and teacher, who created her unique brand of open education with white and Maori children, describes life in her classroom and tells the secret of her technique: "I have found out the (two) worst enemies to what we call teaching. . . . The first is the children's interest in each other. . . . This unseemly and unlawful communication!. . . . So I harness the communication, since I can't control it, and base my method on it. . . . [So] I let anything come . . . within safety; but *I use it*." Photographs of the classroom.

Hawkins, Frances Pockman. *The Logic of Action,* Boulder, Colo.: Mountain View Center for Environmental Education, University of Colorado, 1969. $3.00
    In her journal of a semester's work using lively real-world learning materials with deaf preschoolers, Frances Hawkins continually relates this experience to teaching nonhandicapped children of the same age or older. For instance, commenting on the children's reliance on classroom routine and their lack of initiative, at the start of the year, she writes: "In this again they are not unlike older school children in bleak settings and more dictatorial atmospheres, who rely less and less on the inner and often competent direction they bring from home. In such atmospheres it is as if the open or disguised denigration of who they are and what they bring from poor homes finally destroys or transforms to violence what it has failed to honor." The title of the book refers to Hawkins's belief (from Piaget) that all human beings develop logic from their active experience with natural objects, events, and living things. Photographs of the children at work.

Hess, Hannah S. *The Third Side of the Desk: How Parents Can Change the Schools*. New York: Scribner's, 1973. $8.95.
    An involved parent's story-like account of how white and Black parents in Manhattan's Upper West Side turned their school—P.S. 84—around, working with Lillian Weber's Open Corridor program. The final chapter is a parent's description of open classrooms and testament of belief in this kind of education: "What we are trying to get away from is an education that produces people who follow orders blindly. We are trying to provide an education where people think for themselves, are responsible for their actions, and develop themselves to their maximum potential. . . . That is a tall order, and we have only made a small beginning; but when I first became involved in the school, I would not have believed it possible that we would even make this small beginning, so perhaps the tall order is not impossible either."

Marshall, Sybil. *An Experiment in Education*. London: Cambridge University Press (American branch: 32 East 57th Street, New York), 1963.
    A classic account of informal education in England evolving over several years as teacher and children expressed their interests through art, music, the past and present life of their village. "The essential thing was to grasp every idea that would make learning more *active*. . . ." The book has the quality of a wonder-

ful, inspirational fairy tale but it is believable, given the evidence of the teacher's inexhaustible curiosity, resourcefulness, and dedication to children's growth. She believes the primary school's function "is to create interest, spur curiosity, and open doors through which the children may choose to go in later stages of their growth." Reproductions of children's art. (Marshall's later book, *Adventure in Creative Education* [Long Island City, New York: Pergamon Press, 1968] is an account of her equal enthusiasm and inventiveness in designing inservice education for teachers.)

Murrow, Casey, and Murrow, Liza. *Children Come First: The Inspired Work of English Primary Schools*. New York: American Heritage Press, 1971. $6.95.

Two American teachers' detailed observations of 40 primary and intermediate level English schools during 1969-70. Attention is paid to the reasons for the successes the authors observe—in terms of the organization of schooling in Britain, the supports provided for teachers, the arrangement of classrooms and school buildings, and the curriculum ideas and materials used. For instance: "When we entered the (temporary classroom building), . . . we found a movement class under way. Both boys and girls wore shorts and T-shirts, and despite the November weather, they were clearly warm and unencumbered. Desks, chairs, tables, and equipment were neatly stacked in the corners, leaving the floor open. For lack of enough space, the boys sat on the floor, while the girls danced, exploring the spaces around them, moving between and around one another. There was music playing, acting as a catalyst that sparked them off. Yet, no child followed the beat in any formal pattern. . . . " The Murrows's vignette of this class is followed by explanation of the aims and background of the "movement" movement in England, its importance for children's reading, some success stories, and examples of several different movement programs they saw in other schools. They similarly describe other subject areas.

Paull, Dorothy, and Paull, John. *Yesterday I found*. . . . Boulder, Colo.: Mountain View Center for Environmental Education, University of Colorado, 1972. $3.00

An English teacher's account of two years' work with a class of nine-through-eleven-year-olds in Leicestershire, emphasizing their investigation of materials from their environment—both things brought into the classroom and experienced during field trips. Descriptions of what the teacher did, how the children reacted, what they learned, are interspersed with comments about why such methods produce learning. For instance: "I had a large, woven shopping basket which I took to school every day, usually filled with such things as paper towel . . . tubes, picture cards from teapackets, . . . stones, shells, stamps, and scraps of fabric. Some things I took to give to children who were engaged in a particular activity. Others I collected for possible future use, not knowing exactly what that might be. . . . Nicholas once commented . . . , 'Your house must be like a flipping museum with all these things you keep on bringing.' 'All these things' told the children something important about me and my interests, and when the children also brought things to school I found out more about them." Black and white and color photographs of children at work.

Section B—Rental Films

The British Infant School, Southern Style, 30 minutes, color, sound, 16mm. Agathon Press, 150 Fifth Avenue, New York, N.Y. 10011.
    The principal and teachers of a racially integrated small-town school in Lenoir, North Carolina, describe their concept of open education as the film shows scenes from classrooms at all grade levels. At the beginning there is a brief, interesting description of open classrooms in England.

Children Are People, 42 minutes, color, sound, 16mm. Agathon Press, New York.
    Scenes of day-to-day activities in British primary schools for children aged five through 11. The narration explains the basic principles of open education.

The Informal Classroom, 12 minutes, color, sound, 16mm. Educational Coordinates, 432 South Pastoria, Sunnyvale, Calif. 94086.
    Grape Street School in Watts, Los Angeles, is the subject of this film, made in 1972. The narration is a basic explanation of the rationale for an informal learning environment.

Reading and Writing, 30 minutes, black and white, sound, 16mm. University of California Extension Media Center, Berkeley, Calif. 94720.
    Taken from the BBC television Mother Tongue series on British open education, this film shows the natural development of children's reading through environmental activities, movement, drama, painting, and making their own books. Filmed at Sea Mills School, Bristol; narration is by the head teacher, Doris Nash. Order number 7396.

A Teacher Talks About Her Classroom, 30 minutes, color filmstrip with longplay record. Bank Street College of Education, 610 West 112th Street, New York, N.Y. 10025.
    Sue Monell, a noted open classroom teacher, describes her work with primary children in Bank Street School.

They Can Do It, 34 minutes, black and white, sound. Education Development Center Distribution Center, 55 Chapel Street, Newton, Mass. 02160.
    Starting with the second day of school for 26 six-year-olds in a Philadelphia public school, this film traces the teacher's, Lovey Glen's, development of open education throughout a school year.

What's New at School? 55 minutes, color, sound, 16mm. Murray Benson, CBS Broadcast Group, 51 West 52nd Street, New York, N.Y. 10019.
    A print of the February 1972 television documentary contrasting traditional teaching methods with the gradually evolving open classroom of a University of North Dakota intern teacher, Ken Langton, and his sixth-grade class in Devils Lake, N.D.

Section C—Organizing Yourself and Your Classroom

Biggs, Edith, and MacLean, James. *Freedom to Learn.* Menlo Park, Calif.: Addison-Wesley, 1969.

Hertzberg, Alvin, and Stone, Edward F. *Schools Are for Children: An American Approach to the Open Classroom*. New York: Schocken, 1971. $6.95.

Lorton, Mary Baratta. *Workjobs*. Menlo Park, Calif.: Addison-Wesley, 1972. $5.56.

Ridgway, Lorna, and Lawton, Irene. *Family Grouping in the Primary School*. London: Ward Lock, 1969.

Sargent, Betsye. *The Integrated Day in an American School*. Boston, Mass.: National Association of Independent Schools, 1970. $2.50. Sargent's film of a day in her classroom is called *I Am Here Today* (43 minutes, black and white, sound, 16mm), Education Development Center Distribution Center, 55 Chapel Street, Newton, Mass. 02160.

From the Citation Press (New York) Series, *Informal Schools in Britain Today:*
  Dean, Joan. *Recording Children's Progress*.
  Grugeon, David, and Grugeon, Elizabeth. *The Infant School*.
  Palmer, Richard. *Space Time and Grouping*.
  Probert, Howard, and Jarman, Christopher. *A Junior School*.
  (Available as single books ($1.95 each) or within volume called *Teachers and Classrooms, Volume 3*. $12.50. The books on curriculum cited in the following section are also available all together in one volume entitled *Curriculum, Volume 1*, $13.75.)

Workshop for Learning Things, *Our Catalog*, 5 Bridge Street, Watertown, Mass. 02171.

Yanes, Samuel, and Holdorf, Cia, eds. *Big Rock Candy Mountain: Resources for Our Education*. New York: Dell, 1972. $4.00

Yardley, Alice, *Learning to Adjust*, and *The Teacher of Young Children*, New York: Citation Press, 1973. $2.25 each.

Section D—Curriculum Ideas for Teachers and Materials for Students
(Student materials are marked with an asterisk.)

All Subject Areas

Hertzberg, Alvin, and Stone, Edward F. *Schools Are for Children: An American Approach to the Open Classroom* (see Section A above).

Murrow, Casey, and Murrow, Liza. *Children Come First: The Inspired Work of English Primary Schools* (see Section B above).

Rogers, Vincent R. *Teaching in the British Primary School* (also called *English Primary School*). New York: Macmillan, 1970. $8.25 ($4.25 paper).

Silberman, Charles. *The Open Classroom Reader* (see Section A above).

171

Expressive Arts: Art, Crafts, Music, Drama, Movement, and their relationship to Reading

Blackie, John. *Inside the Primary School* (see Section A above), Chapters 10 and 11.

From the Citation Press (New York) Series, *Informal Schools in Britain Today:*
  Blackie, Pamela; Bullough, Bess; and Nash, Doris. *Drama.*
  Horton, John. *Music.*
  Pluckrose, Henry. *Art.*

Koch, Kenneth. *Wishes, Lies, and Dreams: Teaching Children to Write Poetry.* New York: Chelsea House-Vintage, 1970. $1.95. Also *Rose, Where Did You Get That Red? Teaching Great Poetry to Children.* New York: Chelsea House-Random House, 1973. $7.95.

Marshall, Sybill. *An Experiment in Education* (see Section B above).

Morgan, Elizabeth, *A Practical Guide to Drama in the Primary School.* London: Ward Lock, 1968.

Richardson, Elwyn. *In the Early World.* New York: Pantheon, 1969.

Russell, Joan. *Creative Dance in the Primary School,* Macdonald and Evans, Ltd., 8 John Street, London WC1, 1965.

Spolin, Viola. *Improvisation for the Theatre.* Northwestern University Press, 1735 Benson Avenue, Evanston, Ill.

Teachers and Writers Collaborative. *The Whole Word Catalogue.* 490 Hudson St., New York, N.Y. 10014, 1973.
  A practical collection of assignments for stimulating student writing—personal writing, collective novels, diagram stories, spoofs, fables—developed from experiences of Collaborative writers teaching in Manhattan public schools. The Collaborative also publishes a Newsletter of writers' journals and children's work three times a year ($5.00).

Wiseman, Ann. *Making Things–The Home Book of Creative Discovery.* Boston: Little Brown, 1973.

Yardley, Alice. *Senses and Sensitivity.* New York: Citation Press, 1973.

Reading

Ashton-Warner, Sylvia. *Teacher* (see Section B above).

Balance, Ellen; Cook, Ann; and Mack, Herb. *Reading in the Open Classroom: An Individual Approach,* Community Resources Institute, 270 West 96th Street, New York, N.Y. 10025, 1971.
  A reading scheme telling how to start children reading by having them make their own books from words and pictures about their own experiences. The scheme suggests the Breakthrough Books and Monster Books (see below) for use in subsequent stages in the development of reading skill. *Stories by Kids for Kids* is a mimeographed collection of stories, in children's own printing and drawings, useful as a sampler for teachers.

Goddard, Nora L. *Reading in the Modern Infants' School.* London: University of London Press, 1969.

Johnson, Jean, and Tamburrini, Joan. *Informal Reading and Writing (Informal Schools in Britain Today* Series). New York: Citation Press, 1972.

Lorton, Mary Baratta. *Workjobs.* Menlo Park, Calif.: Addison-Wesley, 1972.
 Resource book of pre-reading and pre-number activities with natural materials, leading to concept development; practical instructions for organizing an open classroom.

Yardley, Alice. *Exploration and Language.* New York: Citation Press, 1973.

Reading Student Materials

* *"Big Boy" Early Reading Program.* Menlo Park, Calif.: Addison-Wesley, 1971, 1973.
 Primers simulating child-made books, vocabulary and stories drawn from common experience of American—mainly urban—six-and seven-year-olds.

* *Breakthrough to Literacy Series.* Glendale, Calif.: Bowmar, 1973.
 Twenty-six paperback readers for five-and six-year-olds using words drawn from experiences common to this age; three stages.

* *Discoveries, An Individualized Approach to Reading.* New York: Houghton Mifflin, 1973.
 Six stages of paperback stories by juvenile authors and children themselves, Bank-Street-designed, for intermediate level.

* *Individualized Reading from Scholastic.* Englewood Cliffs, N.J.: Scholastic Press, 1972.
 Paperback storybooks by juvenile authors, job cards, and student log books; 1-6.

* *Instant Readers.* New York: Holt, Rinehart and Winston, 1970.
 Bill Martin's Storybooks for three primary levels, available as a program or as a classroom library.

* *Interaction.* Boston: Houghton Mifflin, 1973.
 James Moffett's language arts program of storybooks, records, and activity booklets; K-12.

* *Language Experiences in Reading.* Chicago: Encyclopedia Britannica Press, 1965.
 Roach Van and Claryce Allen's program stimulating children's own language and book creation; K-6.

* *MacDonald Starters.* MacDonald Publishing House, 4950 Poland Street, London 1, 1971.
 Very easy paper primers about children's interests—cars, animals, boats, etc.

* *The Monster Books for Beginning Readers.* Glendale, Calif.: Bowmar, 1973.

Stories written by children in New York public schools, edited by Community Resources Institute staff.

* *Sounds of Language Readers.* New York: Holt, Rinehart and Winston, 1970, 1972.
   Reading program based on child's experience of language as sounds first, then print—"a total linquistic experience"; K-6.

Mathematics

Biggs, Edith. *Mathematics for Younger Children* and *Mathematics for Older Children* (*Informal Schools in Britain Today* Series). New York: Citation Press, 1972.

Biggs, Edith, and MacLean, James. *Freedom to Learn: An Active Learning Approach to Mathematics,* Menlo Park, Calif.: Addison-Wesley, 1969.

Charbonneau, Manon. *Learning to Think in a Math Lab.* Boston, Mass.: National Association of Independent Schools, 1971.

Laycock, Mary, and Watson, Gene. *The Fabric of Mathematics.* Creative Publications, P.O. 10328, Palo Alto. Calif., 1971.
   A descriptive directory to active-learning math materials, books, games, keyed to math concepts arranged in a framework; K-6.

Lorton, Mary Barratta. *Workjobs* (see *Reading* above).

Nuffield Mathematics Project. New York: John Wiley & Sons, 1967-69.
   Teacher guides for computation, measurement, algebra, geometry, providing mathematical background and suggestions for student activities; K-8. The fundamentals of active-learning math are in *I Do, and I Understand.*

The Schools Council. *Mathematics in Primary Schools,* Curriculum Bulletin No. 1 (American Edition). Newton, Mass.: Selective Educational Equipment (SEE), Inc., 1973.

Unified Science and Mathematics for the Elementary School (USMES), Developmental Version, Newton, Mass.: Education Development Center, 1973.
   Teacher guides for open-ended class investigations integrating math, science, social studies, communication; mainly 4-6.

Mathematics Student Materials

* *CDA Math.* Washington, D.C.: Curriculum Development Associates, 1972.
   Individualized computation and problem-solving in paper workbooks; 1-6.

* *Elementary Science Study (ESS),* St. Louis, Mo.: Webster Division, McGraw-Hill, 1968-71.
   Teacher guides and student materials for classification, measurement, geometry, probability, etc. See *A Working Guide to the Elementary Science Study* (McGraw-Hill, 1971).

* *Let's Explore Mathematics* Series. London: A. & C. Black. Available

from the Sunflower Source, P.O. Box 2227, Menlo Park, Calif.
> Leonard Marsh's program on number, geometry, metric system, in student booklets, also used as teacher idea sources; 1-5.

* *Mathematics for Schools.* Menlo Park, Calif.: Addison-Wesley, 1971.
> Harold Fletcher's translation of Nuffield materials into paperback student work booklets and teacher guides. From England, metric system; 1-6.

* *Maths & Things, SEE Catalog.* Newton, Mass.: Selective Educational Equipment (SEE), Inc., 1973.

* *Mathematics in the Making.* Boston, Mass.: Houghton Mifflin, 1967.
> Twelve paperback student booklets from England for middle grades.

* *Mathematics Laboratory Materials.* Learning Innovations, 100-35 Metropolitan Avenue., Forest Hills, N.Y., 1969.
> Lore Rasmussen's notes to teachers about setting up active-learning math, plus student worksheets to use with manipulative materials provided by the teacher; K-3.

* *Project Mathematics.* Minneapolis, Minn.: Winston Press, 1972.
> Nuffield-based program from Canada providing paperback student booklets and teacher guides: 1-6.

Science and Social Studies

African Primary Science Program. Education Development Center Distribution Center, 55 Chapel St., Newton, Mass. 02160.
> Teachers guides for ten environmental science activities for primary children. Developed by the Science Education Program for Africa, these units are adaptable to American children. This is the program referred to in Eleanor Duckworth's essay, "The Having of Wonderful Ideas."

Berger Evelyn, and Winters, Bonnie A. *Social Studies in the Open Classroom: A Practical Guide.* New York: Teachers College Press, 1973.

Blance, Ellen; Cook, Ann; and Mack, Herb. *Cooking in the Open Classroom.* Community Resources Institute, 270 West 96th Street., New York, N.Y., 1971.

Caney, Steve. *Toybook.* New York: Workman, 1972.
> Directions for helping children make their own playthings—kites, stilts, etc. —out of scrounged materials.

Dropkin, Ruth, ed. *Science in the Open Classroom.* New York: Workshop Center for Open Education, City College of New York, 1974. $2.00.
> Theoretical pieces by Lillian Weber, Nathan Isaacs, Eleanor Duckworth, and others on how children learn science concepts. Reproductions of children's classroom science projects with teacher commentaries.

Harris, Melville. *Environmental Studies (Informal Schools in Britain Today* Series). New York: Citation Press, 1971.

Nuffield Junior Science; Teachers Guides 1 and 2; Apparatus; Source Book. New York: Agathon Press, 1973.

Paull, Dorothy, and Paull, John. *Yesterday I Found* . . . (See Section B above).

Shaw, Peter. *Science* (*Informal Schools in Britain Today* Series). New York: Citation Press, 1971.

Science 5/13. London: MacDonald, 1969. Available from The Sunflower Source, P.O. Box 2227, Menlo Park, Calif., and Purnell Library Service, 850 Seventh Ave., New York 10019.
> Teacher guides to science projects (especially outdoors). Based on Nuffield Foundation development work, these guides state learning objectives for children based on Piagetian stages; 1-6.

Unified Science and Mathematics (USMES) (see *Mathematics* above).

Yardley, Alice. *Discovering the Physical World*. New York: Citation Press, 1973.

Science and Social Studies Student Materials

* *Elementary Science Study (ESS)*. St. Louis, Mo.: Webster Division, McGraw-Hill, Teacher guides but not classroom kits also available from The Sunflower Source and SEE, Inc.
> 56 units calling for children's active involvement with materials, especially things from nature. Classroom apparatus and kits are available for some, not necessary for most; K-8. (See *A Working Guide to the Elementary Science Study,* McGraw-Hill, 1971.)

* *First Interest Books*. Ginn & Co., Ltd., 18 Bedford Row, London WCl, 1969.
> Several series of paper booklets encouraging children to read for information and discussion. Among the series titles are "Animals," "In a Wider World" (geography), "A Long Time Ago" (dinosaurs, cavemen). About second-grade reading level but interesting to older children as well.

* *Mollie Clarke Books, Observe and Learn* (Second Series). Rupert Hart-Davis Educational Publications, 3 Upper James Street, London WIR 4BP, 1972.
> Paperback library of books about seeds, shells, worms, etc., to stimulate reading for information, active involvement, and discussion. Middle grades. (First series, for primary children, is on math topics, available from SEE, Inc., Newton, Mass.)

* *The Owl Program*. New York: Holt, Rinehart and Winston.
> Information books for a classroom library, available in four stages; K-6. Books about arithmetic, science, social studies, as well as stories.

Section E—Periodicals from Open Education Projects (Relevant to all subjects above)

Insights into Open Education, monthly during the academic year, $3.50 a year. Corwin Hall, Center for Teaching and Learning, University of North Dakota, Grand Forks, N.D. 58201.

Notes from Workshop Center for Open Education, quarterly, $3.00 a year. Workshop Center for Open Education, 6 Shepard Hall, City College of New York, Convent Avenue and 140th Street, New York, N.Y. 10031.

Open Education News, quarterly, $4.00 a year. The Greater Connecticut Council for Open Education, c/o Vincent R. Rogers, U-32, University of Connecticut, Storrs, Conn. 06238.

Outlook, quarterly, $5.00 a year. Mountain View Center for Environmental Education, University of Colorado, 1511 University Avenue, Boulder, Colo. 80302.

Appendix 2

Questions for Review, Discussion, School-Profiling, or Problem Solving

The following exercises are derived from Chapters 2-6. They can be used by an individual reader or by discussion groups as a means of applying the themes of each chapter to a specific school situation. The questions are intended to help readers assess their own prospects for open education, or to diagnose the sources of problems being experienced during implementation of open programs.

Questions about *The Role of the Principal* (Chapter 2)

1. Indicate which administrative staff member in your school, who is not presently a regular classroom teacher, meets the following qualifications. (Place a check mark in the appropriate column after each item, a through h.)

	Principal	Assistant Principal	Supervisor, Resource Teacher, etc.	Other
a. Has had several years' experience teaching in elementary or junior high and still likes to teach whenever there is an opportunity (and teaches well!).				
b. Has been a teacher of teachers; for instance, inservice instructor, curriculum specialist, workshop leader.				
c. Expresses interest (not necessarily expertise) in the developmental view of learning, faith in all children's capacity and desire to learn.				
d. Relates to teachers the way he/she expects teachers to relate to children.				

	Principal	Assistant Principal	Supervisor, Resource Teacher, etc.	Other
e. Feels equal to, unthreatened by, central administration demands; is able to use system resources to accomplish local school purposes.				
f. Welcomes parents in the school, is willing to work with them on educational matters.				
g. Finds satisfaction with his/her present work because it involves children and teachers (rather than because it's on the career ladder toward higher-level management).				
h. Invites teacher participation in administrative and educational decisions, but accepts personal responsibility for the quality of teaching in the school.				

2. As a result of this exercise, how do you view your principal's role in present or potential efforts to "open" your school? Did many or most of your checks fall in the same column—the one labeled "Principal" or in one of the columns *not* labeled "Principal?" If the latter, could this person be assigned to work with "opening-up" teachers? Did many of your checks fall in the column labeled "Other?" Do you have someone specific in mind? Could you enlist him/her? Or does "Other" really mean, in your situation, "No one?"

3. If your principal meets many of these characteristics but is not adept or persuasive in dealing with central office demands for standardization (item "e"), is there someone in central office or in the community who can run interference for your innovation plan?

4. What should be the first step you take to gain, or strengthen, administrative leadership for open education in your school?

5. What should be the first step you take to insure that someone assumes priority responsibility for a specific program to advance the professional growth of teachers in your school?

6. State a long-range realistic objective for your principal's behavior/attitude toward (a) plans for open education in your school, and/or (b) teachers in open classrooms in your school.

Questions about *Creating the Curriculum* (Chapter 3)

1. What rules do you have in your school about the course of study and curriculum materials?

   ____a. Is there a specific course of study spanning several grades? In one or more subject areas, is there a framework of concepts, a syllabus, which all teaching at each grade level is supposed to fit into?

   ____b. Do you have specific textbook series or curriculum programs mandated by your district, from which teachers have to teach? Are teachers expected to cover a specified amount of work in a text or program every year? Are children tested on this work?

   ____c. Are teachers required or expected to teach a specific subject at a specific time every day, or every week, for a specific length of time?

   ____d. Are teachers required to write behavioral objectives on students' mastery of facts or skills? (For instance, "By March 31, 80 percent of the class will be able to recite multiplication tables through six.")

   ____e. Do you have a required program in math or reading, based on a single ladder or "hierarchy" of skills, which allows children to work at their own pace but does not allow variations in learning strategy, materials, or the order in which skills are learned?

   ____f. Are children assigned to classrooms or to reading groups according to achievement as demonstrated by tests?

   ____g. Do you have departmentalized staffing, in which children go to one teacher for math, another for language, another for music, another for art, another for science, etc.?

   ____h. Does your classroom curriculum frequently consist of teaching for the test? Is your school required to use report cards with letter or number grades?

2. If you are a teacher: Would it be possible to get around rules which you consider barriers to an open classroom? Do you see item "a" as a hindrance? Could you consider it a help?

   If you are a principal or parent: Can you plan ways to assist teachers who find such rules a barrier to developing open education?

3. Can you think of an activity (accent on *active* work with "stuff") that could be set up in a classroom (or nearby—in the hallway, an adjacent room, the library, etc.) on a long-term basis, that children could participate in by choice? How would you tie it in with the classroom course of study? How would you justify this activity in terms of *cognitive* learning? How could you organize and supply such an activity? Who would help the teacher supervise the children's work? Could several teachers share such a project? Whose permission would you have to get to set up this activity?

Questions about *A New Resource–The Advisor* (Chapter 4)

1. Rewrite each of the following *erroneous* (some more, some less) items in an imaginary job description for an "Open Education Resource Teacher or In-Classroom Advisor." Make changes and add details necessary to suit your conception of open education and the instructional, social, and administrative realities of your school.

    a. Delegate of the school administration: Installs the district's (or the principal's) new curriculum program(s); evaluates teachers' performance in "Opening up," and reports to the principal.

    b. Curriculum enricher: Upon request will custom-design new learning materials or experiences—field trips, projects, etc.—to teacher's specifications.

    c. Classroom designer: Rearranges furniture and constructs or purchases equipment needed for model open classroom.

    d. Academic expert: Lectures regularly in after-school series for teachers on theory of Piaget, history of Deweyism, techniques for individualization, concepts in new math, methods for "discovery" science, etc.

    e. Efficiency expert: Applies systems approach to educational quality control, insuring that all teachers and all classrooms meet objective specifications of the model for an open classroom.

    f. Liaison agent/Ombudsman: Interprets, trouble-shoots, and mends fences between feuding teachers, between teachers as a group and the principals, between the principal and parents, etc.

Questions about *The Teacher as Learner* (Chapter 5)

1. Find out how well you know the professional *attitudes* and aspirations of the teachers in your school. How many of your staff could be described accurately by the following statements? Before each item write one of the following phrases—"Most of the staff;" "Sizeable group;" "One or two teachers."

_____ a. Is dissatisfied with the progress children are making, in spite of his/her own best efforts. Is unwilling to say that the fault lies with the students—that they can't learn.

_____ b. Basically likes children and teaching, but feels bored doing the same thing day after day, year after year.

_____ c. Has a self-image as a knowledgeable, competent, resourceful teacher. Willing to act according to own judgment, stick his/her neck out, work hard.

_____ d. Respects a child's personal dignity; is sensitive to a child's personal needs and desires; assumes responsibility for each child's intellectual development.

_____ e. Has been reading/talking about/taking courses in/observing in other classrooms, in order to find out more about open education/"British infant schools"/"child-centered education"/Piagetian or developmental learning theory.

_____ f. Likes to—or is willing to—work and plan with other teachers, ask for help and give help, share ideas, though not necessarily to share classroom teaching tasks with another teacher.

_____ g. Has experience as a *self*-directed learner. Pursues personal creative, expressive, or scholarly interests outside of school; not afraid to launch into new studies or projects.

_____ h. Is beginning to see him/herself as a developer of curriculum, not just a user of texts or programs; seeks experience and help in this development, or in integrating student learning in several subjects.

Write your own descriptor(s) which are more accurate characterizations of *sizeable groups* within the staff, or of *most of the staff*.

2. Look at all of the statements labeled "Most of the staff" or "Sizeable group." What do these descriptors suggest as to the *readiness* of a working group in your staff to embark on open education? Can you assess whether open education is an appropriate form of innovation for your school, or for a portion of your school?

3. Can you describe elements of an inservice program that would meet the needs of staff involved in, or working toward, open education? (For instance, should the program include material on child development learning theory? Introduction to new curriculum materials? Practice in making instructional decisions? Training in assessing children's learning level? Concrete-operational level experiences in math, science?) Do you think it would have to be a program for which teachers volunteered? Is one inservice program appropriate for the whole staff?

4. Will you need a workplace available to teachers? Construction tools? "Junk" depot? Library? Lounge area?

5. What sort of skills will be needed in the person(s) conducting the program? (Subject-matter background? Learning theory expertise? Person-to-person relationships? Style of working? Open classroom experience?)

6. Will you need interplay between the inservice course and the teachers in their classrooms? How will teachers have input into planning the inservice program?

7. Should principals, parents, aides, or other school personnel be included in the inservice program?

8. Can you sketch a time line for your inservice program? Do you see it developing through phases?

Questions about *Relationships with Parents* (Chapter 6)

1. Can you characterize your school's relationships with parents (or with several different groups of parents) by selecting from the following descriptors (or writing others of your own)? (If you do not know enough about parents' attitudes to make such a characterization now, can you find out?)

    a. A large bloc of parents—not necessarily having any formal organization or educational platform—is known to be generally favorable toward ideas similar to those of open education and probably would volunteer to place their children in open classrooms—or at least would be disposed to learn more about plans for open classrooms.

    b. An organized group of parents is interested in becoming informed about *educational* matters (as distinguished from fund raising expertise, school district politics and financing, or after-school activities), and this group leans toward an educational position which is favorable to open education.

    c. Some parents are doing volunteer work in classrooms under the direction of the teacher, curriculum supervisor, or principal.

    d. Among the total parent body there is scattered evidence of dissatisfaction with traditional education and a feeling that children aren't learning or that becuase kids dislike school they are "turning off" from learning.

    e. Teachers in your school perceive parents as antagonists and meddlers, or as ill-informed, under-educated laymen incapable of making decisions about their children's educational needs.

- f. The principal (and/or school board) is receiving complaints from parents whose initial observation of open classrooms is that because there is noise and movement there's no discipline, that kids aren't learning academics, etc.

- g. There is no perceivable interest in educational matters among the majority of parents. They appear to accept the school as an unchanging part of the community landscape and approve of it on the basis of the same standards that prevailed when they went to school.

- h. A "community control" movement is enlisting support from parents who believe your school (or the public schools in general) are failing to educate their children and that school officials are not responsive to parents as citizens.

2. Having selected one or more of the above descriptors or written your own, can you verify that they are indeed valid? Do other observers of the parents in your school agree with your assessment?

3. What (if any) is the first step you can take to try to involve parents constructively in plans for open education? When will you take that step? Do some other actions have to be taken first?

4. What is your specific, realistic long-range objective for an average parent's behavior/attitude (a) toward plans for open education in your school and/or (b) toward the open classroom in which his/her child is enrolled?

Index

Accountability, 154
advisors
  in-classroom, 11, 71-98
  characteristics of, 95-96
  in England, 71-72
  evaluating, 91-94
  free-lance, 89-90
  as graduate training, 96-97
  see also Advisory for Open Education; School District 6 Advisory Center; University of Illinois
Advisory for Open Education, Los Angeles and Cambridge, Mass., 32, 85, 90
Albaum, Judith, 90
Amarel, Marianne, 91, 92, 111-112, 113, 151
Andreae, Jennifer, 88
  quoted, 59
Armington, David, quoted, 75

Baker, William E., 90, 109
  quoted, 120
Barth, Roland, 21-23, 60, 47
  quoted, 22, 58, 132, 133
Batchelor, Barbara, 88
Beery, Keith, 35
behaviorists, 51
Bentzen, Mary, 21
  quoted, 18-19, 46
Bereiter, Carl, 74
Blackie, John, quoted, 144
Bloom, Benjamin, 147
Bowick, David, 32-33
  quoted, 32
Brearly, Molly, 103
Brokes, Alfred, 36
Browse, Bill, quoted, 75, 104, 117
Bruner, Jerome, 1
Bussis, Anne, 78-80, 93, 94, 113, 114, 147-148, 150, 151, 157, 158
  quoted, 151-152, 159

Career education, 65, 162
Carini, Patricia, 156
Carnegie Foundation, support to open education projects, 85, 114
carpentry workshops, 118, 120
Center for the Advanced Study of Educational Administration, *see* University of Oregon Center for Teaching and Learning, *see* University of North Dakota

Chittenden, Edward, 75-77, 91, 92, 101, 111, 113, 147-148, 149, 150, 157, 158
  quoted, 37, 44-45, 150-151, 159
City College of New York, 23-25, 118. *See also* Open Corridor
classes, multi-age, 5, 27. *See also* open education
classrooms, *see* open classrooms
Clegg, Alec, 71, 73, 102
  quoted, 41, 42, 43, 44, 72, 101, 130, 144, 159
Coe, John, quoted, 129-130
Collins, James F., quoted, 120
Collins, Mary, 150
  quoted, 114
community control, *see* parent participation
Community Resources Institute, New York, 35, 64, 86-87, 91
Cook, Ann, 102, 111
  quoted, 17, 45, 25
  see also Community Resources Institute
Cooperative Teacher Preparation Project, 108-109, 155
Creative Teaching Workshop, New York, 32, 35, 59, 85-86, 91, 116, 119
Crocker Highlands School, Oakland, Calif., 135
Culture of the School and the Problem of Change (Sarason), 10
curriculum
  change in England, 2, 41-42
  defined, 48-50, 59
  as I-Thou-It interaction, 52-54
  for open education, three aspects, 52-54
  reform movement, 1-2, 12
curriculum materials, 66-67
  criteria for selecting, 58
  natural and environmental, 42, 54-60
  using, 59-60

Department of Elementary School Principals (D.E.S.P.), survey, 19-21
deRivera, Margaret, quoted, 149
Dewey, John, 1, 50, 161-162
disadvantaged students
  cognitive development, 55
  non-English speaking, 62
  see also Follow Through program
Dorn, Miriam, 118-119
Duckworth, Eleanor, 54-55
  quoted, 52-53, 54, 149-150, 155, 156
Durham Child Development Center, Philadelphia, 121
Dyer, Henry S., 147

187

Education
   in England, *see* England, education in
   goals of, Gallup poll, 131-132
   I-Thou-It concept, 7, 52-54
   inservice, for teachers, 11, 30-33, 102-103
   open, *see* open education
   progressive, 50-51, 161
   theories, 50-52
   values, 51
   for work, 65, 162
Education Development Center (EDC)
   advisory, 75, 119
   Follow Through program, 49. *See also* Follow Through program
   USMES, 66
   Open Education Advisory, 91
   parent decision making, 138-139
   Pilot Communities Project, 138, 158-159
educational ideology, 48-52
educational innovation,
   dissemination, informal, 11-12
   Rand Corporation research, 48
educational materials, *see* curriculum materials
Educational Testing Service, 6, 7-9, 75-77, 111, 147, 151
   Development Research Division, 91
   Early Education Group, Princeton, 155
   evaluating advisors, 91-94
Edwards, Babette, 139
Eisner, Elliot W., 143, 154-155
Engelmann, Siegfried, 74
England, education in, 2, 9
   advisors, 71-72
   curriculum change, 2, 41-42
   evaluation, 143-146
   head teacher, 17-18, 45-46, 101, 129
   open classrooms, 1-2
   open education, 2, 36, 42-44
   open schools, qualities of, 42-44
   parent participation, 129-131
   reading, 43-44
   teachers role, 45-46, 101-105
Erikson, Erik, 1
evaluation, 143-162
   assessing learning level, 155-158
   "child outcomes," 150-155
   Educational Testing Service, 6, 7-9, 75-77, 111, 147, 151
   in England, 143-146
   interview instruments, 159-161
   mathematics, 48
   objectives, 154-155
   observation instruments, 158-159
   problems, 11
   science, 48
   teacher, study of, 160
Evans, Judith T., 158-159

Far West Laboratory
   Early Childhood programs, 155-156
   Responsive Education Program, 73-74
Featherstone, Joseph, 42
Follow Through program, 49, 73-77, 79, 91, 107, 122, 138, 143, 149, 157
Ford Foundation, open education projects, 29, 80
49th Street School, Los Angeles, open classrooms in, 31-32
free schools, described, 6-7
Frein, George, 106
Freud, Sigmund, 52

Gardner, D. E. M., 145-146, 155
Gesell, Arnold, 50
Glaser, Robert, quoted, 147
Goddard, Nora, 102
Goodlad, John, 1-2, 20, 21
   1969 survey, 9-10
Grape Street School, Los Angeles
   advisors in, 88
   open classrooms, 28-30
   testing, 157-158
Greater Boston Teacher Center, 109
Greenwood, Marion, 86
   quoted, 86
grouping, student
   family or vertical, 5
   multi-age classes, 5, 27
   nongradedness, 5

Haner, Doug, quoted, 121
Harlem Parents Union, 139
Hawkins, David, 65, 80, 95, 97, 110-111
   quoted, 7, 12, 47, 52, 56-58, 82, 110, 149, 157
Hawkins, Francis, 81-82
   quoted, 84-85
Haynes, Carrie, 28-30, 88, 157
   quoted, 28-30
Hayward, Judith, quoted, 89, 161
Head Start, 80
Hein, George E., 49
   quoted, 50, 54, 54-55, 124, 143
Heyman, Mark, quoted, 17, 45, 129
Holt, John, 1
Howes, Virgil, quoted, 6
Hull, William P., 3, 17
   quoted, 161
Human Resources Research Organization, Monterey, Calif., 105

International Center for Education Development, 29, 89-90

John, Vera, 62
John Muir School, Berkeley, 89

Kagan, Jerome, 55, 65
Kallet, Tony, 71-73
   quoted, 72, 103, 115-116, 124
Kapfer, Philip, 154
Katz, Lilian, quoted, 124, 140
King, Pat, 89
Kirst, Michael W., 46
knowledge, defined, 50
Kogan, Maurice, quoted, 18, 129, 130, 131
Kohl, Herb, 1
Kohlberg, Lawrence, 50-52, 55
   quoted, 53-54, 161-162
Kozol, Jonathan, 1

League for Cooperating Schools, 18
learning
   from children, Piaget's method, 49
   open educators' beliefs, 48-50
   Piaget's three stages of, 53-54
   "skills," 55-56
   theory, developmental, 48-52. See also Piagetian theory
   webs, 65
Learning Institute of North Carolina, 34-35
Learning about Learning, 155
Leitman, Allan, 90
Let's Look at Children, 155
Lowery, Lawrence F., 108, 155

Mack, Herb, 86, 87, 102, 111
   quoted, 17, 45, 125
     see also Creative Resources Institute
McKeown, Pamela, 116-117
Manolakes, Theodore, quoted, 37
Marsh, Leonard, quoted, 130
Marshall, Hermine H., 159
mathematics
   evaluation, 48
   new, 47
   Nuffield, 103, 144, 151
   programs, 64-65, 66-67
   Unified Science and Mathematics for Elementary Schools, 66
Mayer, Rochelle, 50-52, 55
   quoted, 53, 161-162
Meier, Deborah, quoted, 148
Mena, Chuck, 83
Miller, Ann-Marie, 88
Minneapolis Southeast Alternatives project, 97
Morrison, Phillip, 55
   quoted, 56
Mountain View Center for Environmental Education, 80-84
Murphy, Caroline, 135-136

Nash, Doris, 43
National Center for the Improvement of Education, 105

National Foundation for Educational Research (England and Wales), 146
National Institute of Education
   Experimental Schools Projects, 89, 97
   teacher evaluation study, 160
National Schools Council, England, 103
National Study Commission on Undergraduate Education and the Education of Teachers, 105-106, 107
Neill, A. S., 50, 51
New Republic, The, 42
Nias, Jennifer, 129
Norris, Martha, 78-79
North Carolina, State Department of Public Instruction, 34-35, 97
Nuffield Foundation, England, 103. See also mathematics, science

Objectives, cognitive and affective, 76-77, 150-155
   open-ended, 69-70
O'Brien, Thomas C., 143
Olive Elementary School, Arlington Heights, Ill., 88
   open classrooms, 26-28
open classrooms
   in British infant schools, 1-2
   characteristics, 2-9
   Hartford, Conn., school district, 34
   Olive Elementary School, 27-29
   and non-English speaking students, 62
   reading in, 43-44, 60-64, 156-157
Open Corridor, 32, 60-62, 78-79, 97, 119, 148
   advisory program, 96-97
   described, 79-80
   in District 3, New York City public schools, 23
   evaluated, 91
   parent participation, 134-135, 136
   reading assessment, 156-157
   Workshop Center for Open Education, 120-121
open education
   common themes, 160-161
   curriculum, 52-54
   defined, 2-5, 6
   in England, 2, 36. See also England, education in
   role of teacher, 9
   staff development, 30-34
Open Education and the American School (Barth), quoted, 22
open teaching, see teaching, open
Oregon Center, see University of Oregon

Page, Floyd, 85
   quoted, 59, 119

parent participation, 27-28, 122, 125, 131-140
  in England, 129-131
  Harlem Parents Union, 139-140
parents
  decision making, 138-139
  goals for schooling, 131-134
  organized, 24
  school's relationship with, 11
  volunteers in classroom, 5, 62
  see also parent participation
Park South Teacher Center, San Francisco, 121
Perrone, Vito, 60, 66, 138, 154, 160
  quoted, 64, 106-107, 132-133, 138
Philadelphia District 6 Advisory Center, 122, 143
Piaget, Jean, 50, 52-53, 155
  assessments, 156
  "checkups" derived from, 144
  method of learning from children, 50
  quoted, 49
  theory of the learning stages, 53, 156
  see also Piagetian theory
Piagetian theory, 49-50, 53-54, 109, 155, 156
Pidgeon, Douglas A. 146, 158, 159
Plowden Report, 145
principals
  qualities of leadership, 33-34
  role of, 11, 18-21
  support for, 36
  survey of, 19-21, 104
  training programs for, 34-36
  see also England, head teachers
Project Catalyst, 35
Project COD, New Bedford, Mass., study, 113
Prospect School, North Bennington, Vermont, Adjunct Services Department 90, 156
Pryke, David, quoted, 42, 44
P. S. 152, Brooklyn, New York, 32-33, 116

Raggatt, Peter, 46
  quoted, 17, 45-46, 103-104
Rand Corporation, research, 48, 146
Randazzo, Joseph, 88
Raoul, Kathleen, quoted, 114-115
Rasumussen, Don, quoted, 121
Rathbone, Charles, 92, 118
  quoted, 48-49, 153
reading in open classrooms, 60-64
  assessment, 156-157
  in England, 43-44
  see also curriculum; testing
Resnick, Lauren B., 147
Rogers, Vincent, quoted, 110-111, 145
Rouse, Ernestine, quoted, 122

Rousseau, Jean Jacques, 50
Rubin, Louis, 9

St. Paul (Minn.) Open School, 134
Sarason, Seymour B., 10, 20, 21, 30, 33-34, 47
  quoted, 11, 19-20, 34, 73, 104
School District 6 Advisory Center, Philadelphia, 122 143
schools
  architecture, open-space, 5-6
  change barriers in, 10
  innovation in, 10-11
  see also England, education in; free schools
science
  curriculum, 55-56
  evaluation, 48
  Nuffield guides, 103
  programs, 48, 55, 65, 103
  Unified Science and Mathematics for Elementary Schools (USMES), 66
Sea Mills School, Bristol, England, 43-44
"Self-Evaluation of Openness" (Marshall), 159
Shapiro, Herbert, 32-33
Sharkey, Tony, 86
  quoted, 86, 116
Skinner, B.F., 51
social studies programs, 64-65. See also curriculum
Southeast Alternatives project, Minneapolis, 121-122
Spodek, Bernard, 27, 94, 101
  quoted, 9, 94
staff development, 11, 30-33, See also education
  inservice, for teachers
Stitt, Mary, 26-28, 32
  quoted, 27, 28, 139
Stokley, Norellen, 77
  quoted, 91, 119
Strandberg, Warren, quoted, 154
students, disadvantaged, see disadvantaged students
Suchman, J. Richard, 105
Suhd, Mel, 90-92
  quoted, 32, 132
Summerhill, 51
survey of principals, Oregon Center, 19-21, 104
Sweeney, Mayme, quoted, 30

Talmage, Harriet, quoted, 47
Tanaka, Masako, 155-156
Teacher Learning Center, San Francisco, 114
teachers
  attitudes toward innovation, 104-106

authority, 105-106, 124-125
centers for, 109, 114, 120-122
as curriculum developer, 119-120
as decision maker, 45-48, 76, 101-105, 124-125
education, 105-125
English head, role of, 17-18, 45-46, 101, 129
inservice education, 11, 115-122
predictors of success in open classroom, 113
preparation, 122-124
resource, *see* advisors
role in England, 45-46, 101-105
role in open education, 2, 9
see also principals; teaching, open
teaching, open, 3-5
objectives, cognitive and affective, 76-77, 150-155
inservice program for, 11, 115-122
predictors of success, 113
testing, 146-149, 157-158
Metropolitan Achievement Test, 148
see also Educational Testing Service; evaluation
Thomas, Gretchen, quoted, 36-37
Thomas, Susan Christie, 158
Tye, Kenneth, 21
quoted, 46

Unified Science and Mathematics for Elementary Schools (USMES), 66
U.S. Office of Education
Bureau of Education of the Handicapped, 35
National Center for the Improvement of Education, 105
University of California, Cooperative Teacher Preparation Project, Berkeley, 108-109, 155
University of Colorado, Mountain View Center for Environmental Education, 80-84

University of Connecticut, advisory center, 96
University of Illinois
open education advisory, 113
School of Education, 96
University of Minnesota, Southeast Alternatives project, 121-122
University of Nebraska, National Study Commission on Undergraduate Education and the Education of Teachers, "Value Statement," 105-106, 107
University of North Dakota, Center for Teaching and Learning, 64, 106-107
advisor training, 96
assessment, 159-161
parent participation, 137-138
reading programs, 60-62
University of Oregon, Center for the Advanced Study of Educational Administration (Oregon Center)
1971 survey of principals, 19-21, 104
list of principals' commonalities, 33

Values development, 54

Walberg, Herbert, 158
Walker, Decker F., 46
Weber, Lillian, 11, 23, 32, 79-80, 96, 119, 135, 162
quoted, 12, 17, 24, 25, 26, 44, 47-48, 60-62, 97, 104-105, 161
see also Open Corridor
Weikart, David P., 74
Wlodarczyk, Steven, 113, 114
Woodruff, Ashael, 154
Workshop Center for Open Education, New York, 120-121
Workshop for Learning Things, Watertown, Mass., 120

Yale Psycho-Educational Clinic, 20
Yeomans, Edward, quoted, 109, 111